STAY CALM & JOY-UP!

*"The Secret? Love Jesus. Enjoy His Presence.
Have Faith In His Strength, &
Unlock Your Potential, Everyday!"*

–Dr. Candi Dukes

DR. CANDI DUKES

Copyright © 2022
Sagacity Publishing, LLC
Dr. Candi Dukes
STAY CALM & JOY-UP!
The Secret? Love Jesus. Enjoy His Presence.
Have Faith In His Strength, &
Unlock Your Potential, Everyday!
All rights reserved.

No part of this publication may be reproduced, distributed, or transmitted in any form or by any means, including photocopying, recording, or other electronic or mechanical methods, without the prior written permission of the publisher, except in the case of brief quotations embodied in critical reviews and certain other non-commercial uses permitted by copyright law.

Sagacity Publishing, LLC
Dr. Candi Dukes

For permission requests, write to the author, addressed "Attention: Permissions " at cdukes71@outlook.com, drcandi01@sagacitypublishing.shop.
Sagacity Publishing, LLC
www.sagacitypublishing.shop

Printed in the United States of America
First Printing 2022
First Edition 2022

ISBN: 978-0-578-29349-3

10 9 8 7 6 5 4 3 2 1

Table of Contents

Preface 1
CHAPTER 1 3
Joy-Up! Jesus brings Great Joy to the World!
CHAPTER 2 17
Joy-Up: In-Spite-of & No Matter What!
CHAPTER 3 38
Joy-Up: Refuse to be Bound!
CHAPTER 4 56
Joy-Up: Through Introspection!
CHAPTER 5 79
Joy-UP: The Loins of Your Mind & Destroy Negativity When It Spirals!
CHAPTER 6 107
Joy-Up: The Conversation!
CHAPTER 7 146
Joy-Up: For the Fight!
CHAPTER 8 180
Joy-Up: on Your Resilience!
CHAPTER 9 194
Joy-Up: Fulfill Your Fruit-bearing Calling!
CHAPTER 10 208
Joy-Up! Take the High Road!
CHAPTER 11 221
Joy-Up: Repeat the Sounding Joy!
Bibliography and References 239
Reference List by Chapter
Reference List Alphabetically

Preface

Stay Calm & Joy Up, was written to unlock the secret of how to live an abundant life of reigning joy. Although memories fade, let us not forget the hopelessness of job loss, death, sickness, government lockdowns, school shut-downs, social distancing, the termination of front-line nurses, teachers, officers, fire fighters, and others, worship restrictions and ordinances, and the sheer air of desperation that left many wondering if life will ever return to some form of normalcy. Of course, in the natural sense, the loosening of restrictions, mandates, and mask requirements have resulted in a calming effect, but what about the residue of the lingering impact on the spiritual man? Has God's children returned to the pre-pandemic levels of joy and resilient exuberance?

Immediately following the pandemic, a global economic crisis emerged that resulted in afflictions, trepidation, anxiety, and fear as housing costs spiraled out of control, the cost of living dramatically increased; notwithstanding, the rising cost of fuel and a spiked inflation rate that devalued investments and purchasing power, overnight. This book was written after a Christian posed the question, "Are Christians expected to have joy?" Meaning, is it possible for believers to be spiritually restored and thrive in the fullness of joy in a post-Christian and anti-God world that offers little or no hope? The Gospel of John makes it clear; the answer is a resounding yes!

John, a disciple of Jesus, explained how Joy grows on a vine that God often prunes, when it is time for the old paralyzing branches to die off.

This divine pruning process comes through a spiritual, born-again intimate relationship with Jesus Christ. Please consider for a moment, that when Jesus instructed his disciples, he could have recommended multiple sources of joy, but instead he said "these things have I spoken that my joy may be in you and that your joy may be full (John 15:11, 17:1, 24-26). This passage reveals how God is most glorified when he is spiritually engaged with his children. So not only should Christians have joy, but they should also have joy in its vastness and depth based on the inner source. So, even after the dark days of the recent global pandemic; that depleted many of the fullness of joy that saturates his presence; it is necessary to ask yourself, whether it is time to refuel and joy-up? Do you hear the birds chirping each day? Can you refuel with an infusion of joy on the sheer promise that all things work together for the good to them that love God? Trust and believe that joy is our portion, and the joy of the Lord is our supernatural strength, for the journey! To embolden that strength, consider reading "Stay Calm + Joy-Up: The Companion Guide," and afterwards, gather a group of friends and prepare to plunge-into greater depths.

CHAPTER 1
Joy-Up! Jesus brings Great Joy to the World!

We don't speak about the concept of joy enough, do we? It's such a beautiful aspect of life--a gift from God to us that does not need to chip or fade with time or tempering. Joy colors our thoughts, our understanding of God and interpretation of His Word, just as much as a lack of it can turn us into bitter vessels of disillusionment when troubles arise. Most of us imagine joy as a desperate moment of happiness that flashes within our grasp, but it is so much more; it is a deep satisfaction, an abiding contentment with exactly where we are. True joy is to be infinitely excited and fully satisfied with the quality of our lives, and this delight is at its peak when we are in the right place with the right Person.

Think of the joy that poured into the world at the coming of Jesus Christ, God's Son and Messiah. His birth was the culmination of centuries of promise. It was the moment when joy radiated from heaven to earth for the first time since it walked out of the Garden of Eden. For the first time in millennia, all creation could shout out the words of Habakkuk 3:18[1] as one, *"I will joy in the God of my Salvation."* Christ was the source of all good things, and He had come.

---

[1] Habakkuk 3:18 ESV

Joy to the World

"And the angel said to them, "Fear not, for behold, I bring you good news of great joy that will be for all the people. For unto you is born this day in the city of David a Savior, who is Christ the Lord."

-Luke 2: 10-11 ESV[2]

Have you ever stood in the aisle of a store and heard the jingling bells and angelic melodies that signal the season of joy? The annual renditions of *Joy to the World* are catchy and heart-warming, sending us into a tailspin of holiday cheer and fervent preparation. Joy is one of those buzzwords that make for amazing home decor elements, but what does it truly mean for the heart that wants to soar with those angels who celebrated Christ's birth? Are we joyful enough in Christ alone? If not, why not?

Why do we lose focus when life starts to deviate from our plans or expectations? Perhaps, it is because we don't understand the power of joy in our walk with Jesus. The Messiah was the only answer to all that was wrong with the world as it tried to survive losing contact with its Creator. Our holy and loving God could not look upon sin, but thankfully, He also could not endure the thought of cutting us off from love forever. It was God's love that drove our redemption plan, and it was unfailing, sacrificial love that achieved victory over all that sought to destroy our connection with Him forever.

The shepherds would have been shocked at the thousands of angelic voices, worshiping in unison above them as the child of joy came into the world. As men stuck in a lowly career choice under the oppressive Roman rule, it might have been a time of great excitement as the sky lit up with heaven's rejoicing. The mood would have been building as the realization kicked in of what this event meant for the people of that time. Everything

---

[2] Luke 2: 10-11 ESV

leading up to the birth of Jesus was part of a greater story--God's story--and life on earth would never be the same. The Son of Man entered the world, his purpose to bring about a paradigm shift as a long-awaited Messiah. It was glorious, even though what followed did not play out in the way that Israel's descendants imagined.

We all know the story of how the people were convinced that Jesus would overthrow the authorities in a capacity as King, but there was so much more that He had to accomplish in His brief earthly ministry. The King did not leave his heavenly throne for an earthly one that rusts and fades. No, the mission was eternal peace between all men and women with the Living God. Jesus did not need the validation of a generation of earthlings to achieve that peace, or to make it available as a free gift to us. He was God. He *is* God, in authority over all things living and dead in the fullness of time.

Modern life is far removed from first-century Jerusalem, but life then was not simple. It may have been less busy in terms of traffic, technology, and industry, but it was no easier to run a household or build a successful business. Jesus' family were carpenters doing grueling work with blistered hands and none of the modern power tools we now associate with the trade. Carpentry takes hours, but back then it took months or years to complete a project. For non-Romans, it also would not have been very profitable, thanks to the ruling nation's strict laws and taxation policies.

The entry that the Lamb made into the volatile world of the first century was unassuming. Yet there was such a great outpouring of emotion from all in heaven who saw it that it overflowed into the night skies of Bethlehem and gave resting shepherds something magnificent to tell their grandchildren. It was a miracle, and heaven knew how pivotal the humble birth was to the fate of the entire world, before and after. Time divided into before Jesus and after Him. For God's people, it was a stark turning point in history that severed life before the ultimate sacrifice from the hope that erupted after a victory that none of us could have fathomed.

A Joy Reawakened

Before Jesus was born, the last time God walked with His beloved creation was in the garden of Eden, in utter perfection. Sin took that away, shattering the intimacy that we had with our Maker. Joy faded. There was no peace with sin, no rest. Sacrifices had to be made to atone for the disobedience of generation after generation, as cities and kingdoms fell, and time moved on. Humanity's innovations aimed to make life easier, but sin did not have an obvious solution. For those struggling in inhospitable lands and under oppression, there could not have been much to celebrate. Life was hard and hundreds of years had passed since the people had heard from God.

Imagine a young Israeli mother in the time right before Jesus arrived. Picture her in dusty sandals and faded clothes, overworked, subject to harsh marriage expectations (and laws), and doubly undervalued by the overriding Roman conquerors. There would have been so much fear and anxiety as part of her daily life, never knowing whether her children would come home or be forced into slave labor or Rome's military ventures. Did she wonder how to raise kind and loving children? Or was there little time to impart the need to obey a silent, seemingly absent God who was last heard from centuries earlier? There had to have been doubt and frustration present while she cleaned, cooked, fetched water, hosted her husband's guests, and tended to many children.

If her husband was under pressure, it would be easy to imagine her experiencing bitterness, too. She might have felt guilty or sad about how little their faith was doing for the family while she slaved away to keep things running smoothly. Where was the promised freedom and eternal peace? Where was that victory the ancestors had insisted was coming if the people obeyed the law?

In that culture, one steeped in a religion of outward works, the Pharisees' hypocrisy would not have been invisible, either. The people of God in waiting would have noticed their leaders using God's law for personal gain, mistreating others, and pointing fingers. How would a young mother in that world have imparted hope to her children and spouse when she must have doubted often in the silence of a broken heart? How could she have modeled the joy of salvation when she might not have been sure whether the Messiah was real? There were so many beacons of hope in the history of the Jewish people, but beloved and faithful kings like David and Hezekiah died, and idols like Baal faded with the civilizations who created them.

We understand that happiness is a choice, sometimes achievable with gratitude for small blessings. But would that approach have been enough to get a tired young mother through sleepless nights, perpetual poverty, and unanswered prayers? When Israel escaped Egypt, they grumbled still. Joshua's Promised Land was filled with challenges. Esther sacrificed her happiness and almost her life to try and save God's people, and still they disobeyed, killed prophets, worshipped idols, and defiled sacred laws. Before Jesus, the world was blind to its treachery, even in the temples of the people who were named for Him. Something had to change.

Joy-UP!

We live in a different time, but it might not be too much of a stretch to relate to how that young mother or father might have felt. Hope was dim, God seemed silent, and the days still demanded work, childcare, chores, and cultural conformity. Most of us have experienced these demands on our time and energy where our spirits were taking strain. But love came that night, and healing with it.

God is not silent; He has broadcast His great love for all the world in the birth of His Son. So, maybe it is time for us to start thinking about joy as a power-up boost. We might take a path, aim for a goal, but meet obstacles and threats along the way. Sometimes, what is in front of us might feel like an insignificant ditch that we have to jump over, as cheesy video game music keeps us motivated. Other times, it may look more like a spy action movie ensemble, blaring insurmountable challenges that seem to thwart every effort we make to scale the mountain. In either case, a power-up boost could make the difference between progress and pain. Life isn't a video game, but the choice to harness our joy in hard moments is far more powerful than clicking replay options in the corner of a screen.

There are countless moments in life where we throw up our hands in despair, already hearing the death knell as we allow circumstances to overwhelm our character and faith. We might walk away or throw down the reins while there's still an opportunity to see the good that God is working through it. We might even forget about the spiritual arsenal we have at our disposal in the power and blood of Jesus, and his gift to us, the Holy Spirit.

When we think of joy as something we can wield for change and victory, we begin to understand the mysteries of God. We feel ourselves waning, and we take a standby selecting the joy-up option. Perhaps, this is how a young Israeli mother could hold her chin up in the face of looming disaster and disappointment, but it would have taken far more faith while God was still silent.

Today, we don't need that kind of faith--Jesus has come! The promise was fulfilled, the victory secured, and love came down to us in a form we could understand. Joy sparkles once more, and will forever more, and that is truly worth celebrating.

A joy-up moment is one when we can look up to a God who cares for us and know that everything He allows to happen is for our good and His glory. Whether we are facing suffering or trying to help others through it, we can choose to accept that circumstance or trial with joy. Finding a way to pick up joy in the place of pain also turns us outward in the best ways, helping us shed self-absorbed insecurities while bolstering our confidence as joy-filled children of God. It is possible to rejoice, always, even when rising emotions do not correspond to the knowledge, we have of who God is or what He is capable of achieving on our behalf. Those are the moments when the gift of joy is the most rewarding.

I Am the Way

Joy is a shimmering reflection of God in us that surpasses every human experience. It can easily shape how we see the world and our attitude to loving others. Think of how much you enjoy an activity or a relationship when you choose to see the positive aspects of it or fix its flaws. Falling in love provides a glimpse of that kind of mindset, when we find such happiness in the newfound relationship that it seems the person could do no wrong in our eyes. Lasting and biblical joy is more than fleeting feelings of puppy love, though. It is not momentary happiness.

After Jesus was born, there was an awakening of hearts and minds. His beauty and unmistakable purity highlighted the depths of sin each one of us faces in our daily walk. In his letter to the Galatians, the Apostle Paul refers to the fruit of the Spirit, a list of nine characteristics that show who Jesus really is and how we can be more like Him.

"22 But the fruit of the Spirit is love, joy, peace, patience, kindness, goodness, faithfulness, 23 gentleness, self-control; against such things there is no law. 24 And those who belong to Christ Jesus have crucified the flesh with its passions and desires."

-Galatians 5: 22-24 ESV[3]

---

[3] Galatians 5:22-24 ESV

Heartfelt love, joy, and peace are not fleeting, they are how we can live our best lives. As humans in a world that is always dashing our plans or expectations, we tend to look at these nine qualities as something we can consume or discard as needed. These "fruits" don't ebb and flow like emotion or circumstance, though. A more accurate depiction is to look at these qualities as structural changes. As we learn what each one means, and let the Holy Spirit show us how to apply it to our lives, they become part of who we are, how we think, and how we behave as followers of Christ.

If we have grasped the fruit of the Spirit, we don't reach for peace when life is difficult so much as we live it with every step. Joy and love will drive our actions and attitudes because they become a constant theme in our thoughts and dialogue. We can count on these newfound character improvements for every application, a permanent change in perspective rather than a one-time gift.

As the birth of Jesus became imminent, John the Baptist had heralded the Messiah's coming. He told everyone to prepare themselves to receive the LORD, and many people believed his prophecies. At that point, a regime change seemed the only way to escape the rule of the Romans and the people desperately wanted to believe God's promises of salvation. They could not possibly have known that Jesus' victory was only a few years away while the locust-eating prophet foretold of the Messiah's coming miracles. Yet, there was still hope as the crowds arrived to hear the message first-hand. The era of Abraham, Moses, David, Jonah, Job, and every other generation, had also foretold of the coming of the Messiah, the fulfillment of God's covenant. They believed the promise, but it must surely have been difficult to find joy in something so far removed from their daily realities.

Abram and Sarai are an excellent example of how this kind of uncertainty can rob us of joy. Doubt creeps into the mind and inner dialogues burgeon with negativity. When something isn't clear, it's harder to grasp and impossible to relate to our experiences. But, when we realize that joy is real, there's a spark that nothing can extinguish. When we finally realize that joy is ours for the taking, we understand more about how those shepherds in the field felt as the sky radiated with celebration and adoration. When, like Sarah, we are holding a baby in our arms and hearing the little angel cry for the first time, there is no denying the beauty of real joy. We smell that pure newborn scent, and tears flow. Emotions swell, and it is not a moment we need to analyze to understand. Our hearts already know that it is real; we were made for joy.

God's chosen people had seen suffering, been enslaved, endured sickness, and accepted death. Sarai was old and barren, and Abram had sought his own way to garner descendants from a woman not his wife. Yet, God fulfilled His promises to them. Sarai had a child, who became the father of nations, even though she had laughed at the idea when the messenger of God first presented it to her. God's grace covered her uncertainty and brought unquenchable joy to her and all that are called the Children of Promise.

Those who believe in God and look with hope to His promises can feel that joy spontaneously. They can choose to embrace the beauty of what God has created, as Sarai did when she gazed in wonder at her miracle child. It moves from an impressionist sketch to something we can feel or cuddle or see before us, close enough to brush past our fingertips or dig down past our biases.

Promises Fulfilled

When Jesus came, He brought so much more with Him than salvation or justice or freedom. The Messiah also brought the capacity to hope, unfailingly, in the goodness of a loving God. The promise was kept, the price paid, and joy was forever planted in the hearts of those whom Jesus called to himself. Nothing can remove that joy now. The gift of the

Holy Spirit to every believer is the seal of that joy for eternity, but we get to experience it here on earth from the moment we commit our hearts to believing and following Jesus.

The angels brought '*good news of great joy*[4]' the night that Jesus was born. No challenge or trial or disappointment can damage that sense of fulfillment in Jesus Christ. The joy was for the world, not only for Israel or its descendants. The world rejoiced, as all creation breathed a sigh of relief. Centuries had passed of despair, silence, suffering, and no sign of God's promises being kept. And then...He was here. The King had come at last!

That moment in history was a time for celebration because the invisible God had made himself known to all the world in a form we could see, hear, and experience. Heaven and nature sang out praise and awe at the culmination of all the Old Testament prophecies. God's people had waited for so long for redemption and a confirmation of the Word of God. They had fought wars, gone through generations of exile, and fallen into sin time after time. They had wandered toward idols and taken on popular 'gods' when it became convenient, but God was gracious to draw them back with His prophets and kings.

The Old Testament love story is one of tragedy and betrayal from a fickle people with a faithful God. They leave, He pursues them. They complain, He provides a way out for them. He calls them to Himself and showers them with blessings, even when they don't see or appreciate it. It is easy to forget that this ebb and flow might still be how life would look for us still if Jesus hadn't stepped down from His throne in heaven. Our Loving God's plan was moving in the background from the moment Eve and Adam were sent away from His presence. How thankful we can be that His desire was to restore to us the joy of our salvation for eternity, for that is what His coming represented.

---

[4] Luke 2: 10-11 ESV

Our restoration required much sacrifice, however. Atonement is never free, and Jesus Christ, the Son of God, knew that no fallible human would ever be able to repay all that was owed to the holy, righteous Creator of the universe. The only way for us to access true joy as it meant to be experienced was a perfect sacrifice, once and for all. That was why God had to do the hard work of atonement Himself. He loved us so much that He didn't want to see a single drop of our lifeblood spent in the redemption of our dark, dead hearts. He bled and died on our behalf so that all the human hearts He cherished could discern love in all its fullness.

If your joy is waning and hope seems elusive, it might be time to meditate on the magnitude of what God has done for you in that single sacrifice at Calvary. Sin broke the world, and one act in history by the Son of God was the only solution. It wasn't a patch job; it was a complete renewal that changed everything.

The Joy of the LORD

Jesus came for us to know real and lasting joy. It was an opportunity for us to see Him with new eyes and get to know Him in conversation, like talking to a friend. We could listen to Him speak about life, love, and God with authority and truth. Christ Jesus was the beautiful, perfect representation of God on earth because He *was God* in all His fullness. He had the power and presence of God with Him, and all authority in heaven and on earth over suffering, disease, sin, and death. It is no wonder that John the Baptist heralded His coming with such awe.

The Holy Spirit now gives us a powerful sense of how much we mean to God; imagine how much He loves us for Jesus to have gone through all that He did. *We* were the *"joy set before Him"* mentioned in Hebrews 12:2[5]. He came for *you* and me. He came that we may know the

---

[5] Hebrews 12:2 ESV

true joy of an intimate and sin-free relationship with our Maker, as it was meant to be when He first breathed into the lungs of Adam and Eve.

As saved, grace-covered people cling to Jesus for strength, they can come boldly to Him as worthy children of God. They can pray to the Lamb for perspective amidst challenges, tapping into everlasting joy.

Do you need to see the light at the end of the tunnel? **Joy is the secret weapon** and believers in Jesus can wield it by:

- Walking with boldness into the presence of the Almighty God
- Shaking off the chains that threaten our contentment in Christ
- Repenting of all that holds us back from freedom in Christ
- Speaking life to others and to ourselves, no matter the situation
- Girding up our minds against negativity, anxiety, worry, and bitterness, reflecting on who we are as co-heirs with God's Son
- Fighting for the joy that is ours forever in Christ Jesus
- Choosing resilience to match the Savior's as we grasp what it means to be content in all situations
- Spreading joy to others at every opportunity, including our families, communities, neighbors, strangers
- Holding up our heads to rise when there are circumstances trying to keep us down

Pain does feel like war, sometimes. Joy isn't the first reaction for most of us when trouble arrives, and uncertainty thwarts our plans. Christians are not exempt from pain or suffering or illness; they are part and parcel of communities who go through hardship, poverty, and pressure. Jesus understood that people were just people, with all our imperfections, struggles, and habits that needed to be broken. He has the same emotions as we do (remember, we are created in the image of God), but Jesus' perspective is entirely unique because He knows how it all looks at the end.

Can you imagine standing beside Jesus one day and looking back on the life you have lived? I wonder how many of us will see how we reacted to a situation and think "if only I had known...?" Will we stand with confidence beside our Almighty God in heaven and see just how in control He was of every moment we lived, even when it seemed that He was absent or silent? Will we see the chains laying there at our feet and watch the reel of ourselves picking them up again, laying unnecessary burdens on our own shoulders because of unbelief?

Will we admonish ourselves as Jesus points out a few moments where we were so close to contentment that we could have reached out with our fingertips to touch the heart of God? He gives us salvation; all we have to do is accept it and take joy in His victory. Jesus promises to be with us at every step, as a friend and ally. Yet, we so often reject Him for false forms of security, like money and comfort. How many times will we need to watch a clip of ourselves being unwilling to surrender to the Holy Spirit's prompting? Will we have wished that we had stepped out in faith even when we weren't sure about the results?

If we are honest, opportunities for repentance and joy abound in life. Every trial is a chance to grab hold of God's strength and take refuge in His promises. Every failure is an opportunity to repent and know Jesus on a deeper level. We can speak life to others and encourage ourselves with biblical truth and positive thoughts, and we can revel in our right relationship with Jesus if we have chosen to accept His free gift of salvation.

As we explore more about how to joy-up for life on earth, a few things may become clear about how to 'do life' as a Christian when things are not turning out how we hoped. The first new ability that joy gives to us is to conquer our inner struggles, including negativity, anxiety, worry, and bitterness. The choice to harness joy is far easier when our hearts understand how rich we are with an inheritance of abundant life. Our job here on earth is to stand as witnesses, declaring what we have seen of the majesty of God and bringing Him glory. Nothing brings more happiness than the realization that what we are doing is exactly what we were created to do. It is the definition of wholeness, and it brings an unshakeable fulfillment to hearts that were made to find their purpose in the will of God.

John 15:11[6] speaks of a joy that is 'full' and it is worth fighting for. As co-heirs with Christ, believers have complete and immediate access to the joy, hope, and love found only in Jesus. The Word of God continually emphasizes the need for restoration and forgiveness in our relationship with Jesus, and grace abounds in our daily walk with Him. It's this Spirit-fueled joy that gives us resilience in the face of suffering and the right perspective we need to understand the unending love of our gracious Heavenly Father.

The other aspect of true joy in Christ is that we discover the capacity to share it. Joyful Christ-followers can spark a fire of hope and positivity everywhere they go, even when they are hurting or uncertain about how a trial might end. Joy-filled people are supremely rare, too. It's a beautiful gift to be able to look at something devastating and see the love of God right there in the ashes. That's why people notice joy, and it is also why so many Christians step around it. It's hard to let go of the self-pity and gloom that we are so used to feeling in the face of adversity. In fact, true biblical joy would be impossible without the help of the Holy Spirit to show us the way.

The Kingdom Has Come

"Of the increase of his government and of peace

there will be no end,

on the throne of David and over his kingdom,

---

[6] John 15:11 ESV

> *to establish it and to uphold it*
>
> *with justice and with righteousness*
>
> *from this time forth and forevermore.*
>
> *The zeal of the Lord of hosts will do this."*
>
> *-Isaiah 9:7 ESV*[7]

We tend to think of the second coming of Jesus as some kind of goalpost for Christians. It is often expressed as an idea or a visualization technique that gives us the energy to survive each day, but this is not the whole truth behind biblical joy, or happiness, and contentment. Perhaps, it is time for us to realize that we have a supremely flawed view of life with Christ. Real joy is available to all those who love Jesus, on the good and the bad days. And nothing can remove that joy from us. The Holy Spirit reminds us gently of this access, prompting us to rejoice whenever we can and rejoicing alongside us when we seek to spread joy like confetti.

If you need a fresh perspective, joy will get you there. Isaiah 9:7 speaks of the LORD's zeal as the primary catalyst behind His choice to send Jesus. The Son of God's birth "unto us" was packed with the zeal and joyous momentum of God Himself. When the star ascended above Bethlehem, thousands of voices around the world rose in excitement and joy washed over the faded canvas. Life sprang into full color, abundant and fresh at the sight of the Messiah, knowing that the time of His reign had finally arrived on earth.

When generations of silence cracked open, the world was suddenly filled with angel choirs and a bright hope. God's promised one had come, and things were going to change. We have access to true joy today because of the amazing love of God that didn't want us to be left out in the

---

[7] Isaiah 9:7 ESV

darkness. He is wonderful, our Mighty Counselor and the Prince of Peace sitting on the throne of our hearts. He is ruling His kingdom as His plan comes to fruition, and the final days of that unfolding are here.

Isn't it beautiful to behold the sovereignty of God, the One who knew that nations and kings would be moved into place with the swish of the artist's brush? He knew from the beginning that all would be well. A blessed joy arrived with the birth of the Savior, and people everywhere held their breath. If ever there was an opportunity to 'joy-up' and grab onto hope, the birth of the Savior was a great one.

The next few chapters are going to explore this idea of joy as a powerful weapon against adversity, failure, and pain. We'll look at what joy means to a Christian when the Holy Spirit opens our eyes to share in the joy of our LORD. We'll see how it can be like a power-up function to move us forward, making us feel brave enough to forge across the unknown. Harnessing joy isn't dependent on our capabilities, and it doesn't fade when things get messy.

Joy UP with Jesus

Jesus is the perfect example to us of how to harness real joy. He looked to the reward set before Him while enduring His greatest labor of love on the cross, and He didn't give up or bow out. Our salvation was at stake, and Jesus Christ considered us worth the effort. He poured out His life for you and me so that we might share in His joy for all eternity. As believers, we inherit that joy with the gift of the Holy Spirit, and we can access it anytime.

CHAPTER 2
Joy-Up: In-Spite-of & No Matter What!

As a man after God's own heart, King David is, with exceptionality, the one biblical character that learned the power of worship to usher in the joy of our salvation. He knew well that worship was the catalyst of the joyful experience of man touching God and the glory of knowing in faith that God inhabits the praise as we acquiesce. To true worshippers, those moments of joy feel like foretastes of Heaven. As stated by John Piper, "God is most glorified in us, when we are most satisfied in Him." No earthly sensation can compare with the sacred joy experienced in this type of exchange. Although it cannot be easily explained, and our joy-up experience only deepens as we learn to praise and open our hearts to worship God more, while embracing the joy of our salvation like David.

When we praise God with the intensity of all our heart, all our soul, and all our might, we touch God, and He is moved by it. When we extend our hands as worshipers, when we honor, acclaim, and express our adoration of God in His presence; it is how we joy-up in the most effective way possible on earth or in heaven. This is the only way to joy-up from the depths of our souls, honoring and paying tribute to our God who is due so much respect, glory, and gratitude.

David found praise to be the secret ingredient for tapping into real joy. Praise was the antidote, the total fulfillment when Israel's mighty king declared that he would continually praise the Almighty God. It is evident that God knew David's heart when we read of His choice in Samuel 13-14[8], *"the Lord sought him a man after his own heart."* The words in Psalm 34:1-2 also help us to quickly perceive the level of joy that resonates within David's heart as he articulates: *"I will bless the Lord at all times, his praises shall continually be in my mouth, my soul shall make her boast in the Lord, the humble shall hear thereof and be glad[9]."*

Journeying into the New Testament, the Word of God now calls for a new kind of fellowship between us and the LORD, a connection that presents itself to what the Bible terms a 'true worshiper[10].' Our Lord Jesus proclaims that the Father seeks true worship, an act conducted in the Spirit. A true worshiper is one who expresses genuine adoration and participates in the joy of that worship experience long after the words or melody fade.

If joy is available to true worshipers in this way, it makes perfect sense for Christian living to focus almost exclusively on building a relationship with Jesus Christ. However, we cannot worship someone that we don't know. And, what about when life seems to be falling apart? When the chips are down, can we engage in the true worship of our Savior and take joy in the God of our salvation? Wouldn't life on earth be so much sweeter if believers could learn how to tap into everlasting joy at any time? The good news is that we can!

A spirit filled with joy is the product of continuously seeking to know God and to love Him as we embrace the gift of salvation. Habakkuk 3:17-19 puts it this way:

"Though the fig tree should not blossom, nor fruit be on the vines, the produce of the olive fail and the fields yield no food, the flock be cut off from the fold

---

[8] Samuel 13-14 ESV
[9] Psalm 34: 1-2 ESV
[10] John 4:23-24 ESV

and there be no herd in the stalls, 18 yet I will rejoice in the Lord; I will take joy in the God of my salvation. 19 God, the Lord, is my strength; he makes my feet like the deer's; he makes me tread on my high places.

-Habakkuk 3:17-19

Verse 18[11] speaks of the *"joy in the God of my salvation"* as something we choose to look for and find directly in the LORD. In God, we *find* joy. In God, we soak up real love and complete acceptance of who we are as His children. The Almighty God sees every part of us and loves what He has made. In Genesis, God looked at the world He formed and said it was good. When He looked at His final pieces, the man and the woman, the Creator said it was *very good*[12]. When we seek God, it helps us to truly understand how blessed we are to have the opportunity to know Him and be under His favor. Salvation is literally a lifeline, with unending joy as one of the direct benefits when we commune with God each day.

The Christian life should be filled with rejoicing, praise, and adoration of God, yet joy can feel elusive. When we feel disconnected from our Maker, we need to consider how a joy-up experience can realign us with His heart. Habakkuk's words above are a powerful reminder that taking joy in our relationship with the Savior is not meant for a life free of challenges. In this light, verse 17[13] starts with serious ways that life can go wrong for us. In Habakkuk's time, no blossoms on the fig tree meant no figs for eating or sale the following season. Vines without fruit would have meant cutting dead or dying parts of the crop away in hope of saving part of that year's investment and praying for a possible recovery in years that followed. Olive production included valuable oil to be sold or traded; it could feed entire villages until the next harvest. The people of that day also relied on herds or livestock for breeding, labor, trade, meat, wool,

---

[11] Habakkuk 3:18 ESV
[12] Genesis 1:31 ESV
[13] Habakkuk 3:17 ESV

milk, transport, wealth management, and atonement sacrifices. This last category was particularly concerning for devout Jews--if they couldn't sacrifice to the LORD, they could not atone for their sins at the temple or find favor with God under the Old Testament laws[14].

Can you imagine losing everything you own, watching your family starve, not being able to purchase anything, grow crops, work, go anywhere, or trade for essentials, and then being told to 'rejoice?' Yet, that is Habakkuk's message: take joy in God because you are at peace with Him for eternity. He is saying that nothing else matters.

As Christians, it is important to take time to reflect on this idea of a single source of joy. Do you have what it takes to find joy in God alone? Is your life a testament to the residual effects of being in God's presence or is the fullness of your joy more dependent on external factors? Habakkuk understood that true joy does not wax and wane with life's challenges, losses, or trials. Finding joy in our salvation means not dragging our feet when things do not go as we expect or hope in life. We are encouraged to have 'feet like the deer[15]' that navigate thorny pathways with ease and prance about as they enjoy the open fields and sunshine.

The high places mentioned in verse 19 also make us think of how mountain deer or goats balance so skillfully on precarious rocky cliffs to stay out of danger. Habakkuk uses this imagery to describe how God secures our position, no matter the imminent dangers. He steadies us enough to find a safe path as life becomes tricky and we need assurance. It is an amazing picture of how God uses all situations for our good and His glory[16] so that we might know the true meaning of joy, peace, and love in our relationship with Him. The Heavenly Father does not divert us away from trouble when there is an opportunity for us to grow from it or be a

---

[14] Leviticus 1-10 ESV
[15] Habakkuk 3:19 ESV
[16] Romans 8:28 ESV

blessing to others. However, God is always there to give us a sure footing and many blessings as we follow His lead.

Walking life's paths with God brings joy simply because He is with us. He listens, speaks, and moves to reveal Himself to us, as we respond in kind with adoration and obedience. The only way this connection is possible is salvation, and there is so much joy available to us as we mature and understand what God has done for us.

When last did you reflect on the significance of what Jesus Christ did for you on the cross?

How does the idea of 'my salvation' rest upon your soul when you remember how much God loves *you*?

When we seek to know God and learn to love Him as He loves us, we understand the adoration that Habakkuk and David express in their writings. They emphasize a sense of ownership in "the God of *my* salvation." It is a personal and profound experience to know the God of the Universe who sustains all things, and nobody else can experience this revelation on our behalf. It is also a beautiful two-way connection; God loving us and revealing Himself in ways that we can recognize, and us responding in praise, affection, and shared joy. It is like a dance of two hearts, intertwining as they feel the other's rhythm. Think of it like that movie moment when two people are on the dancefloor, and all else fades around them as their connection completely dominates their focus. Being able to tap into the fullness of joy looks like that moment; life can be falling apart around you with money problems, ailing relationships, and global crises, and you can still find full and satisfying joy in the loving God who stands before you.

When we are balancing high on the steep cliffs of risk or uncertainty, the presence of our loving and powerful God gives us a cheerful heart with which to stay the course. If we try to move without Him or find our own way without His guidance, we often feel like the description in Proverbs

17:22 that says, '*a crushed spirit dries up the bones*[17].' Learning how to joy-up is the key to keeping in lockstep with God as we travel the ups and downs of each day. If you are struggling to rejoice in your freedom in Christ, it might be time to learn some new moves so that you can keep up with His lead.

The presence of God is more than a hovering cloud nearby or light in the distance, though. John 17:26 speaks of the blessings that God gives when we choose to accept His gift of salvation; namely, Jesus. When we submit to the rule of God's Son, we receive the love of God and the presence of Jesus Christ[18], right there *in us*. Our Savior not only blots out transgressions for our full acceptance into the family of God, but He also comes to be with us permanently and wonderfully. He grants us the one thing that all human hearts crave: His constant presence. That is why we have joy in our salvation--Jesus is right there in the center of it all.

So, how do we rejoice in the God of salvation? We reach into our own hearts for the Savior that dwells there, holding onto the hand of Jesus, and knowing that nothing else truly matters. It is Jesus we need, and only Him.

What's The Secret to Christian Joy?

In Habakkuk 3:17-19, we saw that the prophet admonishes the believer to look back on the conditions of life. Can joy be found at times where the fig tree no longer blossoms or bears fruit? When there are vines, but no grapes? Or, when it feels as though the olives are void of the hoped-for oil? Habakkuk describes how the days of trouble make it appear as though there is no more grain in the fields, and that stalls are empty. Yet, there is hope.

---

[17] Proverbs 17:22 ESV
[18] John 17:26 ESV

Habakkuk's focus appears to imply that, even when struggles drain our energy and leave us feeling spiritually, emotionally, or physically diminished, dissatisfied, or weak, we can still find joy in the God of our salvation. Our Savior is an ever-present source of help. We can find hope and happiness in Him when life unravels because true joy lives in the God we serve. Since He is eternal, our joy is not seasonal or based on externalities. Believers can joy-up in the God of their salvation whenever they connect with Him, even amid great distress.

The prophet's deliberate use of 'yet' at the beginning of Verse 18 also reveals that rejoicing in our salvation is *always* possible. There are no circumstances whatsoever that can eradicate the fact that God is good. We can rejoice in the LORD because our joy is supernatural, not based on material goods or earthly pursuits. Having the joy of the Lord means embracing an "in spite of" attitude; n*o matter what, I will rejoice and be glad in the God of my salvation.*

The passage also suggests that God is most served, most appreciated, and most satisfied, when we can enjoy Him unconditionally. If our relationship is free of conditions, it doesn't matter what the world outside of that interaction looks like for it to be good between us. God's children can still enjoy Him when provisions appear to be scarce because we do not live by bread alone. When creature comforts dissipate and we reap ruins, we can still praise the God that has liberated our souls. Joy is in the relationship itself.

When Jesus was teaching the people about abiding in His love, He used the analogy of a vine. Jesus referred to Himself as The Vine to which believers attach themselves, with the Heavenly Father filling the role of The Vinedresser. We are the branches, growing and thriving as we take our fill of what He offers. In John 15:11, Jesus ends the lesson saying that He wants us to have *His* joy[19]. He clarifies this idea further with the

---

[19] John 15:11 ESV

reason He wants us to have His joy; because He wants us to have the level of joy that He experiences in His own heart. He wants our own joy tanks to be full or complete. Why would He wish that for us unless He knew that we were missing a crucial aspect of the abundant life we could be living?

In God's presence, there is fullness of joy, and we must realize that we are able to worship Him unconditionally. Why? Because we have the privilege of being in His company, in fellowship. So, joy is not optional if we understand how to joy-up in the God of our salvation. We rejoice in Him, and in return, we enjoy the relationship's numerous benefits. It is the pinnacle of life with God; the crowning glory of knowing who God is and who we are in relation to Him. We can't help but experience joy when we tap into this connection with Jesus, the Vine, who gives us life itself. The wind may blow, and storms may rain down on us, but abiding in the vine--staying connected with our Savior Jesus Christ--is all we need to joy-up and celebrate His goodness.

What Reason Do I Have to Joy-UP in the God of My Salvation?

A chaotic and adventurous lifestyle brought Israel's second king endless challenges, both from external forces and his own temptation. However, David intimately knew the benefits of salvation. He also knew the great joy that salvation brings "in spite of" circumstances, emotions, or trials.

David's poetic wisdom in the psalms provides myriad reasons to feel immensely joyful every time we meditate on our salvation in Christ Jesus. For example, Psalm 103 is an exceptional example of a practical guide on reasons to rejoice. Here are a few of the reasons David lists in this triumphant song of praise[20] to help us take joy in the God of our salvation, no matter the storms raging in our lives:

[20] Psalm 103 ESV

- He forgives our iniquities (3)
- He heals our diseases (3)
- He redeems our lives from the pit (4)
- He crowns us with steadfast love and mercy (4)
- He satisfies us with good [things] (5)
- He works righteousness and justice for the oppressed (6)
- He reveals Himself to His people (7)
- He is merciful, gracious, slow to anger, and steadfast in His love for us (8)
- He does not stay angry or deal with us in the way our sins deserve (9-10)
- His love for us is immeasurable (11)
- He has forgiven our sins entirely and shows us the compassion of a father, knowing that our lifetimes are a speck of dust in the span of eternity (12-16)
- He loves us, and will love us forever (17)
- He rules the heavens and the earth justly and blesses us when we obey Him as King (19)

Perhaps, read through the whole psalm if you have the time. Let these powerful words soak into your forgiven, beloved soul.

The Word of God shows us many ways to joy-up as we meditate on our 'saved' status in Christ, and the Holy Spirit within us helps us assimilate these truths. God has done so much, and all of it culminates in this beautiful, free gift of salvation bought with the blood of Jesus Christ. If life seems to be coming apart at the seams, we need to joy-up in the presence of the God who loves us forever, unconditionally. Our Redeemer wants to fill us up with the delight of His own heart so that we overflow with good, righteous, and wonderful joy!

More About the Joy of Our Salvation

In Habakkuk's day, there was no Savior; only the promise of one in the form of a covenant. We are on the other side of that time now, in an era where Jesus Christ is personally available for us to know. How can we know Him? We do this by reading His Word and growing to love Him. We forge ahead in this relationship, accepting Jesus' gift of salvation to us, that He bled for us on the cross. We also receive the Holy Spirit. It takes time to progress in our relationship with Jesus. Thankfully, His ever-present and powerful Holy Spirit reveals more about who He is, what He has done, and how much He loves us.

Believers can joy-up in Christ Jesus because we now abide in the eternal vine that produces the fruit of joy. This is supernatural joy, radical joy! When the fig tree doesn't blossom, we can still joy-up in the God of our salvation because we abide in Him, like the branch tapping into the life-giving vine. The connection sustains us, helps us grow, protects us from external threats, and keeps us moving in the right direction. It also keeps us productive so that The Vinedresser's work of pruning does not need to remove us. Joy abounds in this relationship, no matter the external forces at play. If we feel like our branch is drying out or losing its will to continue, all we have to do is press into the vine and receive its abundant provision of love, joy, peace, patience, kindness, goodness, gentleness, faithfulness, and self-control[21].

In Psalm 43:4, David hoes in on that kind of joy, the joy that is to be found in a relationship with God as we cherish His gift of salvation. The first line talks of going to the altar[22]. It signifies a sacrifice or giving up something so that we are free to engage with God without hindrance. It might be laying down ego, anxiety, an illusion of control, or a life plan. It might even be willing to give up financial resources, possessions, or

---

[21] Galatians 5:22-23 ESV
[22] Psalm 43:4 ESV

healthy habits. After that, David describes God as his 'exceeding joy.' What a blessing it is to know that when we have laid down every distraction on the altar and handed it all over to God, we are free to approach Him. We are welcomed and fully acceptable to commune with Him as blood-washed, beloved children.

The Joy Connection

As believers seek to understand the source of true joy in life, the Word of God speaks directly into our hearts. The Holy Spirit continuously reveals truth to us and allows us to know God more intimately. Studying the Bible's message diligently is also an excellent way to see how Jesus' fulfillment of the New Covenant brings us greater joy than we ever thought possible. For example, God's Word confirms that Jesus' sacrifice restored our connection with our Maker. The New Covenant (our eternal salvation in Jesus Christ) is also how God fulfilled the old one.

God's promise was to provide a Savior, to redeem all that was broken when sin entered the world. The entire Old Testament pointed people toward hope. They could look with hope as an anchor for their souls[23] in times of trouble, knowing that what was lost would be repaired. The Law and the Prophets emphasized that promise. The Messiah would restore God's people to their rightful place in His Kingdom. The Savior would grant people freedom from sin and ensure unlimited access to the LORD as they had in The Garden of Eden. We can recall when humanity lost this access to God, as the serpent deceived Eve into disobedience. Men and women made their way out of that holy garden into the wilderness, and joy and hope faded as people left the presence of the Creator. However, the death and resurrection of Jesus Christ brought the connection all back within reach and fulfilled God's promise of hope.

---

[23] Hebrews 6:19 ESV

All humans seek happiness in some form, and if we're honest, "fullness of joy[24]" is something most of us would feel ecstatic to discover. Imagine feeling so satisfied, so content with life, that we can choose to be happy all the time and celebrate life. Well, Christians should be doing that because they *have* access to fullness of joy. We have a way to be content like this, through the grace and mercy of God.

Our Creator wants a relationship with us and to show us how exciting it is to be alive in Him. By fulfilling the Old Covenant and ushering in the New Covenant to complete His story, Jesus Christ our Savior has granted us access to a sweet and beautiful fullness of joy through salvation. Humanity is once again invited to connect with God, heart to heart. We can have access to the Living God whenever we want it, a pivotal realization for a great and lasting joy on earth, and beyond.

Remember, people were created to be happy in a perfect world that was in harmony with the Holy God. Throughout history, people have sought to explain and harness the source of true happiness, and we see this prominently in the world of self-help books, trending mantras, and colorful philosophies. Our salvation through Jesus Christ has put us in a relationship with God so that we can be truly happy, no matter how the world around us looks or feels. We *can* be happy with who we are because we belong to God's family, and we harness eternal love and joy in our relationship with Jesus Christ.

If we take up the gift of this connection each day, joy will follow. Isn't it amazing to think that this same joy will be present as the relationship continues in heaven? We will be able to find this ultimate contentment each day on earth, and every day after, without the hindrances of time, tears, or uncertainty. God offers us '*pleasures forevermore*[25]' because the greatest joy possible is to know Him. Christian doctrine encompasses this truth with many Scriptural references and also

---

[24] Psalm 16:11 ESV
[25] Psalm 16:11 ESV

catechisms like *'The chief end of man is to glorify God by enjoying Him forever.*[26]'. It is possible to joy-up in hard times when Jesus Christ becomes a treasure to us that we want to enjoy forever.

> "Where your treasure is, there your heart will be also."
>
> *Matthew 6:21*[27]

We know that the heart finds joy in what we value. If we place value on money, our joy is in jeopardy when we hit financial difficulties or find ourselves unable to accumulate the wealth we desire. If we place value on family, we find ourselves disappointed or heartbroken when children, a spouse, or parents do not live up to our expectations. Where is your treasure? Idolatry is when we value something more than God, and the reason that God outlawed this dangerous tendency is because He wanted to give us the tools to experience true contentment. He knew that the only way for us to be happy was to value our Maker above anything else in our lives. That is the secret to true joy.

If God is our treasure, our supreme measure of value, we will not need anything else to find true and lasting joy. Our walk with Him will be a cycle of joy. For example, it may look something like this:

- We might worship God and understand that He enjoys it when we appreciate Him in this way.
- God will then reveal more of Himself to us by the Holy Spirit and through the truth of His Word
- We will find that God is even more beautiful, powerful, and valuable than we imagined and want to know more.
- As we deepen our knowledge, God will be more glorified as our intimacy with Him helps us overcome the tendency to sin and teaches us how to love others better.

---

[26] Kelly, D. (1986)
[27] Matthew 6:21 ESV

- We will then start to value Him more, above all other forms of happiness, security, or constancy.
- He will continue to celebrate our growth, even if it looks like a *cha-cha-slide* that needs His grace and mercy. He will also encourage us to seek Him even more.
- Then, we will begin to understand how worthy God is of our praise and worship, finding joy in the intimate moments we have with Him while pursuing time in the relationship.
- God will find this worship pleasing as our hearts align more with His, and He will use it to bring even more glory to His throne.
- As He reveals more of Himself to us, we will feel even more valuable and valued in the relationship. Joy will abound as the cycle continues and other pleasures fade.

Isn't it beautiful how knowing God so intimately can open our eyes to His supreme worth? John 17:21 talks of unity with God so that '*the world may believe*[28],' which seems logical given how this relationship will manifest outwardly in our thoughts, actions, words, and life choices. God sincerely wants every person in a 'right relationship' with Himself, through Jesus Christ, the Son of Man. Salvation is the key that opens the door to us knowing our Creator without the chasm of sin between us. As we get to know Jesus, we will see how much He loves us, and that realization will make us feel more worthy of this kind of love.

So, we can take joy in the God of our salvation because that is how we were made to live. We were created to be joyful beings who are deeply connected to God. It is the same idea of joy in the presence of loved ones, family, close friends, or those who make us feel worthy to be there. The only difference is that this relationship is forever--it does not end with death or sickness or betrayal or circumstances beyond our control. God is

---

[28] John 17:21 ESV

fully in control, and He is eternal. He does not change and His love for us will never fade.

Joy UP and Walk in Step with God

Embracing fullness of joy is easy when we feel connected with the God who holds our happiness securely. But what can we do when emotions or doubts draw us away from Him? All Christians describe highs and lows in their relationship with God because humans are not constant. They mature, they learn, they see things for the first time, even when they are old and gray. Only God is constant, and that is where our focus should be when things feel or look challenging.

If we need to take advantage of the joy-up mechanism we have as believers, the first step is to look to Jesus Christ. Our Savior is our supreme connection to all good things. He is the One who holds our salvation and sanctification in His capable hands, fully in control and waiting for us to acknowledge it. Jesus is the God of our salvation, and our LORD rejoices when He sees us looking up at Him, ready to engage. It brings God joy when we show that we want to strengthen our connection with Him as Creator, Friend, and King.

If we want joy, we have to approach Jesus. We have to acknowledge that only He can give us this joy. He has already drawn us a map with a big 'X' on the treasure, but He will not dig it up for us. He knows that we will not be as happy with the exciting discovery if we do not follow the path and put in some effort. It isn't as fun to have a parent or older, wiser person provide the answers to a mystery or complete a puzzle while we look on helplessly. No, it is far more rewarding to find it ourselves, step by step. It is satisfying to struggle through each point with a nudge or a word of encouragement from the person who knows how to bring out our best qualities but lets us choose our own path. How wonderful it is to know that our Creator knows the answers but still lets us participate freely. He knows the best way to get there, but the treasure is all the sweeter when we learn something on the journey.

The joy-up cycle looks like an ongoing journey of discovery as we make Jesus the treasure of our hearts. Verses like Philippians 4:4 are like clues on the treasure map, pointing the way. *"Rejoice, and again I say rejoice*[29]*"* is a hint for how to find our way to the greatest truth in history: only Jesus can bring us the joy we seek. If we are worshiping and exalting Him as we should, abundant joy is the reward. If we listen to the Holy Spirit within us and delve into the Word of God with all diligence, the blessing that comes is the ability to rejoice in any situation. We can meditate on our treasure, Jesus, like we meditate on the idea of finding a great and priceless chest of jewels. It makes our journey smoother when the goal is foremost in our mind. When we sing songs about that treasure, worship Him, do everything we can to keep moving toward Him, and set our hearts on the hope He offers, and life starts to revolve around that focus. If Jesus is that treasure, our lives will start to look as they should; glorifying God by enjoying Him in every moment, whether our circumstances or emotions are conducive or not.

Making Jesus our treasure also strengthens how we see ourselves in relation to God. Our identity starts to align with God's view of us as forgiven children. It lets us approach each day with renewed faith, joy, and the choice to love others because of the love with which God loves us[30]. When we are at peace with God in this way, and pursuing a relationship with Him, we can take joy in all that He asks us to do, obeying Him with gladness. The reason that our joy-up power is so potent is that pursuing God's love only increases the joy we find in aligning with His will. We learn what it means to obey because we love him, not out of fear or a sense of duty. We start to align how our lives look and how our words touch

---

[29] Philippians 4:4 ESV
[30] John 15:12 ESV

others because we realize that living a holy life is right and good and brings everlasting joy.

The Roman church needed this same reminder from Paul, as disagreements rose about the outward working of faith. They were fighting about how Christian life should look and feel, rather than focusing on the fruit of the Spirit that was within their reach. Paul admonished them to turn their eyes away from superficial things that were diminishing their joy. *"For the kingdom of God is not a matter of eating and drinking but of righteousness and peace and joy in the Holy Spirit*[31]*."* Earlier in the letter, Paul emphasized how God works all things for the good of those who love the Lord and are called as He wills (Romans 8:28). Instead of pursuing godly routines or upright lifestyles that could not stand up to adversity, the early church was learning how to turn their hearts toward Jesus Christ and lean on salvation. Paul was pointing them away from entitlements, status symbols, competition, and judgment, and back toward love, joy, peace, patience, kindness, goodness, and all noble things.

Our response to hard times needs us to fully grasp the things competing for our joy and throw them all at the feet of Jesus. Are we willing to give up a strict diet or career if it is detracting from the sweetness of our relationship with Christ? Are we willing to forego prosperity or recognition if it is keeping us from an unencumbered connection with the Savior? What about our possessions, financial security, or comfort, if that is required on the altar?

As we look at life through the eyes of the Savior, worldly pursuits will fade into obscurity. Nothing will matter more than aligning ourselves with the will of God by immersing ourselves in a relationship with Jesus Christ in every way we can. This is the connection that gives us life, and from it stems a joy that will not fade or falter. If we want to know how to walk with God and joy-up in His presence, we need a measure of faith. We

---

[31] Romans 14:17 ESV

must be able to imagine what fullness of joy looks like, and how it will feel to experience its momentum. What will our minds and hearts do when they find joy in the God of salvation? How will it look to praise Him in the storm and worship Him from our deathbeds?

What are you struggling with at the moment? Is there something diminishing your joy or hindering your relationship with Christ? The Holy Spirit helps us to put our faith into action as we focus on knowing God more intimately, even when our lives seem to be an unexpected joyride down the wrong rabbit hole. Sometimes, it is outright sin that makes itself obvious. Other times, it is a noble pursuit getting in the way of what God is calling us to do, like a desire to thrive and pursue riches so that we can help others. It could be an ambition to be the best in our chosen field so that we can achieve amazing things for God's Kingdom. It is not wrong, except when it is the one thing keeping us from connecting with Jesus Christ. If it is moving us away from His will, it is a hindrance in our walk with the LORD.

To joy-up, we need to resolve that a relationship with Christ brings complete joy that ends all other quests for satisfaction or fulfillment. Paul described it as counting '*everything as loss*[32]' compared to the beauty of an eternal connection with Jesus. The Savior Himself promised that, once we took up His offer of salvation and started to get to know Him better, we would '*never thirst*[33]' again. Christ is enough for us, and He is the only thing we need to access true joy. No form of desire, sensual or otherwise, can come close to bringing us the same joy.

Fullness of Joy in Jesus Christ is the Secret to Life

When parents connect with their children, they put down smartphones and kneel down to be on the same level. They look them in

---

[32] Philippians 3:8 ESV
[33] Matthew 6:35 ESV

the eyes and focus on the words they are saying so that they can fully understand what the child is trying to communicate. They care about understanding what is on their children's hearts. God does the same for us, coming down to our level in the same way that loving parents listen, answer, and reassure their children, embracing them in a secure relationship. We connect with God by putting down all that would jeopardize the sweetness of our bonding time. We speak, listen, and connect, basking in each other's company as the relationship forges eternal foundations and takes flight. That is where joy lies. It isn't dependent on anything else but looking God in the eye and letting Him fill our hearts with the joy that comes from knowing Him.

A true and lasting joy depends on us seeing more of who God is, and that takes time and effort on our part. God's greatest joy is to connect with those He loves and see them seeking Him in the same way. It isn't a meditation technique that empties the mind or hopes to find some secret tonic for a more joyful heart. True and lasting joy depends on us seeing more of who God is and realizing that we are filled with the Holy Spirit. Connection with God is what life is all about, and it will bring us the happiness we long to find. If joy seems scarce, take heart; have faith that the presence of God is permanent. He is the source of all joy, and He isn't going anywhere.

If you want to be able to joy-up in any circumstance like Paul, counting all as loss except for knowing Christ, then Jesus Christ should be the treasure of your heart above all other things.

Joy UP with Jesus

Joy is the secret to life, but the only way to know joy in all its fullness is to connect directly with the source of it: Jesus Christ. Our Savior is always with us. If a sense of disconnection has had you cowering in the corner, it could be that you have ventured away from the source of true and lasting joy. The more open you are with God; the more joy erupts through that relationship. It's like stepping onto a live wire and experiencing a joy-up electrocution that spreads into your spiritual DNA once you touch the master.

Jesus Christ has given us the Holy Spirit as a promise. He is the way that we gain the fullness of joy in the presence of God, which is accessible to us throughout our lives. When emotions fail, the joy that we find in our relationship with God can give us supernatural strength, even amid challenges. Nehemiah 8:10 encourages us to think of joy as a boost that's always there for us. "The joy of the Lord is your strength[34]" and that's why we can keep on going, no matter what the world around us has brought to our attention.

The prophet Isaiah also pointed out that the people of Zion who mourned would receive beauty for their ashes[35], a spiritual oil of gladness. In speaking of this oil, Isaiah was pointing to the spirit of Christ as a comforter who facilitates healing, restoration, and joy. He turns or shifts mindsets from mourning into joy.

Compare this to the old story of Rumpelstiltskin. In this children's fairytale, deception takes place when a miller lies to a king about his daughters' ability to turn straw into gold. Eventually, there's an imp that makes an indecent proposition to turn straw into gold in exchange for the girls' firstborn. As the plot unfolds, the girl presents her firstborn to lay claim to what belongs to her, but first, she is forced to engage in guessing games and bet on luck. In Christ, there's no deception; there are no puzzling riddles to solve or threats to navigate. Jesus' offer of a connection is straightforward and free of entanglements.

God turns our mourning into joy so that we have true and lasting gladness through the gift of his Son! Christ is the reason that our weeping may endure through the night, but joy comes in the morning[36]. As the grand weaver of joy and strength, God blesses us with His presence, despite our earth-

---

[34] Nehemiah 8:10 ESV
[35] Isaiah 61:3 ESV
[36] Psalm 30:5 ESV

side challenges. He removes the reason to mourn and provides the joy that we need to turn our situations around.

For us, joy begins with hunger and thirsting[37] after God as our highest priority. The chief end of a man is to connect with Jesus for his glory and enjoy Him in a fellowship that lasts forever. Resolve to refuel and joy-up by spending some time in prayer and petition today so that you can find joy in the truth of God's Word:

- You can come boldly before the throne of grace (Hebrews 4:16)
- God has chosen to love you and that is a great reason to rejoice (Ephesians 1:4-5)
- Strength comes from God, and He delights in sharing His joy with you (Nehemiah 8:10)
- God's children should rejoice, and keep on rejoicing (Philippians 4:4)
- Being in God's presence brings a joy that's complete (Psalm 16:11)
- You can find joy when you connect with God and align with His will (Philippians 2:1-2)
- God's presence uses the intensity of your mourning to spin and weave the situation into an anointed oil of joy and gladness (Isaiah 61:3)

If you need a reminder of what God's presence in your life is worth, read through Psalm 103 again and rejoice. God forgives, heals, redeems, and reveals Himself when people need Him the most. He crowns Zion with all good things, including love, mercy, righteousness, and unending joy. With God's steadfast love for us, we find joy in the freedom we have from sin and death. We rejoice in our relationship with Him as a Father and King because God's love for us is immeasurable and unconditional. He wants to show us just how much we mean to Him, so why not get to know Him better?

---

[37] John 7:37 ESV

STAY CALM & JOY-UP!

CHAPTER 3
Joy-Up: Refuse to be Bound!

We have seen that in the presence of God, there is fullness of joy. This joy that is found when we are in God's presence shows up clearly in the Bible, even back to the days of leaders Exodus 34:29-35[38] describes the return of Moses after his time on the holy mountain as he communed with God.

"When Moses came down from Mount Sinai, with the two tablets of the testimony in his hand as he came down from the mountain, Moses did not know that the skin of his face shone because he had been talking with God. 30 Aaron and all the people of Israel saw Moses, and behold, the skin of his face shone, and they were afraid to come near him.

31 But Moses called to them, and Aaron and all the leaders of the congregation returned to him, and Moses talked with them. 32 Afterward all the people of Israel came near, and he commanded them all that the Lord had spoken with him in Mount Sinai. 33 And when Moses had finished speaking with them, he put a veil over his face.

34 Whenever Moses went in before the Lord to speak with him, he would remove the veil, until he came out. And when he came out and told the people of Israel what he was commanded, 35 the people of Israel would see the face of Moses, that the skin of Moses' face was shining. And Moses would put the veil over his face again, until he went in to speak with him."

---

[38] Exodus 34:29-35 ESV

In this Old Testament passage, the Bible describes how being in the presence of God brought an unusual luster to Moses' face that impacted those around him. He was visibly different, and everyone could see it. We can take from this that, because joy is rooted in who God is, it is also rooted in all of His intentions. The Exodus passage above shows us that experiencing joy in the presence of God in a literal sense would be such a supernaturally profound event in our lives that it would require a veil of protection to allow us to interact with it.

In Psalm 21:6[39], King David described that God is most pleased to make His children eternally blessed and watch His children experience joy in His presence. While we express and experience a complete or full joy in the presence of God, bondage has no place! When trouble does come, all God's children need to do is cry out to the Father for help and experience the uplifting quality of His joy. It is part of why our light can shine in the world; the source of our radiance is in Jesus.

As the world entered wave after wave of the COVID-19 pandemic and its various mutations, it seemed easy to lose sight of joy. It's challenging to focus on tapping into a joy-filled relationship with God amid the stressors that come with burgeoning unemployment, loss of human life, spiking inflation, and other physical afflictions that threaten our wellbeing. As the pandemic situation continued unabated, many people worldwide experienced trauma, disillusionment, pain, grief, and a range of other complicated emotions.

There's no denying that all people suffer in this life. It is heartbreaking to see the pain that families walk through as they address ongoing afflictions, whether physical, emotional, mental, or spiritual. It might be external suffering that has shaped who we are as we go through child abuse or adverse childhood experiences, parental neglect or dysfunction, toxic relationships, illness, racism or other forms of

---

[39] Psalm 21:6 ESV

discrimination, or outright injustice. Others have battled within themselves, as internal threats have given rise to inappropriate desires, a sense of helplessness, or bitterness that makes it hard to forget. Is there freedom to be found when we are so trapped in pain, disillusionment, and suffering? Yes.

Freedom is something that nations fight for and defend at the pain of death. Countries send troops into battle to uphold their right to live as they choose because that freedom of choice is what makes humanity feel whole. Our Creator gives us the freedom to choose how we live because He put that free spirit within us. God does not dictate a command to follow as an authoritarian ruler might; it is a request, an expression of hope that we will choose Him. That means we have the option to decline His gift of love. However, choosing to accept salvation through Christ Jesus is the only way to access peace with God and all the joy that comes with it.

In trying to understand how to access the fullness of joy, we need to go back to the Word of God. David talks so fondly about the joy he finds in God's Word and provision in the psalms. These writings and songs continually remind us that joy is not a byproduct of circumstance. When we are hurting, choosing to lavish the oil of joy over sadness or doubt is only possible as a byproduct of our salvation in Jesus Christ. It is supernatural. However, choosing joy when we are suffering in the very core of our being requires a step from us that we so often sometimes miss--we must *refuse to be bound*.

Restore Joy and Embrace Freedom

Are you bound by something or someone? If you find yourself at a loss at how to answer that, it is helpful to think about things that are eating away at your joy. It might be a previous experience or trauma that has you reeling with guilt, shame, anger, or bitterness decades later.

Maybe, you are facing an ongoing struggle with unhealthy relationships, addiction, sickness, or financial worries.

Bondage is a complicated and controversial topic in anthropological circles throughout history, and Biblical descriptions of bondage include this same idea of restraint, forced submission, or slavery. In that sense, being bound is not something a person could just escape if they felt like it. The slaves of history could not just opt for a career change when they grew tired of the discrimination, work conditions, or suffering. There were chains and circumstances beyond their control that kept them in those situations.

Being enslaved leaves people entrenched in a place and time that they cannot control or change. The Bible often describes sin as bondage because it mires us in disobedience and rebellion against God, even when we have good intentions. For the Apostle Paul, bondage included physical imprisonment to stop him from preaching on the streets of various cities. He also had a rather dramatic conversion[40], from being a persecutor of Jesus' followers to a leading evangelist and missionary in the first-century church. In Romans 7[41], Paul spoke of his exasperation when he found himself doing the very thing that he absolutely did not want to do. It's easy to relate to that infuriating realization as we find ourselves falling back into old habits that aren't godly, kind, or loving. We know that gossip ruins relationships and makes people feel unloved, but our emotions take over and self-restraint goes out the window. In that instance, we are bound by selfish desires, lies, fear of rejection, or simply, a bad habit.

James describes bondage to sin as a result of *'passions at war within you*[42].' Obadiah put it as the *'pride of your heart*[43]' deceiving you. There is

---

[40] Acts 9 ESV
[41] Romans 7:15 ESV
[42] James 4:1-4 ESV
[43] Obadiah 1:3 ESV

much discussion in modern church forums on spiritual bondage, and the common theme is that the more power we give Satan over us, the more he controls us (or binds us) into sinful behavior. It's a power struggle, but only so far as we forget that God is more powerful than anything or anyone, including Satan and his legions.

Salvation is a breaking of chains, as the truth of Jesus' power slices through the lies of the Enemy. Our hearts open to the truth of our freedom, and the binding sin clatters to the ground. Nothing can entangle us like that once Jesus Christ liberates our souls.

As sin and temptation take their shots at us, we need to remember this picture of freedom. We stand before Jesus, the Conquering King, with the chains of sin and death at our feet. We look up to Him and know that He loves us, and we see Him beckoning to us. "Follow me," he says, as He walks away from the pile of dirty chains. He moves, directing our steps toward the light, with hope, peace, love, and immense joy now accessible through salvation. Sometimes, we need to stand awhile and wait for the Savior's signal. Other times, we move forward in faith, running into the open spaces we see before us and trusting Jesus to catch or redirect us if there's a cliff up ahead.

We may also notice some of those fallen chains being cunningly hung around us by invisible hands. What do we do when we see our old, loose chains in the hands of Satan, trying to rewrap themselves around us one by one? First, we pray, confess, and repent. Then, we draw on the power of the Holy Spirit to joy-up and refuse to be recaptured by our habits, sin, addictions, abuse cycle, and anything else that wants to drag us off course in our journey with Jesus Christ.

For David, bondage included physical, emotional, and spiritual aspects. As a young boy, David's place was as a shepherd tending his father's sheep. He was unimportant in the family line of succession, and he did not have the stature or responsibilities of the older brothers. He was bound by his circumstances, duty, and lack of resources. Like so many of us, David's ambitions grew with him. His youthful confidence took him onto a battlefield[44] where he had no business setting foot, let alone fighting giants like Goliath. Yet, God was with him on the journey, strengthening and protecting him. As David realized the path that God had set for him, his boldness grew, but so did his problems.

When David befriended Jonathan[45], King Saul's son, it must have seemed that the lowly shepherd boy had reached heights he could only dream of achieving. Can you imagine him walking into the royal courtyard with a wooden instrument slung over his back and his reddish hair and good looks blossoming into bigger and bigger life goals? Conflict upended his life soon after, as it would many times over.

How surreal it must have felt when David was on the run from Saul[46] the king, fearing for his life. Saul's jealousy continually threatened David's life, especially when Saul realized that God was clearly with the musician, shepherd, and soldier in all his endeavors. God saved David numerous times, including from Saul's years of murderous pursuit. In response, David penned Psalm 57[47], a beautiful picture of joy in the midst of fear and literal bondage as David was trapped inside a cave. While hiding from those trying to kill him, David praised God's protection and comfort. His response to God's mercy shows unconcealed joy and praise as he pours out his gratitude in song and poetry and shouts to '*awake the dawn*[48].'

Many years later, David replaced Saul as King of Israel. His life only became more complicated, but God continued to honor David's dedication to upholding the law and seeking God's will. Psalm 119:45 speaks about being able to '*walk in a wide place*[49]' because of the law being a form of security. In some translations this phrase indicates '*freedom.*' So,

---

[44] 1 Samuel 17 ESV
[45] 1 Samuel 18 ESV
[46] 1 Samuel 20-21 ESV
[47] Psalm 57
[48] Psalm 57:8 ESV
[49] Psalm 119:45 ESV

we can walk in freedom when we are careful to stay within the confines of God's precious law. It's not a contradiction--the law is the boundary that makes our path secure and straight. Without God's will to guide us, we run into briar bushes, steep inclines, snares and dangerous, rocky places. When David felt like he was hemmed in on all sides by threats and trouble, He sought the Word of God and prayed for deliverance. He did not give in to the bonds that threatened to draw him under the waves of despair or doubt.

David spent years on the run from various enemies, outlawed, and always in danger. Even when the way opened for him to accept the position as King and unite all twelve of Israel's tribes, the son of Saul would not give up the throne to the now-elected David or his new followers. Still, God was with His anointed one and David continued to trust that lead.

Later, David had to flee from his own son, Absalom (read about it in 2 Samuel 17). In Psalm 3, David recounts how the Lord saved his life during this terrible experience. Can you imagine having to run from your own son, a handsome and accomplished young man who could have done so much with his talents? David must have felt devastated at the turn of events. Yet, the third psalm ends with a statement of praise that says, "*Salvation belongs to the Lord*[50]." David's writings and life continually show that he understood this connection--it is God who has the right to save us, and if He chooses to do so, nothing can stop it. Whenever David fell into a sticky situation, he called out for deliverance and believed that God could (and would) rescue him from the circumstances, people, or emotions that had him bound and bleeding.

If David had been a different person, he might have chosen to accept fate, give up when obstacles arose, entertain anxiety, or marinate in bitterness. Any of us going through the same crazy life circumstances that

---

[50] Psalm 3:8 ESV

seemed to follow David might feel depressed, terrified, and angry on most days. Yet, the youngest son of Jesse chose to focus on God's saving grace and joy-up with steadfast faith.

Instead of fear and indignation, David focused on God's power to deliver us. He celebrated and broadcasted the Lord's love for His people at every opportunity. The powerful king called out to his all-powerful God when things were good, praising him, using poetry and songs to bless others, and drawing people back to the Living God of Israel. The fact that he did the same when things were horrific helps us understand how he came to be known as a '*man after God's own heart*[51].'

David often chose to insert joy and worship into his writing. Some of the psalms he wrote are raw, revealing a sense of urgency or even fear that must have felt like inescapable bonds. However, David's focus always went back to the certainty that God is in control and sovereign. Not every psalm of David speaks plainly of joy or rejoicing, but the heart of joy looks for ways to glorify God and rest in His salvation, and David did that masterfully.

The king's life didn't get easier as he grew more influential and extended his reach, either. When David's life had begun to unravel, the shepherd who became King reached a turning point. At the pinnacle of his royal career, after a foray into sin with Bathsheba, he returned to his roots and repented. As David confessed his struggles with sin, he wrote the fifty-first psalm, a poem of confession and praise.

In Psalm 51:12 David writes, *"Restore to me the joy of your salvation, and uphold me with a willing spirit*[52].*"* He fully understood that the Lord brings people lasting freedom, and that there is always a reason to joy-up, no matter the pain we are facing. David was a man who had truckloads of

---

[51] 1 Samuel 13:14 ESV
[52] Psalm 51:12 ESV

pain and suffering that seemed to keep him on his toes, but he was also a man who sought the heart of God and rejoiced in divine protection.

If you're going through a hard time, or want to support somebody else who is suffering, the first stop is to tap into the joy of salvation. God saves, and He does so again, and again. His grace and mercy are freely given as we enjoy the liberty of choosing how and where we will walk in life. Rejoice like David because we are free to worship and follow God, no matter how life looks or feels in any given moment.

Here are a few points to grapple with as we shake off our chains today:

- Embracing a spirit of joy is possible during suffering, grief, scary situations, and sinful struggles because Christ's beloved has complete freedom and peace in Him.
- The Holy Spirit is our connection to true and lasting joy because He empowers us. We find even deeper joy as we progress in our relationship and live a righteous life in step with God.
- Jesus Christ provides complete freedom because He broke our chains forever with His sacrifice.
- Nothing can remove His joy from us as we contemplate that salvation and realize our worth in Christ. However, we still have to shake off sin that entangles[53] daily; focusing on being more joyful and grateful is helpful in this challenge.

Setting Joy Free

In Nelson Mandela's *Long Walk to Freedom*[54], the first black president of South Africa, an ex-political prisoner, often spoke of the joy that is to be found in true freedom. He was a wise leader who worked for

---

[53] Hebrews 12:1 ESV
[54] Mandela, N. 2009

peaceful solutions in a country torn apart by racism, greed, and a long history of power struggles. It seems implausible that joy could come from such a place of injustice. There were years of innocent lives in bondage to inferior education, poverty, restrictions on free geographical movement, and many other forms of discrimination in South Africa. Yet, Nelson Mandela and many others throughout history have shown that it is possible to find contentment and celebrate a free life. When we realize that our freedom does not depend on where we are or who the world says we should be, there is much room for a grateful and happy existence. Freedom is a state of the heart and mind much more than it is a physical location.

For many people who have made progress on their journey of healing, the chaos of an ongoing civil war, rising unemployment, or a global pandemic might feel like a significant setback. How do we handle a barrage that threatens to force us back into a '*spirit of slavery*[55]' and fear? These internal and external threats can feel like an attack, and there might be some truth to that when we consider the spiritual forces at play. However, the last place we need to find ourselves is spiritually immobile.

Even Jonah[56] knew that he had a choice as he sat in the belly of a fish. His time there foreshadowed the three days that Jesus would spend in the throes of death. But Jonah's journey had started with outright refusal to obey God's calling, running in the opposite direction and climbing aboard a boat. When God pursued Jonah with storms on the water, Jonah asked the crew to save themselves by throwing him overboard. In God's mercy, Jonah was swept up by a creature for a time of reflection. He did not give up or die; he prayed. Jonah recognized that as a child of God, he was a free man. He saw that he did not need to be bound by fear or pain in that scary, unconscionable situation when God was nearby. Jonah

---

[55] Romans 8:15 ESV
[56] Jonah 1-4 ESV

could not change his circumstances at that moment, but he was well aware of whose power could provide an escape plan.

So, Jonah chose to pray fervently, repenting of his sin, and begging God for forgiveness and relief. He praised God, choosing to joy-up in the circumstances because he understood that, even in a potentially fatal situation, God was still in control. He rested in God's promise and chose to lift up the Holy One's name in worship and reverence. The result was that God gave Jonah another chance to fulfill His calling, and the contrite man then chose to do so to the best of his ability. The unlikely missionary must have found immense joy in taking that path into Nineveh and doing what God asked of him with the right attitude. Jonah's lifetime would still bring further suffering and more lessons that needed to be demonstrated 'the hard way' by his Heavenly Father, but he understood then how choosing obedience took him full tilt into the will of God. Obedience brings joy because it is the moment, we agree to press into God's best for us.

When the Bible recounts joy, it is often with this link to adversity. Perhaps, it is because suffering sweetens the joy we find in peacetime when we know pain. Why is joy even more possible during suffering, grief, scary situations, or 'old nature' struggles? The answer lies in perspective. The freedom that God's children enjoy in Christ is a great place from which to view life.

"There is therefore now no condemnation for those who are in Christ Jesus. [a] 2 For the law of the Spirit of life has set you[b] free in Christ Jesus from the law of sin and death."

-Romans 8:1-2 ESV

The promise that God has given to those who believe in Him and accept Jesus as their Savior is that we are free from condemnation[57]. That

---

[57] Romans 8:1-2

means that all our sins are *forgiven;* our debt is paid. Salvation promises that we will not have to suffer under the punishment due for disobedience and rebellion against God when the gavel falls at the world's final judgment. It is a massive free pass on death and destruction that most of us have not even begun to fathom.

One of the benefits of this liberty is everlasting joy in the presence of God, starting right here on earth. We are free because He has cleared our path to reach Him. He has broken the chains of sin and death that held us back before. Nothing can stop us now. There are no more hindrances when we want to run into the arms of Jesus and find comfort, protection, healing, rest, and unequivocal joy!

Jesus is the greatest example of how we can refuse to be bound by choosing to focus on the joy of our salvation. His story is unique in that He was both fully God and fully man, but His human experience was as vivid as ours. He still felt the nails drive into His hands and the weight of His body as it tried to hold itself together on the cross against the earth's gravity. Jesus' choice was to follow the will of God so that promises could be fulfilled, and people could be saved. It doesn't mean His experience wasn't excruciating, though.

Jesus was not bound by His circumstances as a helpless victim; He could have escaped or changed the course of events with a single word because He was God. However, the God-man knew that there was a plan in place, and He gladly put Himself into the will of God to run that race to the very end. Make no mistake, it was not a pleasant or desirable experience. His human emotion manifested in sweat drops of *blood*[58] as He prayed for strength the night before His arrest. However, Jesus was a willing participant in the suffering He endured because He understood that it aligned with the will of God. He knew that God the Father was

---

[58] Luke 22:44 ESV

with Him in everything that needed to happen. It kept Jesus' eyes on the *'joy set before him*[59]*'* to bring about the furtherance of God's Kingdom.

And, what happened in the moment where He faced the worst pain possible, disconnection from God the Father? Jesus chose to joy-up and remember His freedom. The Lamb of God chose to stay the full three days in the tomb so that His actions could fulfill prophecies, demonstrate God's promises, and free us from our bondage to sin when we could not do that for ourselves. Whether we feel like the target of a well-orchestrated attack or a more subtle trial, joy is a secret weapon. Suffering comes to all, as it did to Jesus when He went to the cross to secure our salvation. Our suffering may look vastly different to being put on trial and crucified by unjust and greedy men. It might look like traumatic events from childhood taking hold of your body and brain while you are trying to thrive in adult relationships. You might be reeling with grief as an unstoppable global pandemic has taken friends and loved ones. In all, real joy is possible when we know that we are truly free in Christ.

So, refusing to be bound is a choice to acknowledge our hard-bought freedom in the midst of a painful moment. Joy is not the first thing we reach for when the tears flow but when we reach for Jesus to lift us out of the mire, it is joy that follows.

The Ticket Out of Dodge City is Joy

When we submit to Christ, our daily struggle to face our sinful behaviors and attitude begins. However, the Holy Spirit's strength and guidance keep us moving forward in our sanctification process, as we learn what it means to shake off chains. It is this quiet voice that helps us to refuse to let anyone or anything wrap these entanglements around us a second or a third or a fourth time. The joyful heart of a child of God cannot and will not be bound by sin.

---

[59] Hebrews 12:2 ESV

This attitude of the heart isn't blind optimism or a peppy outlook toward anything that throws us off-balance in life. In Romans 8:1-2, it states plainly that there is no condemnation for those in Christ. When we look at how Jesus the Messiah set us free from sin's bonds, we understand how His actions saved souls from eternal death and provided an escape plan from sin. In this context, sin is disobedience to God's laws or rejection of His will, which most people do daily in some form or another. For instance, when we choose to cling to our own knowledge or exclude God from our decision-making process, it is sin. When we exhibit hate, racist remarks, impatience, or greed, it is sin. Disobeying God goes against how our Creator has asked us to live, act, and speak. People sin when they put their trust in money instead of God. Children sin when they dishonor their parents. Leaders sin when they put their own interests ahead of the good of the people they serve. We all sin, and we all deserve punishment for it (Romans 3:23 puts it as us falling 'short[60]' of God's glory).

The Apostle Paul had an intimate knowledge of how bondage against one's will test the depths of our souls and diminish our joy. By the time he was killed in an unknown location, Paul's body and mind knew a lot about being in survival mode. If anyone would have been an excellent subject for a study on trauma's brain and body responses, it was Paul. Yet, the Roman's chosen response to unending suffering was an exhortation of joy. He insisted that the church works on its consistency and determination to look for joy in its Savior. Paul continuously reiterates this message when he writes words like Philippians 4:4, *"Rejoice in the Lord always, and again I will say rejoice[61]."*

Later in this same passage, Paul described his newfound ability to be *'content in all things[62]'* He was not downplaying the situations that we come against nor denying the immense pain that we suffer and often have

---

[60] Romans 3:23 ESV
[61] Philippians 4:4 ESV
[62] Philippians 4:9-13 ESV

no choice but to face. Paul suffered, and badly. However, he knew that Jesus Christ walked right there beside him and that it would not last forever.

As we get to know Jesus as our Lord and Savior more intimately, it becomes easier to embrace this new identity. When we confess our sin, repent, and believe in Jesus Christ, our Redeemer breaks every chain that binds our hearts and minds. He also gives us the Holy Spirit's power for the tenacity we need to shake off these broken chains one by one, as we overcome our 'old' nature. The victorious words in 2 Corinthians 5:17 describe God's people as *'a new creation*[63]*.'* The prophet Ezekiel talked about this transformation as turning our hearts from stone to flesh[64], from unfeeling and unaware of how much we are enslaved to darkness into the light of love, peace, and joy.

As our relationship with Jesus Christ progresses, righteousness replaces our old, sinful way of thinking and behaving. It brings immense joy to realize who we are in Christ. It's this joy in salvation and relationship that keeps our heads up in times of trouble, when we can say:

"Though you have not seen him, you love him. Though you do not now see him, you believe in him and rejoice with joy that is inexpressible and filled with glory, 9 obtaining the outcome of your faith, the salvation of your souls."

-1 Peter 1:8-9

The Apostle Paul's stance on suffering was that it was part of life and that getting through it with the help of the Holy Spirit would gain us eternal rewards. When he was in prison, Paul and those arrested with him preached to the guards and sang joyfully in the darkness. Instead of worrying, they worshiped their Lord. When Paul was beaten and stoned and shipwrecked, he prayed, remembering that he was grateful to be alive,

---

[63] 2 Corinthians 5:17 ESV
[64] Ezekiel 36:26 ESV

and praising God with a joyful heart. He had a past, too. It might not be a stretch to imagine that many of the families he ministered to had known him in the past or known of him. His reputation was deplorable as Saul, a persecutor of early Christians. Before Saul became Paul, his hatred for those who followed Jesus was legendary across the Roman empire. Imagine trying to preach to someone whose mother or father or grandmother you killed, imprisoned, or falsely accused two decades earlier. Yet, he preached salvation and repentance, clinging onto the joy of his clean slate in Christ Jesus. *Your past cannot bind you when Jesus has granted you freedom.*

Paul was exceedingly familiar with the concept of bondage, both physically and spiritually. He wrote, *"For all who are led by the Spirit of God are sons of God. 15 For you did not receive the spirit of slavery to fall back into fear, but you have received the Spirit of adoption as sons, by whom we cry, "Abba! Father!" 16 The Spirit himself bears witness with our spirit that we are children of God,*[65]*"* Paul's life is further proof that, if we are to experience the fullness of joy that God so enjoys seeing on our countenance, bondage cannot be part of the story. We have to joy-up and refuse to be bound by circumstance, emotion, uncertainty, and anything that would see our joy in Christ Jesus diminish. Paul reiterates this call across his many letters to the different churches. He also reminds the churches to embrace their freedom in Christ[66] and keep choosing to live as free people even when it feels easier to give up. We should not fall back into the yoke of slavery just because we receive false comfort in the familiarity of brokenness.

---

[65] Romans 8: 14-16 ESV
[66] Galatians 5:1 ESV

Joy-UP For Today: Heaven is Coming

Seeking joy while we are suffering is not a flippant therapy tool or an on-switch for a complete attitude change. It is the ability that the Holy Spirit gives believers to dig deep and press into the heart of God. We cannot talk ourselves into being joyful without a genuine source of joy and hope that we can access when we need it most. That is not to say that there isn't value in uplifting our inner dialogue or choosing to think positively. Sometimes, speaking to ourselves in a kinder way is helpful, but it isn't a lasting solution for a soul steeped in anxiety, fear, self-doubt, shame, or guilt; only Christ's salvation can pour the oil of gladness onto those wounds and heal the hurt.

Choosing to joy-up amidst our brokenness is choosing to take refuge in Jesus Christ as our friend, Savior, and champion. When we know that the source of all joy and peace is Christ, we have the freedom to truly live. There are countless Scripture references about the freedom that believers have in Christ, and this is a cornerstone of Christian living. Freedom is secured by the blood of Jesus because sin no longer has that hold on us, the hold of a slave master who compels us to act or speak or think in a certain way. Isaiah 65:17-25 presents a beautiful picture of the kind of life that God wants to give us if we are willing to embrace our freedom in Christ. It says,

"For behold, I create new heavens and a new earth; And the former things will not be remembered or come to mind. "But be glad and rejoice forever in what I create; For behold, I create Jerusalem for rejoicing and her people for gladness. "I will also rejoice in Jerusalem and be glad in My people; And there will no longer be heard in her the voice of weeping and the sound of crying[67]."

---

[67] Isaiah 65:17-25 ESV

The joy of salvation that David sought so desperately was that first-love joy of connection with *the* Holy One. It sang alongside the joyous celebration of the heavenly host, as David's soul awakened to the beauty and majesty of the Living God. When David called out to God to restore the joy he had in his first experience of salvation, it was a stark realization that the sweetness of his joy had diminished with the advancement of sin. He had known a closeness with God in the beginning of the relationship when he was a shepherd playing sweet melodies in worship of his Creator. However, life got in the way, including when David's own choices landed him in trouble.

An example of how David's own actions caused entanglements in sin was his tryst with Bathsheba[68], the wife of another man. With all that had happened in his life, a worldly viewpoint might have said that he had hit the top of his game. The son of Jesse went from being a poor, simple man in one of the lowliest jobs available to being the second King of ancient Israel with access to riches, power, and anything else he wanted. Yet, there he was, committing adultery and ruining lives. David even had the woman's husband killed, by placing him on the front lines of battle so that he could take her as his wife. It was a low point that might fit the screenplay of a soap opera, yet by the end of David's life, he was a man revered for being in tune with the heart of God.

Every human being falls short of the glory of God in their own strength, even the mighty King David. Sin has consequences and we have to shake it off daily in our attitude, choices, and willingness to lean into God's will for us. We can choose to be grateful for what we have and acknowledge how far we have come in our walk with God. We can also choose to look up in those moments where we need a joy-up boost. God sees our deepest regrets and hurts with us.

---

[68] 2 Samuel 11 ESV

David's first son died as a terrible punishment for his poor choice to stray from the will of God. However, God still brought good from the tragedy. He recognized David's repentant and humble heart and comforted him. God also forgave David and redeemed Bathsheba's part in the story by honoring the promise He made in 2 Samuel 7. He put another one of the couple's sons, Solomon, on the throne to continue the line of succession, and that took future generations all the way to Jesus.

Gratitude and a long-term perspective on righteousness in Christ is an excellent way to feel more joyful when life seems to be unraveling, as it did for David or Moses or Paul. There *can* be honor in the wake of sin because God is merciful and wants us to know unending joy, despite our mistakes. The Scriptural accounts use intense language to describe the way God feels about breaking His people out of bondage. For example, Isaiah 61:1 speaks plainly about the intentions of God,

"The Spirit of the Lord God is upon me, because the Lord has anointed me to bring good news to the poor; he has sent me to bind up the brokenhearted, to proclaim liberty to the captives, and the opening of the prison to those who are bound;[69]*"* The good news that Isaiah spoke of in this passage heralded the arrival of Jesus Christ as God's Messiah. He was the Savior who would break the bonds of those enslaved to sin and bound by death and fear and disobedience. It was news that would heal broken hearts and bring comfort for those who were given the gift of faith. It was a proclamation of liberty because Jesus' sacrifice ended the quest for atonement, once and for all. God put all of this in the heart of Isaiah hundreds of years before Jesus was born to make it happen. Even then, it brought such joy to those who heard it that they spoke of it and passed it down to their children for every generation thereafter.

At Calvary, Jesus Christ restored that full and irrevocable joy that David knew was available. People who were formerly under the control of

---

[69] Isaiah 61:1 ESV

sin and destined for eternal death or disconnection from their Creator were suddenly confronted with an open door and a life-changing decision to walk through it into freedom. The perfect Lamb of God broke our chains forever, and nothing can remove the joy of our Salvation in Him. There is also much to be said about God's grace and kindness in helping us choose wisely when (not if) we walk through temptation, doubt, and fear. The joy we have in Christ is not the opposite of suffering, but *in spite of* that suffering and in the midst of it.

David experienced these kinds of situations continually on his dramatic path to the royal throne, with his suffering only increasing once he became a successful, rich, and powerful leader. If there is a common thread in the stories of Paul, David, and Moses, it is the joy each of these men of God found in doing life alongside Jesus Christ. They each had struggles and unique vices that kept enticing them back into sin, but it was their joy in salvation that kept them coming back to the Joy Giver.

Joy UP with Jesus

Do we have the grit to be like the Hebrews[70], 'joyfully' accepting other people plundering our property and having compassion on prisoners who had done great harm within their communities? Perhaps, they understood the joy that is to be found in salvation in Christ Jesus a little clearer than many of us do today. It shouldn't surprise us that Jesus uses the same language as the Apostle Paul to describe sin as a yoke (of slavery). Letters to the Galatians, Romans, and other churches showed how Paul understood the binding quality of sin and death that seems to hold us back and keep us plowing into bad decisions. When Jesus asks us to take on His yoke, he takes this same imagery and turns it on its head. A yoke has two oxen to plow beside each other, and Jesus' call is to swap out a yoke of sin for a yoke of joy.

---

[70] Hebrews 10:34 ESV

The imagery of a yoke is a beautiful concept in our Christian walk. Brannon Deibert[71] unpacks this idea by describing how Jesus invites us into His yoke as the second 'ox' to labor alongside Him on the path of righteousness. He is the master, and we only have to follow His lead, one step at a time. We get to do this in complete peace, knowing that He loves us and connecting with Him joyfully as we see where He takes us. Life is still labor, still hard work. However, it is so much more rewarding to walk and talk with God beside us. Suffering feels lighter when we can share small and great victories together, hand over our burdens, and ask questions when we are unsure of what to do. Walking beside Jesus lets us tell Him immediately when we are feeling like we need help or becoming overwhelmed. Then, we listen for His reply.

Submitting to Jesus' lead is very different from being forced into bondage on a path that leads to a lonely death. Instead of being stuck in disobedience to God or forced into repeating the same mistakes over and over again, we are called into freedom. The yoke of Jesus keeps us safe and happy, firmly entrenched in the will of God and walking alongside our Lord. Part of God's gift of free will is that we get to choose whether to put on the light, joyful yoke of Jesus Christ or to stay bound in our sin that keeps us from a right relationship with the giver of joy. If we choose to follow Jesus, we have access to the fullness of joy in the most direct way, for our good and God's glory. We can walk daily, building a relationship with Jesus Christ and basking in the joy of our salvation as we achieve all that He has set before us.

---

[71] Deibert, B. 2019

CHAPTER 4
Joy-Up: Through Introspection!

By virtue of our human nature which was conceived in sin and shaped in iniquity, each of us has a story. Although there may be a plethora of awesome plots and unending memories of laughter we cannot escape this sin-prone nature that inevitably results in sin or missing the mark which constantly, diminishes our joy. Whether our intentions failed by trials or unplanned twists in the plot, there are too many to number in the human condition. So, despite our best intentions, there are times when we are robbed of our joy because of the sin within our own hearts.

Paul, a servant of Christ, mentioned the war[72] within us. His anecdote explains the reasons behind our frustration because when we long to do well, evil lurks, and intentions fail. The good news of salvation is that this condition can be overcome by the power of the Holy Spirit that is now a fixture in our lives. He is stronger than any pull toward our old, sinful ways. John, who described himself as the disciple "whom God loves[73]," revealed that God bestows upon His children the power to become legitimate sons and daughters. From John, we realize the truth of the promise that *"all who did receive him, who believed in his name, he gave the right to become children of God.*[74]*"* This section of our joy-up

---

[72] Romans 7:23 ESV
[73] John 21:7 ESV

discussion deals with the experience of drawing from the well of the joy of our salvation[75]. We can become joy-filled individuals, anointed to walk in the freedom of God's presence. We can find a fullness of joy[76] in the presence of our Heavenly Father, and we do it through biblical introspection.

Yet, we do not look within to punish ourselves or evoke guilt and shame. Introspection is not an isolated act of self-degradation or a misguided attempt to motivate ourselves to a better life. No, biblical introspection means to see ourselves in relation to Christ. Through God's Word, we learn that it is God the Father's good and perfect will includes His desire to work in us and help us act to achieve His purpose. We find this type of promise in passages like Philippians 2:13, "**for** *it is God who works in you, both to will and to work for his good pleasure.*[77]" This means that as life typically throws us into temptations to stray from the joy of our salvation, we must recharge. We must choose to seek and receive many "fillings" or re-fillings of joy as the Holy Spirit works in us.

Those that abide in the True Vine[78] have the Father's pruning hands working continuously for our good and His glory. The Holy Spirit has a special purpose assigned to each one of us, a divine purpose that brings us closer to Jesus. It is His will that we walk closer to Him each day by dwelling on the Word's power in our lives, including its discipline. When the Holy Spirit convicts us of spiritual depravity, it is to bring us closer to Jesus through forgiveness and a fresh start. His purpose is not to guilt-trip us into action but to give us a clear picture of how loved we are by our Heavenly Father. He loves us, and calls us sons and daughters, co-heirs to the throne.

---

[74] John 1:12 ESV
[75] Psalm 51:12 ESV
[76] Psalm 16:11 ESV
[77] Philippians 2:13 ESV
[78] John 15:1 ESV

Introspection is a crucial part of the joy-up process. When we delve into the Word and look for specific details about our identity in Christ, we make introspection a valuable tool in our sanctification. We should typify this personal self-contemplation with the Word of God as our yardstick. It should be a joyous occasion for us when we clear the way to become better recipients of joy--the same joy that Christ wants to share with us. The power to "become" more joyful is a transformative process that looks and feels more like Christ-centered introspection. What does Christ see when He looks into our hearts? We need to go deeper into His Word to find out.

When life throws us challenges that rob us of our joy, we must choose to look for the opportunity to humble ourselves so that the Holy Spirit can work in us. He reveals God's will and acts on God's behalf to make us look and see things more like God does. He does this so that we can enjoy Him more, as is our life's purpose. Isn't that amazing? The Holy Spirit seeks to show us our sins, our attempts at self-sufficiency, our pride and selfishness, and our spiritual complacency so that He can lead us to a more profound, radiant, and joy-filled sufficiency that is found in Christ alone. In God's presence, there is fullness of joy and at His right hand there are pleasures evermore[79]; endless blessings and joy await when we look into our redeemed hearts to see what God sees.

It is also helpful to think of joy in the context of 'percolating,' which refers to the process of being filtered to greater osmosis. When God's children enter His space, where there is fullness of joy, that jubilation begins to percolate within our very souls. It isn't stagnant, even though it may appear to be so in the beginning. Oh, it is working, through heat and pressure from deep within. When our joy becomes stagnant, it might be because we have wandered and strayed outside of His presence. To joy-up, we need to delve into our relationship with God through His Word and reconnect with the source of our full and unending joy: Jesus Christ.

---

[79] Psalm 16:11 ESV

Finding joy through Word-based introspection is not a new biblical concept, but neither is it an insignificant one. The Bible mentions the idea of motion in Heaven over just one soul that repents of its sin and turns back to Christ. Repentance is the force that sets the joy-up process into percolated motion, but most believers do not do it as often as they should to open the way for joy. Oddly, we often fall into numbness, which becomes the new normal until we find ourselves in a big mess! We were meant for joy, and numbness detracts from this God-given freedom to enjoy life with Him. When we find ourselves going through a cycle of falling in and out of fellowship with God, the first thing we need to do is to recognize our sense of loss and turn back to Him.

According to Luke 15:7, the angels in Heaven experience joy over our one soul reuniting with God, compared to ninety-nine other souls who do not need that specific moment of repentance. Why? Because Heaven is amazed to see our freedom in Christ, knowing that we are not likely to be condemned to darkness if we accept God's gift of salvation and redemption. Instead, we are more likely to enjoy the display of God's splendor and His own excitement to reconnect with us on that level. The Father loves to see us coming back to a place where we are actively seeking a relationship with Him. He longs to see us ready to enjoy a father-son or father-daughter relationship in all its fullness. Isn't God awesome?

What an amazing revelation of the atmosphere of Heaven it is to think about how our own repentance and relationship with God brings joy to everyone watching the plan unfold. God's love for us is moving so many hearts to joyful celebration. When we embrace more of God's presence in our lives, each move we make toward Him inspires jubilant responses in heaven, as the people of God celebrate our discovery alongside us. It reveals how much God loves us, in spite of the situation. God's love for us is indeed awe-inspiring!

When a person repents, the very act of humbling themselves before God brings a full and lasting joy to all those who witness it from heaven.

As Christ's followers, we want there to be constant joy in heaven. We want repentance to become a welcomed and typified experience in our lives, don't we? Whether we like it or not, every person is a sinner without the Redeemer's gift of salvation, and the wages of sin is...death[80].

In Luke's gospel, the lost coin[81] represents all who need to be found; this includes everyone before Christ takes hold of their hearts through His gift of salvation. We are out of the purse, so to speak, and we need to be found by the Person to whom we belong. Only He can put us in a place where we can find our rightful purpose and rejoice in the acceptance we find there. There is another small but significant idea in this story--the lost coin needs *someone* to find it and put it back where it belongs. Human beings are born lost, thanks to sin. We find ourselves outside of the Kingdom, and we need the Faithful One to find us for that to change! We cannot repent of brokenness or embrace purity or save ourselves; we need the Holy Spirit to awaken us into a new joy of repentance.

"The wind blows where it wishes, and you hear its sound, but you do not know where it comes from or where it goes. So, it is with everyone who is born of the Spirit.[82]" We can be born again by a mighty act of intervention that, thankfully, God blows our way! Each one of us needs that new birth, and it starts with a contrite heart. Repentance brings the radical change of turning away and making massive changes as we are born again into a new creature, with a new heart and a new spirit.

In the same way that Jesus imparts the parable of the lost coin's discovery and redemption, we need Him to find us in the darkness and sweep us into the light. It is even more than picking up a shabby old coin for collection and distribution, though. Salvation is the Holy Spirit's powerful act of plucking us out of guilt and shame and blowing new life into our deadened hearts. He admires our new form, rejoicing over us as

---

[80] Romans 6:23 ESV
[81] Luke 15:8-10 ESV
[82] John 3:8 ESV

He shines up every part of who we are so that we can reflect God's glory more effectively. He wants the shimmering joy He radiates to penetrate our souls and then bounce right back off of us. Whoever sees us will know that Our Rescuer brings abundant life and real joy, as He works His purposes in our hearts. After the rescue, we do not look or feel the same way ever again. We are alive, and our joyful reunion with the One to whom we belong becomes the only thing that matters in life.

The Joy of Reunification

Whether we are a coin that has just been found or one in the process of being shined up, there is a process that has started within us. When we aim for joy through biblical introspection, the Holy Spirit begins this work of salvation by drawing our eye to the obstacles that are keeping us from the joy we seek. We can't help but notice these dark shadows on our souls as we see the light of salvation.

When Jesus begins the well-known story about the Prodigal Son in Luke 15:11-32, He highlights a few critical components of this introspective process. He also shows how humility ultimately leads to the inheritance of joy through the gate of ongoing repentance.

When the younger son asks for his portion of the inheritance, the father grants the request without hesitation. The son leaves a few days later to seek a life of adventure with his newfound wealth, savoring pleasures along the way and soon running out of money. His lifestyle leads him further down the path, with poor choices ruining his financial independence and landing him in a position where nobody is willing to help him with work or food. The son's last hope is to take a menial job as a pig herd, a smelly, thankless position that would have stripped him of his last threads of dignity (especially if he were Jewish).

At that point, the penniless pleasure-seeker was so hungry that he contemplated stealing the pigs' food, until '*He came to himself*[83]' and realized that pride was no longer a good reason to remain in those circumstances. The son could go home to his father and brother, even if he planned to offer himself as one of his father's servants. His indignity had reached such a low that he could not fathom the idea of pompously reclaiming any position as an heir or equal.

As the son looked into his own heart and measured its worth, he saw a problem. His choices had led down a path he never intended or imagined, and he found himself doing grievous, disgraceful things along the way. Taking time to look into how we got to where we are is never easy. It requires us to look past our blind spots and expectations to the reality of how we appear through the eyes of the LORD. That yardstick is the only true measure of our heart's worth, and our meditation on God's Word is the only way to delve into that truth deeply. The wayward son might have looked into his heart and seen mistakes, pain, unhealthy obsession, and a tendency to pursue instant gratification. When he looked at the reality of those qualities against the purity of His father's love, he knew that going home remained an option. He also knew that it required a humility he did not possess at the start of his fateful journey.

However, what that humbled soul did not yet know was just how completely that kind of love would cover '*a multitude of sins*[84].' The reunion looked entirely different from the son's expectations of seeing his family again. Instead of contempt, the father's reaction was one of complete and utter joy at his son's return. There was no blame, no lecturing. There were no questions about how the son could have squandered such vast wealth on the kind of lifestyle that other families in that culture would have been justified in shunning or even punishing. As the disgraced heir lifted his eyes toward home, all he saw was his father running toward him so that he could wrap him in a long-awaited hug. Instead of bitter, angry words, the return was met with unadulterated

---

[83] Luke 15:16 ESV
[84] 1 Peter 4:8 ESV

jubilation and ostentatious celebration--the lost boy had returned and everything was going to be alright!

Jesus provided a joy-up revelation for us in this striking picture of grace and love. The Father's arms are wide open and waiting for us, ecstatic that we have chosen to return to Him instead of wallowing in the dirt. No act or choice can keep us from the love of God. There is always a way back, and there will be joy in the return.

The wayward son's foray to a far-off country and subsequent fall from grace is also confirmation that the emotion of happiness is fleeting. The search for joy brought the son to poverty because he looked for fulfillment in physical pleasures, knowledge, friendships, entertainment, and many other sources of instant gratification. His choice was the same one that so many of us make when we pursue joy in fleeting pleasures. It leads us to misery, depression, and despair until we come to our senses and realize that we have the choice to turn around.

We can go back home.

We can return to the Heavenly Father, no matter what we have done to land ourselves in trouble. As forgiven and redeemed children of God, we have the option to reunite with the One who has brought us abundant life. All of heaven will rejoice alongside our Abba Father at the sight of our homecoming--all we have to do is point our feet in the right direction and take one step at a time. We have to fix our eyes on our Father and take another step.

As Jesus relayed the story of The Prodigal Son, we see that the context is also one of deep introspection. The young man-made choices that led him into troubled waters without a lifeboat. As he sat in the mud, starving, bankrupt, and drowning in self-pity, he realized that he had a decision looming. He recognized his desperation and that he had lost his way. As he pondered the situation and the choices that led him to that point, he also recognized that the only way to find what he needed was to go back to where he belonged. This is a profound climax to Jesus' lesson--

it is our choice to leave, and it is our choice to return. So many of us miss this truth when we are chin-deep in the tumultuous waves of challenges or pain or grief or depression, feeling more panic rising with every breath.

Take heart; God has created us with freedom of choice. However, He has also given us the tools to exercise that freedom in the way that gets us to where we need to be. God's Word is a lamp to our feet[85] when the darkness seems to be closing in; it is that lifeboat we need when we choose the freedom of returning to higher ground. When we wallow in self-pity or feel trapped by our past, the choice to return home is ours to make. We might decide to turn around, flee, cry for mercy, or cry out for a pardon from the God we have disobeyed. Whatever we do, it remains solely our responsibility to choose that freedom in Christ, and only ours.

If we do choose the path back home, it is only possible to make the journey with a heart that knows where it went wrong. We have to acknowledge and confess our wrongdoing to be able to change the trajectory of our lives. The prodigal son returned home humbled and ready to bear the weight of his transgressions; he knew that being home was the key to accessing joy, even if that meant accepting the role of a servant rather than a son. Repentance is required for joy, but God is also merciful. He pours grace upon us when we choose rightly. It doesn't matter what you have done--joy awaits your return to the Father.

This concept of reunification is clearly framed by Spirit-filled joy. All of heaven rejoices at the returning of one lost soul, even with ninety-nine already saved[86]. The Prodigal Son's father rejoiced at the chance to reunite with his beloved son, despite the mistreatment of the family or terrible life choices. When we look at the prodigal's audacious request to receive the inheritance early, we must also realize that he was treating His Father as though he was already dead. The relationship was broken, and the son was writing off the father's life as unimportant; the man was of no value to his

---

[85] Psalm 119:105 ESV
[86] Luke 15:7 ESV

own child. Imagine the heartbreak at hearing this request from your son or daughter in that ancient culture where family meant everything.

Today, we still live for legacy, wanting to give our children the lives they "deserve." Imagine giving all of that and receiving such bitter rejection in return; the child you raised, looking at you as though you were dead to them. The story does not say whether the father begged and pleaded with his son to stay or what reparations he tried to make to the relationship. Jesus' anecdote does not tell us how the son came to be so ungrateful or even hateful toward his father. All it shows is the father granting the request, and the son's subsequent choice to leave.

The son knew what he was choosing. He understood that leaving home in this manner was akin to disowning the family. He would not likely have planned to return because what use is a benefactor who has no other resources left to give? It seems harsh, but that's all the son seemed to want out of the relationship with his father, material wealth. He went to great lengths to get it, offending the cultural practice of looking after and respecting one's parents in their old age. We can easily look at his actions and shake our heads in disbelief, warning our own children never to treat us in such a disrespectful or unloving way. However, our sins against our Heavenly Father are just as grievous. The Word shines a light onto our choices, illuminating the path we have taken, and it isn't pretty.

The Prodigal Son realized that he had reduced himself to humiliation (the pigs were the lowest point he could have reached as a respectable Jewish man). However, that didn't stop him from realizing that he wanted to return home. Even at his worst, he knew there would be room in his Father's house. As he made the choice to get up from the dirt and start walking, this action dictated his future. We might feel humiliated against the backdrop of an unfeeling and uncaring world, but still, we are able to return to Jesus and rejoice at the prospect of reunification.

Enter Into Joy

The Prodigal Son was never reduced to a servant. Instead, the real servants prepared a feast in his honor at the request of an ecstatic father. God loves us like that. We are His children, and He does not begrudge us for our sins when we return to Him in repentance. God does not point fingers at us and click His tongue; instead, He sees us from far off making the right choice and runs to meet us with a loving, joyous embrace. The Heavenly Father looks for His child's return and waits eagerly. He greets the son or daughter with unconcealed joy. If we open our hearts in humble repentance, the joy found at this celebrated reunification can replace any doubt or shame that might still try to lodge itself there. When we repent and return, we find joy waiting on the doorstep.

Today's Christians want to be affirmed and comforted, but if we are lost coins or lost sheep, repentance is the key to finding our joy-up moment in Christ. Even as the older son becomes upset, the prodigal's father reminds him that everything the father has is already the oldest son's inheritance; his worth in the eyes of the father did not diminish because of a lost brother's return. The older son's faithfulness was acknowledged, and his reward remained intact. When we see sinners coming to repentance and receiving new life, we have to realize the same truth. It is fitting and appropriate that we celebrate the return of a lost soul with joy. *"He was dead and is now alive forevermore!"*[87] and that is truly something to celebrate when we realize that we were ALL lost and found, and we all still need daily repentance.

Introspection leads to joy because it reveals our darkness against the light of God's Word. We can pick apart our failures with joy because we have a Savior who is strong enough and kind enough to help us change. However, the first step is always ours to take. Repentance is ongoing because sin is entrenched in our habits and tendencies while we are still on

---

[87] Luke 15:24 ESV

our way home. We must repent, and often. We must add these acts of confession and confrontation to our daily experience, asking the Holy Spirit to help us see the truth. How can we replace those choices with godly, righteous ones if we do not make repentance a part of daily life? Hesitation or pride will only lead us to a greater risk of returning to a life of chains.

In Chapter 3, we explored the concept of choosing joy while refusing to be bound by temptation, habits, worldly idols. Nothing should have the power to draw our gaze away from Jesus Christ, but all of us will continue to have weak moments. The Holy Spirit's role here is crucial, making it possible for us to exercise our freedom of choice. We can return to God, or we can move further into our disobedience, ingratitude, or outright rebellion. In those moments, the key is to repent and rejoice in Christ's salvation.

Whether we find ourselves at the end of our ropes or just stopping for a sideshow, we must remember the choice. We can choose to go into the tavern and squander our inheritance or we can choose to turn around, look toward home, and take one step after another until the temptation is behind us. Even if we find ourselves entering the diversion, sitting down at a table, and becoming immersed in the distractions, we can still escape. We can always choose to do what is right with the power of the Holy Spirit and a revelation of God's Word.

Do you need to stop, get up, and walk out? Look at your heart and ask the Holy Spirit to help you put your feet firmly back on the path in a posture of genuine repentance.

There is no greater joy than knowing that we are headed to where God would have us go. All of heaven will rejoice in that decision alongside us. If we obey God faithfully, from a heart of love and adoration, the reward is the joy of the Lord. In this choice to follow him, step by step, day by day, we find an abundance of blessings. When we finally reach home at the end of that journey, there will be a feast awaiting us as our

Heavenly Father exclaims, *"Well done, good and faithful servant. You have been faithful over a few things; I will set you over many things. Enter into the joy of your lord.*[88]*"*

In Jesus' parable, there is also an important note about the reunification that we should not miss. Jesus calls all people to repent and return to God with humility, even respectable people like the older brother. Understandably, the older brother showed indignation at the father's request for a feast in honor of the family traitor. He was upset at the grace shown toward his younger brother. He may have believed that punishment was more appropriate, but the father gently reminds him that the same treatment would apply if it were him coming home. A holy transformation of the heart is always a cause for real, Spirit-filled joy. Even 'respectable' Christians need to repent of their assumptions that they are more deserving of reward or recognition than others who have done "worse" things or failed to please God in some way. This is a false and dangerous belief--Jesus says that every single lost soul is valuable, and each of us was lost before grace and mercy found us.

God's Word reiterates this point in passages like Philippians 2:1-2, calling His people to participate in the Spirit of affection and sympathy and being unified in joy and love. We all need repentance, and we can all be joyful, whether we are on the path, or already home. Christians who are truly saved will rejoice at the repentance and salvation of every soul, celebrating in the very same way as when they themselves received that eternal blessing.

The Wells of Joy

When God finds the one lost sheep, he doesn't look at the tally and say, "Well, I have ninety-nine and that's good enough." No; He rejoices in the prospect of finding the one lost sheep and bringing it back to the

---

[88] Matthew 25:21 ESV

flock[89]. The shepherd cares for each one, including you. He leaves those who are safe in the fold and actively pursues the soul that is lost, looking through rocks, ravines, thickets, forests, and rivers until He finds the sheep that needs help. He doesn't give up! When He finds the lost sheep, He doesn't beat it with a rod for running away or being unfaithful. Instead, He picks it up and carries it back to the fold where it can recover in peace, knowing it is loved beyond measure.

When Jesus brings us home, He says, *"Rejoice with me because my lost sheep is found. Be glad with me!*[90]*"* There is joy in heaven over the one; the angels rejoice, and a great cloud of witnesses join the celebration! God's people that have reached heaven--brothers, sisters, uncles, aunts, friends, relatives, and neighbors--rejoice over each soul that was a breath away from destruction and is now safe in the fold of the Good Shepherd.

When Jesus imparts the story of the woman at a well[91], we see this concept of 'being found' even more powerfully. A Samaritan woman with a sordid reputation draws water while the well is quiet, and Jesus engages her in a stunning conversation. Firstly, she is surprised that a Jewish man is asking a Samaritan woman for a drink of water when this was highly counter-cultural. However, He then tells her that His own Living Water would ensure that she would never be thirsty again. It is not a trick, a magic show, or a proposition to start a business venture. She bravely calls him out on the practical implications, saying, *"Sir, you have nothing to draw water with and the well is deep.*[92]*"* But, when she asks Him for this Living Water, Jesus cuts to the heart of the matter and asks her to call her husband. She does not have one, and the perfect stranger then tells her what He knows about her love life. It is a test to see whether she will be truthful about her life choices.

---

[89] Matthew 18:10-14 ESV
[90] Luke 15:6-7 ESV
[91] John 4:5-32 ESV
[92] John 4:11 ESV

Stunned, the woman dares to look into her own heart. She confesses her sin to the Savior and passes the test. Jesus then speaks plainly with her about His role as the Messiah and tells her what will happen when God's promise of salvation comes to fruition. She is so honored by the exchange, and excited about what she has heard, that she runs straight to town and urges others to come to Christ. Her joy at meeting Jesus was so full that it overflowed; she went into the place where she had known shame and rejection, boldly sharing the life-changing news with everyone she met.

Jesus pursued a connection with this woman of questionable ethics and encouraged her to open her heart. He asked her hard questions, forcing her to look into her life and recognize the sin that lay beneath the surface. She had to see what was broken before she could understand that what Jesus offered was the opposite--a perfect wholeness and joy in a relationship with the Savior. Jesus did not condemn or ridicule her as she was probably accustomed to experiencing in such a traditional and religious society. Instead, Jesus offered her an opportunity for introspection so that she could access the everlasting wells of joy that He holds out to all who believe in Him. The woman's jubilation was clear, and she drank so deeply from the wells of joy that Jesus provided. She was so filled with the Savior's love and joy that she could not wait to go and tell others where they could find the same blessing.

The story is profound in many ways, but one of the key elements is how Jesus pursued that encounter at the very moment the woman would be able to experience the Spirit's transformative power. She was ready to hear Jesus' message as she drew water by herself, working hard in the midday sun. She was thirsty and probably physically and emotionally tired. Yet, all this culminated in an opportunity. Her circumstances prepared her heart to receive God's Word, for His pearls of truth to break open her soul and grant her everlasting joy.

Jesus did not have to go out of His way to go to Samaria, but He considered it a need to go that way. When He did connect with the woman at the well, He used the setting to emphasize the message He wanted to share with the world. For example, Jesus compared the well of water to the depth of everything He knew about this woman; He knew what would satisfy her thirst. She was looking for fulfillment in all the wrong places, like the Prodigal Son, and Jesus' solution was to bring her back to introspection with the backdrop of gospel-based truth. Jesus, the Messiah, let the woman know that He was everything she needed in no uncertain terms. She only had to accept His Living Water to come to a place of complete and utter joy.

In essence, the Son of God offered this sinful woman a joy-up moment. In doing so, He revealed the secret of how all who believe can keep accessing that joy forever. When the woman responded to Jesus' questions and call, He seemed totally unphased by the state of her soul before God. His focus was on what He could offer her, as He looked beyond her faults to her thirsty soul. He does the same for each of us, as we lift our eyes and engage with Him in holy conversations.

Jesus offered the woman Living Water, and she received her fill of joy alongside a newfound desire to return to the well with her LORD. Just as Christ found the woman in that dusty place, this book has reached your hands. You might not be in the same state of darkness or despair as this woman, but God's Spirit will indwell your heart in its own quiet space if you seek that connection. He does not offer condemnation, only love. The Lamb of God does not offer guilt or shame as you engage with Him, only eternal joy. Look into your heart and see what He sees, and then let the Word of God wash over you with Living Water as you open your eyes to how much Jesus loves *you*.

Why does the Father wait for the wayward son?

Why does the Son of Man seek out the sinful woman at the well?

Why does the Good Shepherd seek the lost one when there are ninety-nine perfectly reliable sheep in the fold? Because joy is in the recovery.

Joy is to be found in the turning and the returning, and in the hard choice to look at the real state of our souls. Joy is there when we seem to be at rock-bottom because Jesus is there, too. Take His joy with both hands, like a refreshing drink of cool water on a beautiful summer's day.

Everlasting Hope and Joy in Christ's Reign

In all these stories, we see an element of hope. What does the prodigal's father reveal by his reaction? Jesus uses this parable to demonstrate that there is only joy in the return to Christ, not condemnation. When we misuse our freedom and then turn away from those choices, God is more concerned about showering us with joy and affection than expressing displeasure. Our loving, kind Heavenly Father is ready to indulge His children and celebrate their homecoming.

Sin is always going to drain us because it is a state of brokenness that hinders our connection with God. Moral sin is always going to place us in a worse state than when we began because it moves us further and further away from the will of God. We were not made to thrive outside of a relationship with God--we need Him, and He wants to welcome us back into the fold with jubilation. It's where we belong, and we should never resent coming back to the Father or seeking the Father's own joy for our lives!

Seek to experience a joy-up moment when you need it; imagine it and embrace it. Picture a most gracious and dramatic celebration in all of heaven each time you come to realize that your sin needs to be handled. The angels rejoice with you when you pluck sin from your heart and swiftly place it under the blood of Jesus. God's people cheer as you return to embrace the Father, knowing to whom you belong.

That realization of seeing our joy diminish as we move away from God is the Holy Spirit's reminder to stop, repent, turn around, and then keep moving toward home. When we evaluate what we think about Jesus Christ through the scope of God's Word, we see what our hearts want to hide in the darkness. If you are seeing your joy wane, take a moment to stop and immerse yourself in the Living Water, the Word of God, for some biblical introspection. Ask the Holy Spirit to speak to you and reveal the way back home so that the celebrations can begin.

The prodigal thought of home and felt that glimmer of hope rising in his chest, despite dire circumstances. The woman at the well looked into her soul as Jesus spoke and realized that she needed the joy and fulfillment he offered. When we open our eyes to what our hearts need, the only possible source of joy, hope, and unconditional love is Jesus Christ, our LORD and Savior. Paul puts it well in Romans 15:13 when he says, *"May the God of hope fill you with all joy and peace in believing, so that by the power of the Holy Spirit you may abound in hope.[93]"* The Spirit gives us hope enough to seek that joy-up moment. He reminds us of how valuable we are to the God who made us, and He encourages us to repent of the sin in our hearts and return home to the joy that awaits.

Joy is the Answer to the Heart's Cry

We could speak of King David's joyful connection with Father God all day long, but the story would not be complete with a reminder that even great men and women fall short of the glory of God. When he sinned and sought an illicit relationship with Bathsheba[94], a married woman, David fell into patterns of sin that stunted his joy and made life immeasurably more challenging. He was the king but using his freedom to

---

[93] Romans 15:13 ESV
[94] 2 Samuel 11-13 ESV

pursue unholy endeavors drained his joy quickly. He was the height of his reign, and yet, it was the place where he fell hardest.

By the time the ordeal climaxed in the death of David and Bathsheba's son[95]--a consequence of these poor life choices--he was completely devoid of the joy he once had. As David realized that it was time for a change, the king turned from his terrible sin and lifted his eyes to the promises of God that seemed such a long way off. He took the first steps toward home and didn't look back. There were still consequences that followed this time in his life, and hard things going on, but David's heart was back to where it needed to be in returning to the Father's embrace.

Psalm 51 was the culmination of David's repentance as he cried out to God from arguably his lowest point in life.

51 Have mercy on me, O God, according to your steadfast love; according to your abundant mercy blot out my transgressions. 2 Wash me thoroughly from my iniquity, and cleanse me from my sin! 3 For I know my transgressions, and my sin is ever before me. 4 Against you, you only, have I sinned and done what is evil in your sight, so that you may be justified in your words and blameless in your judgment. 5 Behold, I was brought forth in iniquity, and in sin did my mother conceive me. 6 Behold, you delight in truth in the inward being, and you teach me wisdom in the secret heart. 7 Purge me with hyssop, and I shall be clean; wash me, and I shall be whiter than snow. 8 Let me hear joy and gladness; let the bones that you have broken rejoice. 9 Hide your face from my sins, and blot out all my iniquities. 10 Create in me a clean heart, O God, and renew a right[b] spirit within me. 11 Cast me not away from your presence, and take not your Holy Spirit from me. 12 Restore to me the joy of your salvation, and uphold me with a willing spirit. 13 Then I will teach transgressors your ways, and sinners will return to you. 14 Deliver me from bloodguiltiness, O God, O God of my salvation, and my tongue will sing aloud of your righteousness. 15 O Lord, open my lips, and

---

[95] 2 Samuel 12:18 ESV

my mouth will declare your praise. 16 For you will not delight in sacrifice, or I would give it; you will not be pleased with a burnt offering. 17 The sacrifices of God are a broken spirit; a broken and contrite heart, O God, you will not despise. 18 Do good to Zion in your good pleasure; build up the walls of Jerusalem; 19 then will you delight in right sacrifices, in burnt offerings and whole burnt offerings; then bulls will be offered on your altar.

Let's take a closer look at David's walk of repentance:

- David's acknowledgment is clear in verses 2 and 3. By introspection, David reveals his own sin that needs to be dealt with, expressing it as a prominent fixture in his thoughts. He describes it as something that is in need of a cleansing intervention. David knew that what he had done was wrong, and the problems were still there causing him pain as they tainted his connection with the Good Shepherd.

- In verse 4, David makes a pointed statement that his sin is against God, and God only. This is important because his sin has indeed hurt other people, but the affront is most grievous against God.

- David's reference to the 'secret heart' in verse 6 reminds us that God intends for introspection to happen in our lives. He honors our efforts to examine our hearts for sin by coming into our 'inward being' and pouring truth over our wounds and mistakes.

- Verse 7 uses a similar analogy to that of the well, asking God to wash him clean of his guilt and pour joy into his heart instead.

- By verse 8, David cries out for a purge of this weight. Sin seems to crush his bones and he wants relief. But more than that, he wants to hear that God loves him and hear God say it aloud so that he can feel the 'thrilling joy[96]' of the favor of God. David

---

[96] Pulpit Commentary (2010)

wants a new joy, and to hear the sound of rejoicing in heaven as his heart breaks free from this sin.
- Verse 11 references how God removed His spirit or favor from Saul because of the first king of Israel's unrepentant heart. David acknowledges that this could be his own reality and prays for deliverance, confessing his sin outright.
- In verse 12, he reiterates this desperate plea for real, lasting joy. David wants the joy he had upon his first encounter with the Living God, and he wants God to help him hold onto it forever.

David's revealing message in Psalm 51 was part of a repentant heart's cry. He fervently prayed and asked God to restore his joy after sin had taken him in the wrong direction. He wanted to experience that sense of jubilation and connection once more, and he begged God for a joy-up moment as he laid his sins on the altar.

Verse 17 promises that God will not despise a 'contrite heart.[97]' He blesses us through our repentance immeasurably. When we take the time to look deeply into our own hearts in a spirit of repentance, we watch as God washes away those surface spots. It's like a lake covered in water weeds that reveals shimmering wells after the trawler's sweep. There is Living Water beneath, when we wade through the sin on the surface and ask God to remove us from its entanglement. As we pull up those tangled handfuls, we suddenly see the wells of joy emerging. Then, we understand more clearly how to be filled to the brim under the favor of our Heavenly Father.

Psalm 32 follows this same train of thought, imploring us to inspect the depths of our hearts and acknowledge the forgiveness that awaits us in Christ Jesus. There is no condemnation for those who believe in the Son of God and choose to walk the path that leads them home. *"Blessed is the one whose transgression is forgiven,*[98]*"* because they have been invited to

---

[97] Psalm 51:17 ESV
[98] Psalm 32:1 ESV

return home for a grand celebration of love, hope, and everlasting joy. The Father opposes the proud[99], the self-righteous, the defiant; but when we fall, He offers us a hand of support. If we are humble enough to acknowledge our fall, humility brings repentance, and that act of turning toward home brings joy.

That is why, like James, we can say that we count all trials as a joy[100]. Life is hard, and Jesus promises that following Him may make certain experiences challenging. However, He also promises to be there with us on the road, encouraging us in the right direction and leading us home. There is joy in the return to God, especially where we have lost our way and then been found by the Shepherd himself. Both trials and discipline strengthen our faith. When we lead a life of humility, acknowledge our sin, and pray to God for His Living Water that heals and fulfills, He leads us to joy.

The LORD hooks his elbow into ours and walks with us straight to the Father, embracing us as we run back to Him with great rejoicing. Our introspection leads us to embrace who God is and who we are in Him. It helps to secure our identity by reminding us that we are still in Christ, even at life's lowest points. Joy is possible in any situation because we know where home is and who waits for us there.

Joy UP with Jesus

The jubilant call in 1 Peter 2:9 describes believers as part of a "chosen people, a royal priesthood, a holy nation, God's special possession," Remember who you are; you were made to glorify God and enjoy Him forever[101]. He has chosen you so that you may "declare the praises of him who called you out of darkness into his wonderful light.[102]" David's heart knew to whom it

---

[99] James 4:6 ESV
[100] James 1:2 ESV
[101] Douglas, K. 1986
[102] 1 Peter 2:9 ESV

belonged, even when temptation and trials threatened his joy. Does your heart know its Good Shepherd? Does it leap for joy at the thought of learning more about Him as you meditate on His Word?

When we take the time to look into our own lives and recognize how God's Word cuts to the truth of who we are, miracles start to happen. Biblical introspection reveals all that holds us back from our freedom in Christ. It shows us the truth behind our trials, stressors, and concerns, and allows the Holy Spirit to encourage us to 'count it all joy[103],' because of who we are in Christ Jesus. This is how we access a joy-up moment in the midst of hard conversations, deafening thoughts,

and the sin that threatens to bind our fallen chains around us once more.

We have the choice to rejoice, and that is a beautiful thing. It's important to acknowledge this idea of free will because the only way we feel good about our decisions, in general, is to know that we weren't forced into something we didn't feel invested in pursuing. God knows how important it is for us to feel secure about our prospects in life. When men and women sense that they are restricted or expected to perform under threat, they can't relax, learn, or dream. If we feel controlled or manipulated, we respond with anger, indignation, sadness, and fear.

Where do humans feel happiest? For most people, it is in those moments where we feel completely ourselves. We feel joyful and at ease when we are doing what we most enjoy with the people who love us. Parents often come to understand this crucial idea: even little humans need to feel like they have options to be happy. A toddler might throw themselves on the ground when a mother offers them one solitary morsel of appropriate food. They'll cry and scream and perform as though they were expecting a round of applause. However, if the mother puts that same item on the plate with another one or two less desirable morsels, the toddler is likely to snap it up without a second thought. Even as toddlers who cannot yet express themselves verbally, they

---

[103] James 1:2 ESV

recognize the power that comes with the freedom to choose. We can say no to God, to anything that He asks of us, but we should use our freedom wisely.

Teenagers lament their limitations, whether it is restrictions put in place by loving parents or laws regarding adult privileges, like drinking alcohol or driving. It's a frustrating time in life when it seems as though the world wants you to grow up but doesn't want to let you. In this case, the boundaries are there for the protection of the young adult as they find their feet and fully develop their brain's decision-making center. That's the idea with God's law given through Moses on Mount Sinai. It's like God was seeing us still developing the ability to make God-honoring decisions and putting boundaries in place to help us choose the best path.

Here, My People, I am giving you a few boundaries to help you stay safe and happy while you learn about who I am. I don't want you to jeopardize our relationship, because I love you. I want you to know the joy, peace, and love that comes from doing life with me, but there are some areas that still need some work before I can open your eyes to all that is coming. I know that you are not yet fully aware of all that is going on in the background, but as and when you are ready, I will reveal my will to you. I love you. Please try to make good decisions based on the boundaries I have given to protect you on your journey to joy.

A teenager hates to be left out of adult business, even though their brains are literally not ready to handle its burdens. In the same way, God puts safety rails up for us as we navigate life so that we will not step out into something we cannot handle. 1 Corinthians 6:12 describes it as the knowledge that, "All things are lawful for me," but not all things are helpful." The second half of that verse is even more important in our journey of biblical introspection and joy-seeking. It says, "All things are lawful for me," but I will not be enslaved by anything." Freedom is a powerful motivator for us; we cannot abide the idea of bondage because we were made to be free.

God knows that we need to choose how we do life--it is why he created us with imagination and the ability to learn. As our Creator, God the Son gives us the option to follow Him, and that is the best course of action, but it remains a personal choice. The woman at the well chose to receive the Living Water. The Prodigal Son chose to return home. David chose repentance and praise. All of these examples are why Jesus chose to die on our behalf; He looked into His heart and decided that we were worth it. He bled so that we may know everlasting joy in heaven with Him.

All of heaven and earth rejoices as a new believer comes through the door of salvation into eternal life, like the feast that erupted at the Prodigal Son's return. However, God the Father also wants His beloved children to make that choice for themselves. He is patient[104] as He waits for all to come to repentance. Wouldn't it be amazing to think of our role in the Kingdom as a joy-bringer simply by pursuing a relationship with God as we were meant to? We fulfill our own purpose this way, and we bring glory to God as others celebrate our choice. We also get to see how God enjoys us 'enjoying' Him and that is perhaps the most satisfying well of joy we will ever find.

---

[104] 2 Peter 3:9 ESV

CHAPTER 5
Joy-UP: The Loins of Your Mind & Destroy Negativity When It Spirals!

As we bear witness to the wells of joy and hope that Jesus offers to us, amazing clarity begins to take root in our hearts and minds. Salvation penetrates our way of life, and our focus shifts. We om empty earthly needs in the daily work of fetching water to magnificent eternal joy as we drink deeply from the Living Water.

What happens as the love of God starts to bloom in our perception, and He reveals His everlasting love for us a little more each day? All kinds of good things. It also becomes easier to see how the Apostle Paul could be so passionate about unity with Christ. In Philippians 2:1-2[105], Paul describes how excited he is to picture all God's people coming together to *"complete (my) joy by being of the same mind, having the same love, and being in full accord and of one mind."* This is the gift of the Holy Spirit: an uninterrupted connection to the mind of Christ. We get to share in His perspectives, just as we share in His joy[106], forging ahead in a blessed and eternal relationship with our Redeemer. In the chapter that follows, Paul moves even further into this idea that our knowledge of Christ--truly knowing who He is and what He has done for us--is all we need for everlasting joy.

---

[105] Philippians 2:1-2 ESV
[106] John 15:27 ESV

In the eighth verse of Philippians 3[107], Paul describes how his relationship with the LORD has made him consider all else as a "loss" (some translations put this as 'rubbish'). Nothing else can compare to the supreme value we find in knowing and loving Christ Jesus, and knowing that we are loved by Him, beyond measure. It is a transformative notion, and one that penetrates deeply into our Spirit-awakened mindset.

Modern literature has an almost morbid fascination with 'the mind,' from emerging mindfulness techniques entering mainstream business and educational sectors to psychological researchers making headway into concepts like 'chatter,' our relentless inner monolog. When we think about our fast-paced existence and the impact it is having on our minds, it is easy to see how quickly things can spiral out of control without a handle on our thought lives. Is it possible to access joy-up moments we need when we are at the height of self-doubt? Can we shake off negativity for happier thoughts or is it all an illusion?

The Bible is clear in its stance on our thoughts--we must take every thought captive[108]. Our minds are a key component to how and when we seek to restore the joy of our salvation, as David did[109]. Authors, preachers, and counselors have provided ways to do this through the centuries, but biblically, a key component to bringing our minds under control is to let the Holy Spirit do most of the work. The Spirit gives us freedom[110] and this includes liberation from thoughts that have taken hold of us. We have the freedom to choose redirection, to think on all that is noble, true, right, lovely, pure, admirable, and praise-worthy[111]. Joy is possible because we have the power of the Holy Spirit giving us strength, the freedom of Christ girding our souls, and the love of God telling our hearts to be still[112].

---

[107] Philippians 3:8 ESV
[108] 2 Corinthians 10:5 ESV
[109] Psalm 51:12 ESV
[110] 2 Corinthians 3:17 ESV
[111] Philippians 4:8 ESV

So, if we want to access that joy-up boost when we are at our lowest, the Bible only has one requirement: that we go 'all in.' As we think more about how our minds affect our ability to rejoice in tough circumstances, we see more about what Jesus meant by His call to love God with our heart, soul, mind, and strength. For example, when Moses addressed the people of Israel in the desert, he delivered God's commandments to them after a vivid encounter with I AM. The joy of that meeting shone visibly on Moses' face; an outward show of God's glory reflected on a man who had come through so much trouble in life. After Moses read out the Ten Commandments, he began to clarify some of the principles behind these rules and regulations created to help God's people live a holy, joy-filled life on earth. The leader's stern reminder in Deuteronomy 6:5 began with, *"You shall love the Lord your God with all your heart and with all your soul and with all your might.[113]"* Moses put this phrase to the people as a clear and non-negotiable commandment, not a suggestion, guideline, or vague insinuation of what holy living looks like. In one simple yet powerful sentence the man who saw God in the flames uttered a life-changing command encapsulating how we are to love the LORD.

Imagine being in that crowd. What might your response have been to hear this daunting directive from a religious leader for which there was no equal at the time? Centuries later, when the Pharisees asked Jesus for His opinion on the greatest commandment of all time, this is the verse the Son of Man chose to quote. In the English translation, Jesus' use of the Hebrew term seems to add one more aspect--the mind--but the meaning remains identical to Moses' language. John Calvin's commentary[114] explains the semantics from the Hebrew, correcting any assumption that Jesus was making "additions" to God's Word (opposing God's law against 'adding' to Scripture[115] in Deuteronomy 4:2). In the English version,

---

[112] Psalm 46:10 ESV
[113] Deuteronomy 6:5 ESV
[114] Calvin, J (1555)
[115] Deuteronomy 4:2 ESV

Moses' sentence included only heart, soul, and might, but the purpose of this phrase was to signify a holistic love for God. It describes a love for God that should flow through every fiber of our humanity, including all of our emotional, physical, and spiritual aspects. The mind is included in Mark's Gospel[116] specifically because the English translators felt the need to add the full Hebrew insinuation of the words spoken by Jesus. Calvin confirms that this was not 'adding to the gospel' but clarifying the totality of the commandment for each person who seeks to love the Lord. Both verses send an identical message: go 'all in' on how you love God!

The three corresponding verses in the New Testament quote Jesus as including four aspects--the heart, soul, mind, and strength. The references to Jesus' words as He answered the sly lawyer's question stem from:

- Matthew 22:37,
- Mark 12:30, and
- Luke 10:27.

Calvin's stance on why modern translations includes this word 'mind' in these descriptions seems very reasonable; the idea is to love the Lord with everything we've got.

Unsurprisingly, our way of thinking is something that comes up regularly in Scripture. God fully understands that our minds only sometimes manage to overrule emotions as we learn habits, test theories, and form opinions about the world. God knows our pain as we experience moments of doubt, and when our minds play tricks on us or cloud our judgment. The LORD understands how a thought life rules outward actions and can steal decades from us with simple misunderstandings in relationships and much else; after all, He made our minds, crafting each synapse into being.

Doesn't our mind seem to run the stage production that is life? It tells us how to live and runs background commentary while we do its

---

[116] Mark 12:30 ESV

bidding. Sometimes, when the heart interjects, harnessing the power of the mind can nullify that emotion or send us in a different direction entirely. God knew that we would need all the encouragement we could get to love Him in the middle of our weakness, anxiety, and fear of the unknown. He knew that we would question our faith and mistrust our feelings, that we would want to test our soul's deepest convictions that tell us God is real and that He loves us. Sin has jaded us, sometimes just enough to help our minds convince us that joy is gone forever. However, our omniscient Heavenly Father knew that every Christian would have these experiences, more than once. He planned for the time where we would need a heart-soul-mind-body reminder of God's love. He is faithful, and He loves us.

Love the Lord with All Your Mind?

Let's delve deeper into God's command through Moses to love the LORD with ALL our heart, soul, and might or strength. Jesus confirmed the 'entirety' of this command to love and glorify God with everything at our disposal--heart, *mind*, soul, and body. Perhaps, He knew that the world would need a modern reminder that the mind is not the enemy of faith; it is a catalyst of faith. Jesus did not say 'just believe' and move on. In God's Word, He gave anecdotes, reasons, truths, examples, miracles, and the gift of the Holy Spirit to ensure that our minds could be satisfied with the terms of salvation. We are tasked with thinking through all Scripture. We are encouraged to meditate on it, as we apply our minds to its spiritual, emotional, and physical implications. Christianity isn't a blind faith; it is a mind-engaged faith. The truth is available in written form as well, to mull over, memorize, and apply logically throughout life's twists and turns.

Why all this focus on mind engagement and logical reasoning? Because when we can love God with all our minds, we can more readily experience His joy!

So, if we want to truly let 'nothing separate us from the love of God[117],' we must guard our thoughts. Believers must develop an affinity for enjoying intimacy with God, in the fullness of joy[118]. Reveling in the relationship we have with Jesus Christ means constantly engaging in spiritual activities, prayer, worship, and meditation on Scripture. The Bible, God's written Word, is particularly His way of speaking truth into our minds so that we may grow in our knowledge of Him. To harness full joy, we have to be absolutely convinced that substitutes will not work. Not only is there joy in God's presence when we seek to build our relationship with Him, but there is exceeding joy[119]. In this case, a deeper knowledge of God leads to love, and in that connection, there is more joy than we could ever imagine.

It is also important to understand that God created joy as something that emanates from the Holy Spirit, along with love, peace, patience, kindness, goodness, faithfulness, gentleness, and self-control[120]. In Psalm 94:19, we see how joy or, in this case, a sense of delight[121] bubbles up within our souls when God comforts us *'in the multitude of (our) thoughts.'* Is it possible to experience joy in the midst of a spiraling, anxious train of thought? Yes. If the Holy Spirit is within us, so is the source of the joy we need.

We instinctively understand that joy can comfort us when our thoughts start to sow doubt, fear, or confusion in our lives, but practical experience is more likely to make this concept real to us. Proverbs 17:22 takes the idea further, looking at the delight we find in the Spirit's presence not only as comfort or kindness, but as a salve that heals like "good medicine[122]." Accessing joy brings vitality to our whole being,

---

[117] Romans 8:39 ESV
[118] Psalm 16:11 ESV
[119] Psalm 43:5 ESV
[120] Galatians 5:22-23 ESV
[121] Psalm 94:19 ESV
[122] Proverbs 17:22 ESV

including a healthier frame of mind that touches every other part of our lives. Letting our thoughts get out of hand has the opposite effect, where a lack of joy makes us feel crushed, like the crumbling of useless old bones, a dust that blows away when the wind is strong enough. David echoed this pressing need for joy when he was feeling pressure from all sides, including from his own sinful choices. When David's soul was afflicted, he cried out to God *"Let me hear joy and gladness; let the bones that you have broken rejoice.*[123]*"* He wanted spiritual healing and he knew that this was to be found in a more joyful life.

The power of the mind is incredible. God has given us the ability to wield our minds as a tool, a mechanism that can turn around our emotions, help us make godly decisions, and teach us to see the world differently. Much research has emerged as to the manner in which these thoughts can cause problems for us humans: various eating disorders, depression, anxiety, and other ailments manifest both mentally and physically. What we think is a catalyst for our changing moods, emotions, and attitudes as we go about our days. If so many of our thoughts are negative, it is easy to see how we might feel sadness, anger, confusion, irritation, or frustration more than we feel a sense of real joy during our waking hours.

The Word tells us that God wants to typify thoughts based on things that are true, honest, and of good report. It seems that as humans who naturally think cynically about life, we need a daily reminder that supernatural joy is being offered to us by the Spirit. God gives us good and perfect gifts from above[124], including the ability to harness joy when life is hard. In a dynamic world that opposes Jesus Christ and His way of life, Christians need to be ever mindful. We need a daily sense of focus to keep our thoughts anchored in the fruit of the Spirit, not negativity, shame, or anger. But what does a mind that loves God need to look like?

---

[123] Psalm 51:8 ESV
[124] James 1:17 ESV

A mind that loves and honors God might take time to audit its thoughts. We might need to sit back and consider the ideas, questions, and 'chatter' that dominates our train of thought. When you look at these habits of thought, what does it reveal? Are you experiencing joy in your thought life? Surely, we cannot have a joyful thought life without an abiding connection to God, the True Vine. We desperately need this anchor point of joy and gladness. When our minds start to drift in the sea of doubt and despair, we need to cling onto the Word of God. We need to call out to the Holy Spirit who speaks to us of the Word's mysteries. We need to cry out to God like David, *"Speak joy over me, Lord. I need to hear you tell me of happy, wonderful blessings so that my mind can regroup. I'm overwhelmed, Holy Spirit. Restore joy to my soul!"*

Have no doubt, the Holy Spirit will answer your call. Joy and gladness will come if you submit your mind to the power of God, the One who gives Living Water. He is a safe harbor.

God's Word can cut through our thought life if we invite Him to do His work. At the same time, the Holy Spirit reveals this Word to us so that we can understand it, synthesize it, and let it powerfully transform our minds into a joy-filled place. A mind trained on Jesus has returned to its rightful focus. There are so many good things that find their way to the surface in that mind-based transformation, including great joy as we rein in our thoughts and bring them back to Jesus Christ. For this reason, it is important to gauge our spiritual condition by the infectiousness of our joy. It does not seem illogical to say that proximity to the LORD brings ever-rising levels of joy. The closer we are to God, the more we experience joy because of His presence. We have seen that there is fullness of joy when we walk in step with God, safe and sound and learning to love Him better. If we love Him with our heart, soul, mind, and strength, our level of joy should be increasing on a daily basis as we move ever closer to our Savior's heart song.

Our level of joy might even be considered a barometer for the amount of access God has given us to Himself. His love penetrates through our whole being, but especially our minds. The brain is important in this discussion of joy because we are emotional beings but also rational ones. God has created humans with a broad, malleable brain that allows us to think, read, question, and grapple with what we know about the Triune God. It controls so much of who we are and what we do, from mechanical bodily functions to the miracles of healing, innovation, creativity, problem-solving, and the capability to love. Gauging the state of our minds is so important because we must joy-up for battle if we are going to survive the chaos ahead of us.

Jesus has warned of impending trouble in this world for those who love God. So, we are to gather up the loins of our minds[125] as for battle, taking up the quest to destroy negativity before it spirals into dangerous, soul-crushing territory. It is the talk of war, and for a good reason. When the Enemy is close, we will need a sober mind to be able to experience God's joy.

> *"Therefore, preparing your minds for action, and being sober-minded, set your hope fully on the grace that will be brought to you at the revelation of Jesus Christ."*
>
> *-1 Peter 1:13 ESV*

Believers must take time to meditate on the state of their thoughts to guard against a double-minded approach to Christianity. We cannot do it alone, though. Seeing things through the lens of God's Word helps us make more objective observations about how and what we think when nobody is watching. A mind trained on God is a healthy one, but that does not mean that it won't need daily, even hourly, assistance to ignore

---

[125] 1 Peter 1:13 ESV

distractions and keep us fixed on Jesus' steps before us. It takes work, it takes the power of the Holy Spirit, and it takes tremendous courage.

Girding up our minds for action happens through the authority of the Holy Spirit who leads us. He will guide our thoughts "into all truth[126]." How? Through the Word of God that cut like a double-edged sword[127]. As human beings, we have no power to joy-up and ready ourselves for action--we must seek this joy-up boost on the authority of God's Word. We can rewrite the narrative that our thoughts tend to produce, but we cannot begin to reimagine the thought life of a 'new creation' without the illuminating knowledge of God's Word to address falsities. As untruth runs rampant, the truth of God's Word offers us a way to clear our heads through a more positive internal dialogue. We can cut the negativity short and switch the narrative to one that confirms the sovereignty of God and our place in His Kingdom. However, this task is more complicated without a solid foundation in the Word of God--we need to read it with all diligence to know the way forward!

Joy-up and Skip the Mind Games

One of the most powerful life lessons we learn is that we cannot control the events or circumstances of life. However, we can control how we respond to these events with practice and the Spirit's aid. If we consider our minds in the context of Jesus being the Vine, and ourselves as the branches, we soon realize that inviting God into our thought life is something that should become second-nature to us. His constant presence offers a flow of life-giving joy to us, including at times when our 'branch' is in distress. All we need to do is stop, redirect our thoughts, and accept the joy and gladness that the Vine offers.

---

[126] John 16:13 ESV
[127] Hebrews 4:12 ESV

We also do not need to look to any other source of comfort or joy--Jesus is enough. The True Vine has explicitly stated that He is ever-present. He sustains us as the Vine sustains the branch, and He will never leave us nor forsake us[128]. Talking to Jesus "in our minds" often begins with a childlike conversation and a childlike trust that He is with us. If we believe that He knows us, created us, and longs to have fellowship with us, we can give any doubts into His capable hands for reexamination. This is the chief end of mankind, to love God and experience the joy of a deep and abiding relationship with Him in the secret places of our minds. We 'feel' God's love because our minds understand that He loves us. We 'feel' joy because our minds submit to God's presence in faith and pursue a righteous, beautiful relationship with Him through His Word.

Through the incredible work of the Holy Spirit, the mind has the potential to behold the beauty of holiness and experience joy as a direct result. If we want to truly experience this infectious spiritual joy, we have to seek an attachment to God that is supernatural, radical, and higher than any other attachment we have to the world. When David asked God to "make (him) hear joy and gladness,[129]" he was putting this request directly to the One who gives joy. At this point, David perceived that sin, despondency, and disenchantment had stained the allure and beauty he once saw in life. He understood that his life choices had threatened the joy he once found in a personal relationship with God, and he wanted it back.

When we have enjoyed the beauty of communing with God, it is impossible to go back or settle for anything less. We cannot be happy with less than the unparalleled, unprecedented, unchallenged, and welcoming experience that brings such joy and gladness to our hearts and minds. It is powerful and tangible, like hearing a clear affirmation from God of our worth. Our mind 'hears' this joy and gladness through the utterances of the Holy Spirit, as the truth of God's Word confirms its framework.

---

[128] Hebrews 13:5 ESV
[129] Psalm 51:8 ESV

God's joy is to be enjoyed and it is found in a space of liberty to enjoy Him, but He does not compel it. God knew that to command us to enjoy Him would have diluted its potency. We would not be responding out of our love for Him, though it might be out of fear, respect, or a search for righteous living. Following a command to rejoice would not be the spontaneity of love. If we do not love God out of choice, we cannot enjoy Him in the full and beautiful way that He has made possible through Jesus' sacrifice. However, if we do love God and seek to enjoy the relationship with our Creator, we might find ourselves more readily immersed in unspeakable joy as we savor that precious spiritual connection.

It might be joy during times of worship or meditation on God's Word. It might feel most tangible in the observation of God's natural wonder, and countless other opportunities for us to know more of Him. Whatever our experiences, the essence of this joy comes when we see Him with newly opened eyes. Our amazing God loves His children unconditionally, beckoning us to come and love Him back. He wants to show us what true joy looks like, and for that He gives us eyes to see.

If our minds hinder this connection because they are stubbornly stuck on autopilot when a negative cycle kicks off, we miss out on that joy. Instead, God wants us to learn to enjoy Him more. He wants us to share in His promised fullness of joy; our minds need a way to stop the rot. Joy is heavily contingent on the quality of our thinking, and our connections are very much like cultivating that Vine-branch relationship that Jesus uses to explain the Creator-creation relationship.

Our Minds Can Choose to Cultivate Joy-producing Roots

Like a tree that has its roots in just the right balance of water, soil, nutrients, and room to grow, our joy often requires improved conditions in the mind. It's why leaders like Paul are so adamant about transformation and renewal[130] when it comes to thinking. The right mindset leads to a holier life, better choices, and a deeper understanding of the Joy Giver.

But how can we ensure that our minds focus on cultivating joy-producing roots? First, we must seek to understand what causes joy as we think, reason, and question the course of our lives. One way is to embrace Psalm 100's first four verses:

1 *"Make a joyful noise to the Lord, all the earth!*[131]

Verse 1 says that we should be making a joyful noise to God, which describes giving Him praise and adoration. However, it is more than acknowledging His power or worthiness as 'even the demons[132]' might do. Rather, we are to appreciate His majesty in a real, undeniable declaration that produces a joyful garden of thoughts. Demons who see God's power do not experience this revelation because they do not love Him. It is love that drives true worship, and spiritual joy is steeped in us recognizing God's goodness and being truly in awe of it. If we really believe that He is wonderful, we will shout it out to all the earth because we will not be able to contain the joy, He shares with us.

2 Serve the Lord with gladness! Come into his presence with singing![133]

The second verse goes on to talk about serving. If we love God and want to guide our thoughts to more joyful ideas, we need to be serving God with a glad willingness, not drudgery. We love others because He first loved us[134]. He died for us and brought us love, grace, redemption, and fellowship. Have we forgotten that Jesus has served us in the most

---

[130] Romans 12:2 ESV
[131] Psalm 100:1 ESV
[132] James 2:19 ESV
[133] Psalm 100:2 ESV
[134] 1 John 4:19 ESV

wonderful way possible? When we reflect this attitude of service into the world, joy is sure to follow.

3 Know that the Lord, he is God! It is he who made us, and we are his; we are his people, and the sheep of his pasture.[135]

In the third verse, David encourages us to 'know' that God is at hand, not a God far-off, and to believe that He is sovereign. Our creator is a Good Shepherd who leads us to green pastures[136] for rest and the kindest care. This is the knowledge we need--to know who God is and who we are in relation to Him--so that we can find joy in that relationship. David's words are jubilant and outwardly expressive. His state of mind is one of seeking knowledge and confirming beliefs, but the results of those thoughts are a joy that is inexpressible, except to dance, sing, shout, and honor the Lord.

4 Enter his gates with thanksgiving, and his courts with praise! Give thanks to him; bless his name!"[137]

The mind is the tool we wield to know God, through the catalyst of His Word, and the activating agent of the Holy Spirit. Without logical reasoning and a thirst for this knowledge of God, all we have are feelings that change and fade as life's challenges come at us. If we have a right mind, we can enter His presence with thanksgiving, praise, and blessings abundant.

Another way to embrace joy-producing thoughts is to act on passages like Psalm 1:1-3:

"Blessed is the man who walks not in the counsel of the wicked, nor stands in the way of sinners, nor sits in the seat of scoffers; 2 but his delight is in the law of the Lord, and on his law, he meditates day and night. 3 He is

---

[135] Psalm 100:3 ESV
[136] Psalm 23:2 ESV
[137] Psalm 100:4 ESV

like a tree planted by streams of water that yields its fruit in its season, and its leaf does not wither[138]*.*"

This psalm describes a more active role in deterring our negativity; not just the taking on of joyous wonder, but the casting off of toxicity to make room for better things. It talks about the Word of God being a joy and "delight[139]" to us, which starts as a seed. That seed of delight needs a bit of attention to get going into full-blown joy under pressure. Thoughts start that way, too; small, unassuming, unthreatening. However, if we cannot identify the toxic seeds from the joy-producing ones, we let the wrong kind of thoughts shoot up and cause entanglements in the garden of our minds. The more we let the sin grow, the more complicated it is to eradicate.

Our Minds Can Choose to Cultivate Toxic Roots

There are toxic roots that stay dormant within our minds for years under the right conditions. When we become Christ-followers and receive our 'hearts of flesh[140],' those toxic seeds still lie within our minds unless we take an active stance to find them and handle them. Brokenness is part of our humanity on this earth, and we need the love and forgiveness of Jesus Christ to make us whole. Our walk is toward perfect restoration, but there is some work to do first--our sanctification. This is work done by the Holy Spirit in our heart, soul, mind, and strength, and our part is to follow His lead.

The parable of the Sower (Luke 8:4-15) is well-known as a favorite children's story, but this is an important message from Jesus about how to cultivate a joy-producing thought life. Gardeners know well the pointless exercise of pulling out a few blades of grass or breaking off the tops of the

---

[138] Psalm 1:1-3 ESV
[139] Psalm 1:2 ESV
[140] Ezekiel 11:19 ESV

weeds--it is the roots that count. These roots foster newer, more resilient weeds in each new season if you don't yank them out the first time. Sanctification takes just as much work as cultivating a garden, especially if we want to know a joy-filled life rather than a discontented half-life that embraces compromise.

"And the ones on the rock are those who, when they hear the word, receive it with joy. But these have no root; they believe for a while, and in time of testing fall away. 14 And as for what fell among the thorns, they are those who hear, but as they go on their way they are choked by the cares and riches and pleasures of life, and their fruit does not mature. 15 As for that in the good soil, they are those who, hearing the word, hold it fast in an honest and good heart, and bear fruit with patience."

-Luke 8:13-15 ESV

Clearly, a mind with toxic seeds or lingering roots in sin is susceptible. It might be that the good seeds have not yet taken root in the heart or that the mind has not explored or grasped how salvation needs to transform an old way of thinking. A mind filled with the toxicity of the old nature makes no room for new growth. It is unproductive in terms of cultivating an understanding of God's Word. However, the more chilling result is its unproductivity in seeking a deeper relationship with the One who offers clarity, maturity, and the joy of growth.

If our minds are brimming with toxic thoughts, our perspective cannot bring forth the fruit of joy. There is no place for the good, joy-producing ideas to establish strong roots. Negative thoughts come more naturally to the human heart tainted with sin and darkness, and we need supernatural intervention from the Holy Spirit to keep us looking onward and upward towards joy in every circumstance.

Jesus' analogy of the mind as a field or a garden is poignant when we think about how nature works. There is the aspect of the seeds being intentionally thrown or pressed into the soil, but there is also a natural (and supernatural) dependency on rain and sunshine to germinate that seed into new life. If our minds are the soil, immersing ourselves in the Word of God is like throwing good seeds of salvation onto the same soil where bad seeds of sin may still linger. We need to pull of the bad seeds at the same time as we fill the soil with the good ones. However, the gardener (us) still needs the power of God to send down rain and sunshine to spring up the abundant life we seek from those joy-producing seeds. Joy is a process, and we need to do our part to see God's handiwork[141] come to fruition.

If we are abiding in God's presence, clinging to Him for life, good thoughts will germinate. However, we also need to deal with the seeds of sin waiting to choke these delicate seedlings at their most vulnerable. If we haven't uprooted sin and burned it on the altar, it is still waiting in the recesses of our minds. It is always ready to strangle our hope, quench our ability to love, and extinguish our joy. Instead of the fruit of the Spirit and the joy-producing seeds of God's Word, our thought life could develop nasty strains that seek riches, fleeting pleasures, and selfish ambition.

So, if we are serious about living more joyful lives, our mind gardens need a makeover. The Word of God leads to greater joy as these seeds of life are given a chance to flourish. We need spiritual power both to embrace joy and to shirk off negativity before it becomes lethal.

Joy-Up and Create a God-honoring Thought Life

So, how can we curate this mind that honors and exalts God? There are two sides to the coin that we need to consider: putting on a new thought life and putting off the old one. It is a fine balance that requires the skill of the Creator who both sows the seeds and sends the rain.

A good starting point is to really think about who we are and what we believe about Jesus Christ. These two concepts are intricately related. If

---

[141] Ephesians 2:10 ESV

we believe that Jesus Christ is the Son of God and that He died as a propitiation for our sin[142], then we cannot be unmoved by the gift of salvation that is on offer. If you have already accepted that gift and committed your life to Jesus Christ, then you cannot be unmoved by the sin that still tries to wrap itself around your thoughts and actions, either through habit or deep-rooted toxic issues that you have not yet handed over to God. Do you believe that you are saved by grace[143] and that your sins are forgiven[144]? Why are your thoughts still telling you that you're worth nothing or that you are inadequate in some way?

The proverb "As a man thinks...so is He[145]" comes to mind. We need to be intentional about redirecting our minds to the truth of who we are in Christ when our focus wanes. When we get into a weird headspace, "all into your feelings" and driven by relentless cycles of negative emotions or God-dishonoring thoughts, the only solution is to ask God for the grace to help us stop that toxicity in its tracks. Ask Him to help you see yourself through His eyes, a child covered by grace and acceptable and pleasing to God. We are loved beyond measure, but only God's power can bring that vision to life in our mind's eye when sin threatens to crush our joy. If we think we can have a joyful life, God will help us fulfill that expectation as He offers us wells of joy through Living Water.

Thoughts also affect how we see others, whether this perspective is through God's eyes or not. Why does Jesus ask us to pray for our neighbors *and* our enemies[146]? Perhaps, it is because He is offering us a tip from the Gardener's handbook on how to uproot hate, hurt, and injustice. It's God's 'woke' solution. We cannot think good thoughts about people we hate while the roots of those thoughts are still strong. Even if we chop off what is visible on the surface, the roots will still be there. When Jesus

---

[142] 1 John 2:2 ESV
[143] Ephesians 2:8-9 ESV
[144] 2 Chronicles 7:14 ESV
[145] Proverbs 23:7 ESV
[146] Matthew 5:44 ESV

encourages us to pray for our enemies, we have a picture of Him saying, *"Put your hands together, wrap it around that sin, and close your eyes. Pray with all your might as I stand beside you. I will give you the strength to handle this sin. Uproot it. Pray hard, don't give up."*

We must pray for our enemies and feel the arms of God wrap around us and help us uproot that sin forever. As we pray for the strength to love our enemies in this way, something amazing happens mind transformation. God honors our efforts by helping us clear the way for good thoughts and more joy. Once the toxic roots are drying up in the light of the Son, there is space for us to focus on those delicate seedlings of love, joy, and peace that are popping up all over the garden of our minds. It's a partnership of care and cultivation, a joining of two minds in unity toward the same goal.

The Garden of Joy

In the physical garden, Eden, there was this same kind of intimacy between God and creation. God created man for fellowship with Himself, in a garden that was thriving, beautiful, and filled with things to nourish the man and woman, including fruit. He also made man an intelligent being, one who thrives by thinking and learning about how to enjoy life and enjoy God. The man and woman were also made in the image of God, which meant that the way they looked, operated, and thought had qualities very much like God Himself. Why did God give us minds that bend and buckle with negativity but also brim with hope, love, and joy? Because God wanted us to love and enjoy Him forever. To do that, we need to decide that He was worth loving and enjoying.

There are three gardens we see in God's story that are helpful for understanding how to seek a joy-filled life through a connection with Jesus. The first garden, Eden (which means "delight" in Hebrew) was the starting point. God sowed seeds, crafted landscaping, and cast visions.

However, there was a betrayal, compromise, and temptation to sin, and some bad seed from Satan took root.

In the New Testament, we see the second garden, the Garden of Gethsemane (which means "oil press" in Hebrew). This was about 4,000 years later, with a second betrayal as Satan sowed his bad seed into Jesus' disciple. It distracted the thoughts of Judas Iscariot to sell out his own friend, the Son of God, for some money[147].

As Jesus wept in Gethsemane, He also prepared to uproot the sin of the entire world by the sweat (and blood) upon His own brow. He bowed low, asking God whether it was going to be worth it, and sensing a nod from above that the roots of sin needed handling. Jesus, our Creator, bent His back and broke His body, spilling His own blood on the altar to cleanse us from all the seeds of sin scattered throughout history. His blood flowed from the nails driven into the very trees He created, covering a multitude of sins[148]. It sank into the soil that He brought about with only a word and killed each and every toxic root of sin in us, His garden, His bride.

Now that the blood has cleansed the third garden, our minds, it can be restored to a place suitable for fellowship with God. God would not walk where sin's thorns lay, so Jesus cleared the way. The spiritual garden of our minds can now connect to the True Vine, Jesus Christ, unencumbered. It bears joy as a result, a fruit of the Spirit that now indwells our garden. Christ's blood covers all, and the only thing we need to do is respond rightly. How? By embracing joy-producing seeds and eradicating toxic ones. The choice is ours. If we believe in Jesus Christ, our Savior, we choose life. And isn't life better with abundant joy driving our experiences and perspectives? As we fellowship with God, learning more about who we are in His presence, Spirit-given joy springs up in the same mind where Jesus' blood once flowed.

---

[147] Matthew 26:36, 46-50 ESV
[148] 1 Peter 4:8 ESV

In the garden of our minds, there are the same choices as in Eden and Gethsemane. We can still choose betrayal, even without realizing it. The roots of sin run deep, and we need to let the blood of Jesus penetrate those toxic, negative, sin-driven thoughts at their very core. If we hide or bury roots, they will grow. If we ignore them, they will overwhelm us. If we let it, sin will choke all the good work that the Holy Spirit is doing in our new 'hearts of flesh' and transformed minds.

May God hear our prayers and make us more like Him each new day. After all, how can we expect to reap joy when we have sown seeds of doubt, criticism, negativity, or ingratitude? If we want to become a tree of joy and righteousness, our thoughts must be planted by the river[149] of Living Water!

"For those who live according to the flesh set their minds on the things of the flesh, but those who live according to the Spirit set their minds on the things of the Spirit."

-Romans 8:5

Paul's warning in Romans 8:5 points us to the value of choosing to submit to the Spirit's filling rather than letting sin continue to grow from old roots. If we choose to eradicate sin as we recognize its growth, and make room for new growth by the Spirit, we make the choice to honor God's work in us. Thoughts set on things of the Spirit produce God-honoring results[150], but thoughts set on things of this world lead to betrayal. Through Jesus Christ's shed blood, we can choose to use our minds to seek the presence of God where there is fullness of joy, or we can lose our joyful response and disconnect or disengage from that fellowship. The seeds we cultivate in the garden of our minds represent those choices at ground level.

---

[149] Jeremiah 17:8 ESV
[150] Romans 8:5 ESV

The infectiousness of our joy will depend on the richness of the seeds and the type of nourishment. Quality seeds produce quality results, so we need to be sure that the seeds we are planting or allowing to grow are the joy-producing kind, not robust sin. If we plant the right seeds (putting the Word of God into our minds through reading it and asking for the Spirit's enlightenment), we can grow the fruit of the Spirit. To germinate and develop in a way that reaches our hearts (our emotional response), those seeds need the right soil and God-sent blessings, but it starts with the mind.

William Wordsworth wrote, *"Your mind is the garden, your thoughts are the seeds, the harvest can either be flowers or weeds."* It is true, and we need to remember that our minds are not masterfully trained to honor God in an instant--it takes a lifetime to grow a garden. We need to abide on the Vine[151], allowing the Holy Spirit to nourish our minds with all good things. A God-honoring mind is one that is accessible to God so that it can produce a harvest of joy.

Destroy Negativity and Take Every Thought Captive

If the garden of the mind is such a vital part of a joy-filled life, we need to also remember the tougher side of gardening: weeding, pruning, and composting. The Bible describes this process as taking 'every thought captive[152]' in the same way that Jesus did when tempted by Satan. Jesus used the Word of God as a defense against the subtle tactics that threatened to plant doubt instead of joy. Jesus' answers to these dangerous offers of wealth, power, and immortality began with "It is written..." God's Word is a powerful tool that keeps the garden of our mind free of sin that binds. We need to wield it with courage, following the example

---

[151] John 15:4 ESV
[152] 2 Corinthians 10:5 ESV

that Jesus set for us in the face of relentless temptation and grueling challenges.

However, before we can embrace the joy of fellowship as God's love and peace flourish, we need to eradicate negativity. Destroy negative and God-dishonoring thoughts. Look out for them and learn to recognize them while still in their weakest form so that you can quickly pull the roots out of the ground. When pernicious weeds invade the flower beds, we must gird up the loins of our minds with effort, focus, and intentionality. The Bible says that '*nothing shall separate us from the love of Christ*[153]' and that includes our own thoughts. If what we are thinking is taking us further away from God, that line of thought is part of a weed-producing sin. Negativity is a forbidden fruit that robs us of joy and threatens to take us out of the garden for which we were made: the place of joy-filled fellowship with God forever.

So, how do we approach negativity when it is such an overwhelming force within most normal human beings? One helpful thing to remember is that temptations are an illusion. A tempting proposition comes to your mind dressed as relief, but it is actually a thief that will rob you of joy in Christ. Temptation entices, tricks, and subtly draws us away, almost quietly enough so that we don't notice our course has altered. It's a seedling masquerading as something we think we have planted but that we do not really recognize until it is full-grown. Yet, by that point, it could be too late to stop the effects. It is far better to yank it out, examine it against the field guide of God's Word, and see whether it is something to keep or burn.

Oleander is a magnificent flower, but it is dangerous. It can kill, even though it looks like something that might make life in the garden more beautiful. We might even compare Oleander to the false beliefs we fail to recognize germinating in our minds, bad seeds masquerading as gorgeous

---

[153] Romans 8:35 ESV

additions or fruitful offerings. How do we handle these seeds of toxicity? By tearing down the altars built on these false beliefs. We need to look deeply into the Word of God to find what is true, noble, right, pure, and admirable[154]. We need to address the false narratives that tend to run rampant in our minds and replace these dangerous notions with all that is true, honest, of good report, praiseworthy, and virtuous.

The dangers of plants like Oleander include the appeal of these 'negative seeds' as they grow. We think to ourselves how innocuous the seedlings look, and then start to admire the flowers as the plant produces deeper roots. As it strengthens, our resolve weakens because it becomes more of an effort to pull out the roots. Pulling out established weeds leaves great gaps in the garden, and the weed's flowers often seem rather beautiful, don't they? However, part of destroying negativity as our thoughts spiral is to learn to resist temptation as Jesus did. Cling to the Word of God, the light to our path[155], and resist the temptation to 'go with the flow' of contemporaneous thoughts and wild emotions. These elements often contain no factual basis or representation of reality under the scope of God's Word. Rather, we need to take a stand against conforming in this way. God's people are called to be holy, set apart for Spirit-filled joy, because they are not to be bound by the 'herd mentality' of the culture in which they live; they are liberated by the truth, God's Word.

Joy UP with a Sound Mind

Embracing Spirit-given joy requires us to be bold in our approach to life's challenges and our attitude toward sin. Comfort is not a helpful goal; neither is compromise. As our love for God grows and we begin to meditate on His Word, our minds mold into more beautiful vessels that

---

[154] Philippians 4:8 ESV
[155] Psalm 119:105 ESV

can be filled to overflowing with the joy of Christ. When our mind is pitted with sin, there is less room for the fruit of the Spirit. However, it takes courage to tackle inconsistencies head-on. For this, the Spirit gives us power, love, and a sound mind, not a spirit of timidity[156]. As we root out each of our stubbornest sins in turn, there is more opportunity for us to sow good, wonderful gifts from God's Word. After that, our minds start to transform like a gratifying landscaping project. The final result is the Spirit's gift to us, a sound mind rooted in God's Word, beautified with the fruit of the Spirit, and overflowing with the joy that comes with from the Creator Himself.

What is the secret to regulating our minds with the truth? Being intentional about walking in agreement with God's Word. Remember, John 15:11 assures us that Jesus wants to present us with His own joy.[157] It is His will for our joy to be complete, which means that one more drop would push our stocks to overflowing. There is no need to seek any other source of joy when we cannot possibly fit in anymore! When we accept the truth of who Jesus is and what He has done for us, we accept this Living Water and experience a "filling up" of joy in the process.

Self-discipline, a sound mind, is unshakeable in the face of challenges because it knows how to reach out for a joy-up boost in God's Word. Tuning in to the truth necessitates an effort to understand with all diligence[158] who God is, who we are because of that love, and how we can cultivate our minds into more beautiful representations of that relationship.

We looked at the passage in Philippians 4:8 earlier in the chapter, and this is a great start for seeking that mind-based change when we connect with God's Word. It describes thinking on, *"whatever is true, whatever is honorable, whatever is just, whatever is pure, whatever is lovely,*

---

[156] 2 Timothy 1:7 ESV
[157] John 15:11 ESV
[158] Proverbs 4:23 ESV

whatever is commendable,[159]" and tuning into things that represent *"excellence"* and *"anything worthy of praise."* What are the results of training our minds to focus on these virtuous notions when negativity threatens to derail us? Peace, love, joy, patience, kindness, and all the other Spirit-given gifts. We receive these gifts with a mind that's growing stronger and more beautiful in its relationship with Christ Jesus.

Sometimes, we have to switch up our armor or tactics. David knew that Goliath needed to be destroyed, but he also felt the need to take off the heavy armor given to him by the doubtful king. David chose instead to trust God, knowing that the Faithful One would direct his weapons. Our giants come in many forms, and when we know how to joy-up, we can conquer negativity, anxiety, and every other mindset that threatens to put us down.

As you prepare for action, gird up the loins of your mind by choosing to:

- **joy-up** when negativity, fear, and forces of darkness rally
- **search** the Scriptures and begin to see yourself as victorious in God's finished victory
- **resist** temptation or the tendency to 'go with the flow' when thoughts and emotions become overwhelming
- **measure** reality against the Word of God and the truth that the Holy Spirit reveals to your mind as you learn more about His perfect will[160]
- **stop** thoughts that are drawing you away from joy in Christ--give those thoughts an expiration date so that you can dwell on what is true and worthy instead.

---

[159] Philippians 4:8 ESV
[160] Romans 12:2 ESV

As we learn to handle our negativity in this way, we become more conscious of the God who holds us together. Then, we can start to train our minds and prepare for the way of life He intended for us.

Joy UP and Move Toward Worship

Christians embrace a radical and hopeful faith, but we need to preach the truth to ourselves over and over again. Think it! Speak it! And let the truth of Christ draw you to a wider yet clearer understanding of who it is that deserves your worship. We live in a world where evil seems to prevail, but the weapons of our warfare are mighty through God's power and authority. The Almighty One is the only worthy recipient of our adoration, and that act of worship is why He created us. If we learn who He is and seek to build that relationship, the natural response is to praise the Living God. We worship Him for all that He is, all that He has done, and that He will do as this story ends.

Preach the Word of God to yourself when you need a dose of Spirit-given joy to address negative thoughts and emotions.

Flame your imagination by aligning your thoughts with the Word.

Build your confidence by delving into a deeper understanding of who you are in Christ Jesus.

The sheer glory of belonging to Jesus is captivating... coheirs, adopted sons and daughters of God, cleansed from sin, saved from death, victorious over evil. That fullness is what the Holy Spirit wants to sow into our mind, heart, soul, and body. What happens when we see the amazing joy to be found in Christ Jesus? We want more of it. In God's presence there is fullness of joy, and the internal work of the Holy Spirit throughout our lives helps us to maximize our capacity to receive more and more and more joy from our generous Heavenly Father.

Joy UP with Every Fiber of Your Being as You Love the Lord

Have you ever watched those cake tutorials where the mass of random, boring cake shapes transforms into a hyper realistic form, like a tiger? What makes it look real? It's the light in the eyes. Once they add those tiny white specks into the deep recesses of the eyes, the dark form seems to spring to life. Light does that; it represents life. Death extinguishes the sparkle in the eyes, but life lights them up. Joy is the same; our countenance shines like the face of Moses did when we meet God on the mountain or in the valley or right in the midst of the fire, and joy literally shines through us for all to see. It dances in our eyes, no matter their color, age, or point of view.

When we dig up the weeds of negativity and sin in our minds, we let in the light. It penetrates the soil, awakening all those good and wonderful seeds that the Spirit has sown in us. As we let the Creator's tender loving care bring those good and perfect gifts to life, our minds bloom with more Christ-like positivity and start to recognize sin more clearly. The light of God's Word shines into our transforming minds to show us where to focus our efforts with each new moment or challenge.

The way that we love God matters! We must love him with all our minds, hearts, souls, and bodies because He is worthy. We can honor Him with thoughts that are steeped in His Word, and we can sow seeds of truth, love, peace, and joy. If we plant joy, we can expect to produce a joy-filled life. First, we need to tune in, acknowledging the many ways in which God has set life and death choices before us. We must practice choosing thoughts of joy based on God's Word and ask the Holy Spirit to reveal the truth of these joy-producing seeds to us. We must also target the Word, putting specific ideas or verses before God when we talk to Him in faith.

Only you can find what stirs your heart, but we can all start by connecting with God in a way that feels most natural to us. The guideline is that all interaction with God needs to be rooted in the Word of God, the Bible. For example, The Word explicitly tells us to bring thanksgiving into our fellowship with God in Chronicles 16:34, 1 Thessalonians 5:16-18, Psalm 28:7. We might choose to embrace gratitude by approaching God through a song when others prefer a walk in the countryside, but it is still grounded in the truth that meaningful fellowship with God requires thankfulness. In a continuously growing relationship with Jesus, the connection is driven by the Holy Spirit's power and confirmed by His written Word. Sometimes, we can see His wondrous works through our minds as we give ourselves over to consistent worship. We come alive as we let the Word dwell richly in us through songs or meditation on His Word. So, we must do whatever it takes to necessitate "all vigilance[161]" and cultivate a mind trained on true, right ways of thinking.

As the transformation starts to penetrate our thought lives more deeply, those changes will show up in more concrete ways. Joy will intensify through the fulcrum of a strong, radical relationship with God as we 'abide on the Vine[162].' In God's presence is true joy, and He is the light by which our minds navigate out of negativity. There is no other way around it; joy-up moments that transform the mind require feeding our souls on God's Word, cultivating a habit of prayer, and communing with God. It is supernatural and unparalleled.

If we develop this approach and let the Holy Spirit help us through challenges, before we know it, consistent thoughts of joy will begin to mold us into more joyful people from the inside out. The work of the Holy Spirit manifests fruit, like joy, and we should long for this *"as the deer pants for the water[163]."* If we hunger and thirst for God, He will honor

---

[161] Proverbs 4:23 ESV
[162] John 15:4 ESV
[163] Psalm 42:1 ESV

this faith by allowing us to joy-up and gird up the loins of our minds to repel negativity when it spirals.

Joy UP with Jesus

Renewing our minds comes as a direct result of communing with Jesus Christ. It is that union of souls that creates a positive connection and redirects us away from negativity into the life-giving wells of joy. We need a reservoir of positivity to deal with our mind's tendency to jump to worst-case scenarios, and we find it in the Word of God, our yardstick of truth. However, embracing joy and cultivating a more Christ-centered mindset does not mean that we deny the problems that exist in our lives. It just means that we can rejoice while we resolve those problems because we serve the God that can help us triumph over adversity.

We serve the God who walked into the furnace with three Hebrew boys to keep the flames at bay (see the story in Daniel 3:16-28). They had so much joy that they were confident enough to say that, even if God did not rescue them (as they believed He could), He would still be there for them. They had faith that He would show up in the midst of their struggle, not that the struggle would disappear. They curated an attitude of joy because of the power, love, and self-discipline they knew the Spirit had given to them. We can have that kind of confident joy if we know God and live out the implications of His Word.

Sometimes, developing a more joyful thought life is about having a sanctified mindset that focuses on God's providence. It is knowing that God is working all things together for the good of those who love Him[164] *and rejoicing because of this truth. We know that challenges will come to Christians and non-Christians alike. We know that all human beings will face heartache, stress, and even tragedy. However, a view of life that emphasizes sanctification understands that those circumstances are just part of the journey. What truly*

---

[164] Romans 8:28 ESV

matters is our response, and our growth in the knowledge and faith we have in Jesus. Bad things happen to good people, too, but there is always a joy to be found in the midst of those adversities when we know where to run. Ripping out sin and negativity in our minds and sowing the fruit of the Spirit in its place mean that our minds will be more prepared to 'keep us safe' and more joyful in Christ Jesus when challenges test our resolve.

How do we embrace a renewed mind? The first step is to be open to what the Word of God and the Holy Spirit have to show us. Are you ready to accept the thoughts sourced from the Holy Spirit rather than seeking 'intellectualism' or puffed-up knowledge? Are you ready to deny yourself in ways that the Spirit reveals are necessary to get you moving in the right direction? Joy requires a step back from wrong thinking, argumentative attitudes, and thoughts that oppose God. The Bible describes us as lost sheep, and sheep are prone to wander into dangerous curiosities or loss of focus on reality. The world is one big distraction, and our test is how well our minds can help us navigate what is true and what is a lie. If we want to stay the course, we need the Holy Spirit's supernatural guidance and the yardstick of God's Word, two powerful resources for those who follow Christ.

If you notice your mind deflecting to ignoble untruths that make you feel despondent or disengaged from joy, it is time to recalibrate. Stop those weeds, and 'recall to (your) mind[165]' hopeful, joy-filled truths in the same way that the prophet Jeremiah recalled God's faithfulness. As the writer of Lamentations (which literally means "deep sorrow or weeping"), Jeremiah is not the first person we think of when we want to exemplify joy. Yet, even the man that God used to deliver awful news to Israel found beautiful joy-up moments at the feet of His Heavenly Father. When he mused over how good God was and how His compassion renewed our capacity for joy each morning[166], even Jeremiah rejoiced. He understood that it was by God's mercy that we are not consumed, and that was a great reason to celebrate, no matter the situation.

---

[165] Jeremiah 3:21 ESV
[166] Lamentations 3:22 ESV

When our minds immerse us in guilt, shame, anxiety, condemnation, and other forms of negativity, we must remember God's wonderful faithfulness; remember His mercy and love. We must think compelling thoughts about truth, light, and eternal life with Christ to shift our focus back to God's love for us. We need a great memory, soaked in God's Word.

Pray that the Holy Spirit would help you remember the truth. May we always recall to our minds that:

- The LORD is on our side---we have eternal hope (Hebrews 13:6)
- God chose us before the foundations of this world (Ephesians 1:4)
- We are chosen, and nobody can lay a charge against God's elect (Romans 8:33)
- God has a purpose for our lives, including plans to prosper us and not to harm us (Jeremiah 29:11)
- We know how it will end and there is eternal life for those who love God (John 10: 28-30)
- In the fullness of time, God sent Jesus to be your personal Savior (John 3:16)
- Weeping may endure for the night, but joy will come in the morning (Lamentations 3:22)

When the enemy comes against us like a flood, we can recall the seeds of hope, love, and joy in God's Word. Like David, we can ask God to let us 'hear joy and gladness' again as we meditate on God's Word and hold it in our minds, ready for action. The greater the quality of our call, the greater the measure of assurance we will walk in. God has placed us in a secular, uncaring society for a great purpose: that we may reflect joy in every circumstance, even when it is hard. Renewing our minds is part of that process.

If you want to have joy, you need to be deliberate about producing God-honoring worship, conversation, and Word-based meditation. There is room for doubt, but only until we fall back in step with the Great Comforter. The by-product of our diligence to cultivate joy-filled patterns of thinking and gratitude will be an increasingly fulfilling life, overflowing with joy.

CHAPTER 6
Joy-Up: The Conversation!

Have you watched a seed's green birth as it readies itself for that first kiss with sunlight? Growth is slow and steady at first, but it gains impressively once it connects with the right elements. If ⁾d soil and the right amount of sunshine, that seedling's expansion continues until it has reached its full purpose. It blooms right there in the spot it has been planted.

The garden analogy lends itself well to seeds of joy that help us uproot negativity and fill our minds with what is good. If we follow that train of thought, the blooms those seeds produce might be compared to the full-grown words we speak. Our conversations are the evidence of what we sow in our minds, the place where our words gather and build momentum with every seed we allow to flourish. Once these ideas bloom, they can no longer be contained. They burst forth into the open air to fulfill their purpose and there is no way to get them back again. As words emerge from the mind's cultivation and fly out of our mouths, they also tell a story. If we are honest, that story might not be the most flattering picture. Do the words we speak glorify God? If it were possible to measure these spoken words, reactions, and ideas, what percentage of our dialogue would seem to bring honor to God?

Bringing joy to our conversations is a crucial growth curve on our journey with Jesus Christ. The more we get to know Him, the more we reflect His love in the words that we speak to others, to Him, and to ourselves. As we draw near to our Savior, we also feel the tug of the Holy Spirit in meaningful ways. For example, if our words are in conflict with the truth we have seen in the Word of God, we may feel uneasy. Our hearts know when our talk is not God-honoring, when our words are not tokens of blessing, peace, and joy. We experience a sense of disconnection when our words turn into arrows that wound or weapons that destroy. A Christ-follower is bound to have many such experiences, where they feel in conflict with the words that they have spoken aloud or to themselves. However, the Holy Spirit hides God's Word in our hearts—seeds within the gardens of our mind—so that when sin taints our words, we can recognize it.

Think about the words that you have spoken lately. Is there some tension between what you've uttered and how the Holy Spirit is leading you into a deeper understanding of God? Do you pray about these tensions or ignore them? Do you let the words flow or try to override them?

Discord indicates a problem. If our words as infallible humans are not glorifying God, we will soon recognize that these words have a negative impact on our joy. Most of us don't take much time to really listen to our minds' dialogue, but it is good to be aware that those seeds grow rapidly into full-blown words ready to be released into the world. So, how do we joy-up our conversations and ensure that God gets the glory He deserves from us? One way is to consider being more intentional about cultivating the fruit of joy from our lips; it isn't easy. The Bible talks about our hearts and minds being the source of the words we speak, and in the other direction, our speech being a revealing picture of what truly lies in our hearts. Maybe, the answer to more joy-filled conversations lies in seeking out a deliberate connection with the Great Gardener Himself. If our soul is so deeply rooted in our relationship with the One who gives us joy, surely, we will see exciting growth as we walk with Him to identify, root out, and replace what we allow to flourish within us.

Minds that love God and honor the Creator-creation relationship need more care to ensure that joy has space to bloom. It is hard work to sow joy-producing seeds each season. We need to be prepared for a continuous process of weeding and planting, as we move around the rows and rows of sin and allow the Holy Spirit to show us the next task. We need motivation to continue this work of sanctification alongside our Savior, and the Word of God is very clear about the need for us to abide[167] in Jesus (the Vine). Abiding in Jesus Christ is the only way to be able to produce the fruit of joy while we grow.

Our words are like a litmus test, showing up the core beliefs on which our soul resides. If we are not paying attention to the quality of the words we are flinging around, we may find ourselves horrified at the mud we manage to get all over those who see first-hand what's truly in our hearts. Part of the Holy Spirit's work is to help us cultivate a joy-filled mind so that we can speak words of life. This is particularly important when it comes to conversations with those who are yet to meet with the Savior, Jesus Christ, but it applies to all other exchanges, too.

The words that roll off our tongues are often the visceral manifestation of how much we are abiding in the Vine. If we want a golden tongue that brings glory to God by revealing the joy of our salvation, then we need to joy-up the conversation with urgency. The first step is to ensure that our connection to the Vine is secure. If it holds, we will be learning more about God's character and will for us each day through His Word, the Bible; joy will follow.

---

[167] John 15:4 ESV

The Words We Share with The World Should Reveal the Joy We Have in Jesus Christ

It's true that no man can tame the tongue[168], so we can be extremely grateful that Jesus wasn't just a man. The Son of Man was also fully God, even as He navigated human existence in the family of Mary and Joseph. Jesus' ministry was one of both words and actions, but His message of love was always clear. The Messiah came to seek and to save the lost[169], and He sought peace. He also scattered joy like confetti; it was part of His character. Those who met Him and heard what He had to say about God's love for us could not help but praise the Father who sent Him.

Jesus' message included the idea that we are the 'salt[170]' of the world; flavoring it, preserving it, and making it more appealing to those who taste the goodness of God for the first time. Why is it necessary to joy-up the conversations we offer to others? Because we are tasked with making life better for all who hear our message as we point them closer to the truth. Our mouths should be spreading Good News, and that means we have to make a joyful noise to support our mission. If what we say makes others feel robbed of joy, the Good News we have to tell them will be drowned out by resentment, anger, sadness, criticism, gossip, complaints, and hypocrisy.

When we submit to Jesus Christ and let Him renew our hearts, one of the most noticeable changes will be the way we speak to and about others. However, it takes some practice to break bad habits, like cursing or gossiping or complaining. Often, new Christians find themselves in a radical place of excitement to meet with Jesus and tell others what they have found and finding the right words might feel challenging. We should

---

[168] James 3:8 ESV
[169] Luke 19:10 ESV
[170] Matthew 5:13 ESV

not be a stumbling block for others, but salt and light. Keep going, the Holy Spirit is at hand and change happens gradually sometimes.

Once we realize that we are living for eternity, our focus shifts toward long-term goals and eternal hope. We start to see the value of storing up treasures in heaven[171] where nothing cannot corrupt our joy. A renewed heart values joy highly because it is something that we can only fully understand once Jesus opens our eyes to His love. Before, we lived a temporal life; now, we live an eternal life. Our words must be born out of unity with our eternal God so that He can grant us the joy of our salvation and help us speak words to mirror that precious gift.

Words matter. God's Word endures forever, and our words are intricately connected with that eternal perspective. Words are the reason we sing and why we purchase greeting cards, read books, and write poetry. Humans believe in the power of words to develop a better world because that is how God created us. If we want to experience the power of a joy-filled life, there is no better way to express that than through the words we speak to others and ourselves. God has given us powerful words to shape so much of our lives on earth, and the desire to use that power for His glory should drive everything we say. Our love for God has a significant impact on this intentionality, making it a powerful catalyst in being more thoughtful about producing God-glorifying words. If we are focused on getting to know Him and love Him better, God will reciprocate with an increasingly generous outpouring of joy and other spiritual fruit.

Words are also powerful because they can change our perspectives. It is not uncommon to read books that topple our entire worldviews; perhaps, none more so than the Bible. God's Word is how we know that He loves us and remember what He has done for us. So, if we want to be having conversations that reflect our joy in Christ, there are two

---

[171] Matthew 16:19-21 ESV

important Biblical perspectives we need to consider; love is at the center of each.

The first is loving who we are because of *whose* we are. We need to appreciate that we were made a certain way because God loves us and wanted us to love Him back. God made us exactly as we were meant to be, but we need to see ourselves through His eyes to grasp it. He loves us so much! We need to allow ourselves to feel this truth deeply. If we understand God's love better, we will likely want to sing for joy every time we open our mouths. It truly is Good News that brings tidings of great joy to all, and Jesus is right there at the epicenter of it all. We need to give ourselves permission to be fully engaged and intentional about honoring God with our words. Speak encouragement, love, and blessing upon others and watch as the conversation fills up with Christ-centered joy.

The other perspective we need to adopt is one of faithful sharing. Jesus wants us to share the reason for our joy whenever the opportunity arises. There is really no other way to do that than through words. When we speak joy, our hearers will also be more likely to question how we got to that point and seek to understand our hearts. That kind of curiosity opens many doors for joy-filled conversations that revolve around hope, love, and how much Jesus has done for us. Christ's directives were clear about loving a neighbor as ourselves, and this includes being intentional about producing words of joy in our neighborly conversations. Intentional, joy-filled words during conversations creates a chance for us to speak about how and why we embrace the joy of salvation; it is also how we share Christ with a gentle, loving approach.

Truthfully, filling our conversations with joy seems easier when we are talking directly to the LORD. There is true humility in that exchange as we see how much He loves us, even when we are in desperate need of His grace and mercy. Yet, loving ourselves and our neighbors seems to bring more entanglements. There are far greater complexities in the equation when we are acting from human-based perspectives on both sides. For example, it isn't easy to talk joyfully to someone who likes to complain. It isn't easy to speak words of joy and peace to someone when life seems to be taking us through one disaster after the next, and the person we are addressing may not seem to care or understand. All of us naturally like to complain, criticize, and corrupt joy, thanks to inherent sin. We also continually seek confirmation or acceptance from other people. Perhaps, that is why we tend to draw each other into negative or God-dishonoring conversations for the sake of conformity or a false sense of belonging. Speaking joyfully is also harder when it seems like what we are saying is just not resonating with the other person; we feel alone.

In the previous chapters, we have explored how to access joy through the presence of God, breaking the bonds of sin, and accepting God's gift of a clean slate as we turn back to Him. We also saw how destroying negativity and planting joy in its place takes close collaboration with the Holy Spirit. Then, if we are finding that our words are not bringing God glory, it may be time to take a step back and remember who we are in Christ. We are never alone when we are in relationship with Jesus Christ. We do not have to wax lyrical to impress God, and we do not have to rely on acceptance from other people through what we say.

That last statement might be worth repeating we do not have to find acceptance from other people. Quite the opposite, a blessed and happy life is already ours to enjoy because we are already accepted and well-loved by our gracious Heavenly Father. Our joy is secure in our salvation. We have the presence of God in our renewed hearts of flesh, and He isn't going anywhere. So, if we want to produce a golden tongue that persuades others of the authenticity of our salvation, there is much to be done.

How do we start to season our conversations with a more intentional joy that comes solely from our connection with Christ? We have to stay focused on cultivating the fruit of love and weeding out sin. We also have to let love motivate us in the quest to show others what they can have if they follow Christ. The freedom that believers have in Christ should be inflaming an earnest intention in each of us to produce a golden tongue that glorifies God. Why? So that we can bring many others before the throne of grace.

The truth presented in 1 John 4:18 describes the idea that *"perfect love casts out fear*[172]*,"* and this is in the context of our salvation in anticipation of Jesus' return. Those who know God and have accepted Christ as their Savior can rejoice on the impending Day of Judgment without fear of punishment or retribution. It is wise to fear God and keep His commandments[173], but it is our love for God that draws us near to Him, not fear. There is no need for us to fear God's wrath or wonder whether our sin will tip some invisible scale; it won't. Instead, we are a new creation in Christ Jesus, and love reigns. This freedom catapults us into good works that will glorify God, including a tongue that honors the LORD at every opportunity. Love and joy gird our hope and orientate us toward others, as Spirit-given gifts that remove obstacles in our relationships by keeping us grounded in Christ alone. We don't have to worry what others will think of our choice to use God-honoring words filled with joy and power--God's glory is all that matters.

The fear of God is wise, but that it isn't the same as a fear of judgment. We are free of judgment because our Redeemer has assured our salvation by His sacrifice. However, it is still wise to recognize the might of the God with whom we are so intimately connected. The Creator inspires reverence and worship because of who He is, even though we are free to approach the throne with confidence under the blood of the Lamb. God's creation is also a testament to His preference as a God of order. He knows the time for each new season, spring, summer, fall, and, yes, winter. So it is with our words; joy can be found in all seasons because our Redeemer never changes, and He is the source of all joy and love. If we truly want to love God and please Him, we have to realize that a joyful

---

[172] 1 John 4:18 ESV
[173] Proverbs 9:10 ESV

tongue is a reverential one. It is born out of a God-honoring and God-fearing heart that treasures the Scriptures.

In Chapter 5, we looked at what it means to love God with all we have--heart, soul, mind, and strength[174]. We know a tree by the fruit it bears, and words are a very clear picture of the truths or lies we have adopted. Are we overcomers, praising God in the storm, or are we failing, cursing, blaming, or criticizing where there could be joyful conversation instead?

Life is a test of our character in many ways, and joy-filled words show whether we are making progress in the endeavor to be more like Christ. Most of us are well-aware that our words can build or destroy a relationship on any level with a spouse, parent, child, church, community member or work colleague. If we are to be joyous followers of Christ who speak righteousness and peace into the lives of others, things have to change. It is time for us to think about how we can realign our words to reflect the sanctification that Christ is working within us. How can we show that we are born of His spirit and abiding in Him? We start by asking Jesus to season our words with love and joy and show us the way.

Jesus-focused Hearts Speak Joy in Every Circumstance

When Jesus invites us into His Kingdom, and we accept that amazing gift, there is rejoicing across heaven. This call into spiritual awakening is intricately woven with the words that will now populate our thoughts as we learn more about the One, we serve. The Word guides us in this walk, by the power of the Holy Spirit. As Scripture penetrates the dark corners of our minds and illuminates the lingering lies and sin that need attention, we slowly start to see a change in how we see ourselves and others. For most people, life before Christ was eating and drinking and

---

[174] Mark 12:30 ESV

finding ways to be merry. However, when we have The Living Water[175] and the Bread of Life[176], we move into a life that seeks righteousness and peace[177] as its portion. Our goals change, and the sweetness of our connection with Christ is enough to satisfy our souls, deeply and forever. As we harness the joy of our salvation and tap into the Vine, it also becomes clearer when our words are not doing justice to Him.

A wise king (Solomon) once said that "a word in season[178]" brings great joy to us. Likewise, "A soft answer[179]" can prevent an angry exchange as we calm things down and lace our words with good. If we look at the world today, these timely reminders seem apt. Everyone seems offended by something because, well, nobody is perfect. We all say the wrong things or inflame situations where we could have brought peace. We all have those frustrating moments where we realize that what we have said has saddened or disappointed someone instead of bringing them joy and excitement. That's because no human has the complete ability to bridle what we say--only Jesus could do that perfectly. So, when we find ourselves at a loss for how to joy-up the conversation, that's the first port of call: a prayer to the LORD of our lives who always knows what to say.

As believers, every day is about learning that only Jesus can fill us up to overflowing with real, lasting joy. Only His work in us can ensure that our speech reflects an uplifting tone when we speak. "Positive thinking" is one product of a heart filled with joy, but Jesus remains the source of it. He gives us a tongue that has the power of life and death[180], and we need to realize that our mouths can declare miracles over our own lives and those to whom God sends us. Wholesome talk builds[181] others up and

---

[175] John 4:14 ESV
[176] John 6:35 ESV
[177] Romans 14:7 ESV
[178] Proverbs 15: 23 ESV
[179] Proverbs 15:1 ESV
[180] Proverbs 18:21 ESV
[181] Ephesians 4:29 ESV

creates opportunities for us to mirror the love and glory of God. How can we keep our way pure[182]? By guarding the Word in our hearts and cultivating an entire repertoire of joy-producing seeds. When we have joy in our hearts, it manifests in our words and sparkles in our eyes as we speak about how much God has done for us.

A word needs to be said about keeping our speech wholesome, but this might require another book to cover all the nuances of cultural and social gray areas that ensnare us. The best place to start is in prayer and communion with Christ. We can tap into the Holy Spirit's power to either speak boldly or hold our tongues. God-honoring conversations that are filled with joy will build others up and show them the love of Christ through our gratitude, sincerity, and infectious joy. The result of our salvation in Jesus Christ is a bubbling joy that seems to overflow as the Holy Spirit works through our whole being. Big or small, each change begins to make us think and look more like Jesus Christ. We start to value what He values and look at people with the same kind of love. We also start to speak more like Jesus as we learn to talk in His language.

God Speaks the Language of Joy and Peace So That We Can Embrace Life

Do you speak God's language? Jesus said, "(my) words are spirit and they are life[183]" and this is a powerful truth. If we speak in that language, the one that brings life to others, imagine how strikingly it could shape our conversations. Nothing can bring more meaningful discourse to life than a word spoken 'in season.[184]' Indeed, every word we speak has the power to change lives for better or worse. Proverbs 18:21 mentions that there is the power of life and death[185] in the tongue. The wise choose

---

[182] Psalm 119:9-16 ESV
[183] John 6:63 ESV
[184] Proverbs 15:23 ESV
[185] Proverbs 18:21 ESV

godly words because the tongue that goes unchecked is like a fire that doubles in size each minute; destructive, dangerous, and indiscriminate in its assault.

Instead, it is vitally important to speak righteously and lovingly. We should be cultivating words of joy that encourage, uplift, and inspire other people, believers or not. However, this can only happen when our spiritual condition is bolstered by its freedom from sin. As the Holy Spirit works in us, and we start enjoying an intense and committed relationship with the LORD, joy filters into our conversations more regularly. Unsurprisingly, the more purposeful we are about speaking joy into the hearts of others, the more satisfying we will find our exchanges with family, friends, communities, and coworkers. Those joy-filled conversations may even lead to more meaningful relationships with those to whom we would like to speak openly of God's love and kindness. If we love God, our chosen words will be intentionally joyful and God-glorifying, dedicated to speaking 'life' to others.

In 2 Kings 4:8-37, we are introduced to the Shunammite woman. One lesson we learn from her story is how to speak joy into situations that do not feel or look fine in the slightest. Her experiences show how we can still speak words of life when we are in distress because we have a God who is nearby.

The story begins with the woman's household providing great hospitality to Elisha the Prophet whenever he passed through their town, Shunem. Elisha wanted to repay the hospitality and asked God to grant the woman a son, though she did not ask him for this or believe his prophecy until the son was born a year later. Sometime after that, the boy died. The woman lay his body down and rushed out to find Elisha in the wilderness. Her husband saw her going and asked if all was well, and she said it was. Elisha's servant also asked her this question as she approached, and she gave him the same reply, "*All is well*[186]." However, upon reaching

Elisha the truth of her grief came out. It was very evident that she was not alright, and Elisha was shocked to see her grief pouring out before him. His servant had reported that the woman seemed composed, yet all was not well.

The woman's strength was not in her composed reply to those she saw along her path; it was in her realization that only Elisha (or God) could help her. She did not waste a breath explaining the situation to anyone else. She went straight to Elisha and would not leave until he had answered her cry for help. We could imagine that the Shunammite woman could have spent that time mourning or complaining to others about the unfairness of life. She could have railed against the prophet who, unbidden, had asked God to give her a strong and handsome son and then taken him away. She could have told her sad story to others or questioned the love of God in ways that made others doubt it, too. Instead, the strong, God-fearing woman held her tongue. She composed herself until she reached the only person who could potentially help her boy, and then she released it all into capable hands.

It's a beautiful picture of how we can say 'It is well' with us amidst the storms of life. These kinds of choices ultimately bring us joy. The Shunammite woman's son was raised, but she had already demonstrated that she knew the value of uplifting, God-honoring words when life's challenges seemed insurmountable. We need to joy-up like this woman, embracing a confidence that God *can* make all things well. There is no need to speak to anyone but Him about our most difficult experiences; He is enough. When circumstances become troubling, we can joy-up and revel in the fact that God still loves us. We need to do what David did and "bless the LORD at all times," allowing His praise to continually be in our mouths.

---

[186] 2 Kings 4:26 ESV

God is sovereign and His perfect plan for us is in motion. The Shunammite woman's life turned upside-down, first with the unexpected conception, and then with the tragic death of her little boy. Imagine the emotional turmoil that must have arisen; the anger and sorrow mixed into desperation to have her child back. Yet, she was able to gather herself and focus on her destination without distractions from those she met along the way. Instead of digressing or disturbing those who asked after her, she said that it was well with her soul, and carried on to the place of comfort, rest, and miracles. The woman must have had a deep-seated sense of God's power for her to interact with such outward joy when her heart was torn open and bleeding. A God-honoring, God-fearing heart like hers bears witness to the peace that surpasses understanding[187]. It guards us when our hearts feel broken or thrashed about by the storms that come to all in good time. That's why a golden mouth speaks God's Word and encourages others in their walks; it is a well-maintained tongue, doing its best to speak 'destiny' to others, with hope, through faith. A golden tongue avoids controversy and offense, saying too much or too little when the occasion calls for spiritual upliftment. It takes practice, and the guidance of the Holy Spirit to know what to say and when to say it, and thankfully, we can be confident that God will always show us the way.

Not only does Jesus Christ want to share His joy with us for eternity, but He also wants us to pass it on to others, to pay it forward in a sense. Jesus fills us to overflowing with Living Water so that our unending joy might spill over onto those we meet on our journey. The overflow does not stop when things go wrong for us or when we suffer. In some cases, it may even seem like our portion increases during these times, as the Holy Spirit ministers to our broken hearts. He washes away our tears and binds our wounds for healing. We do not need to be afraid to approach Him with our pain, or to pour out our grief on the altar of love.

---

[187] Philippians 4:6 ESV

Joy-up conversations come when we intentionally put words into our mouths that emanate from an intense agape love, the 'fatherly love of God for us and us for Him[188]'. This is the highest form of love and sometimes described as unconditional or immeasurable." *Love bears all things, believes all things, hopes all things, endures all things.[189]*" We have joy when we answer with a spiritually discerning and loving mouth that captures the essence of God's unconditional love for us. It sparks joy because it brings Him glory, and others notice when our words reflect this kind of wisdom. When we love and fear God as we should, out of that wisdom comes a timely word that gives grace to the weary. When we love God with all our heart, soul, and mind, with a fiery passion, we anticipate ways to share that love and joy with others. We speak with excitement and hope, words that elevate moods, season tough conversations, and bring light to dark spaces at every opportunity.

If we develop a wholehearted love for God through His Word, the Holy Spirit, and daily fellowship with Him, a God-honoring dialogue is bound to develop. Why? Because our hearts and minds mature in our knowledge and love of Christ. How do we get there? Well, joyful words start with joyful thoughts. We need to meditate on the Word of God, allowing the truth to infuse with our worldview and permeate our souls. It can ignite a blaze within us, a passion for what is good, right, and holy. Then, out of this spring, living water will flow, life born of the Spirit. It will gush over us, bringing with it renewed hope, love, and of course, joy.

How do we know when there has been a radical transformation of the heart? The Biblical message our mouths utter will reveal this change. If it doesn't, we need to run to the Holy Spirit for eyes to see and ears to hear the words that God is placing in our hearts and minds.

---

[188] Britannica (2021)
[189] 1 Corinthians 13:7 ESV

Joy is Produced Through One Resolve: to Speak Life Only

Have you ever marveled at the centrality of language in almost every culture in the world? Words are how we learn, live, and love. It should not be surprising then that Jesus asked His followers to 'tell' others the Good News. Evangelism through relational connection is a mainstream idea in modern churches, but even these love-based actions will need clarification with words (our own or God's Word) for a full understanding of the truth.

Words are a gift entrusted for righteousness and joy, and we can apply the laws of sowing and reaping to this area to curate more joyful conversations. Remember, God places people in our paths and it is never by coincidence. The people we meet are there so that we might speak words of life to them and then leave the Holy Spirit to do His work. So, what might be the result of more intentionally joyful words in our time with others? Hopefully, they will feel more positive about life, and we will feel exceedingly joyful knowing that we have brought glory to God through the exchange. There is powerful transformation potential as the sowing and reaping repeats its cycles. We may even find that 'speaking life' to others becomes easier with each new conversation.

The other result of joyful words is that God will be glorified through these types of conversations. He has given us the ability to understand His Word so that we might share its benefits with others. When we speak joyfully about life, faith, and everything else, God gets the glory. We honor Him when we appreciate our blessings, and we can imagine that God and his heavenly hosts would be thrilled when a person we are speaking with starts to comprehend our life-giving words. Undoubtedly, heaven gets ready to celebrate the return of one lost sheep.

When we put joy on our lips, we are sure to reap what we sow. For example, we may receive joy in the form of more positive relationships.

People gravitate towards positivity, and joy is infectious. We may also increase joy when our words become a source of evidence for our connection with God. It's impossible to tame the tongue, but the more we get to know God and love Him, the easier it is to speak life as the norm. God is a God at hand; He is not far off[190]. He takes our words seriously and He listens carefully to everything we say, think, and feel. He has chosen to use words to bring us life--the Word of God was there in the beginning--and we are made in His image. So, when we are transformed into a new creation by the Spirit, we will start to look more and more like God. That also means our words should sound more and more like His own. A new creation should be spewing words of joy, love, peace, and hope to all people; God hears it all.

So, how do we speak words that are seasoned with salt and purposed to preserve? We practice:

- using words justified by the Word of God (as a yardstick)
- choosing words that hold up to reason or dispute (like in Isaiah 1:18)
- crafting words in the spirit of God's Word (to glorify Him)

Our choice of words can only bring joy if it springs from the river of life. If we want to joy-up our conversations, our words cannot assassinate the character of others or wallow in sinful gossip and malice. Joy comes from the light, and that is where we find it. How do we joy-up the conversation and speak life to all those with whom we interact each day? We start by making a commitment to using God's language to paint a picture of our world. His brushstrokes are evident in every part of our lives and embracing joy as a daily goal helps us truly appreciate the vivid beauty of the love that surrounds us.

Below are six considerations that may help you curate words that speak life to others:

---

[190] Jeremiah 23:23 ESV

#1 Joy Resides in Being Slow to Speak and Slow to Become Angry

It is difficult to forget the account of when God became angry with His people yet again. It happened when Israel began complaining in the desert, speaking out against Moses and God about their apparent lack of food and home comforts. They were tired of eating manna everyday, even though Exodus 16:31 describes it as having a taste of '*wafers made with honey*[191].' As a result of this unrest, God responded harshly by sending poisonous snakes among the people. Some people died from the bites, and the rest repented, asking God's forgiveness through the intercession of Moses.

It's easy to gasp at this story and gloss over the nuances of what was really happening here but let's tread carefully; we can't see into the mind of God. The first observation is that these people were exhibiting slightly more than ingratitude. They were actually grumbling against God and the man He had placed over them. In essence, they were questioning God's love for them and accusing Him of unholy intentions. Imagine the audacity of the people to complain about their circumstances. Doesn't it give you chills thinking about it?

Here is a recap of what they had come through:

- Israel had received their freedom from the Egyptians' rule without lifting a finger; God did all the work through Moses and Aaron. The people literally walked right out.
- The whole multitude of people had walked *through* the Red Sea as God held up the waves for them and parted the waters. That experience included witnessing the pursuing Egyptians drowning in the waters behind them as God protected them once again.

---

[191] Exodus 16:31 ESV

- God had provided them with a cloud by day and fire by night to guide them through the desert. They only had to follow it.
- God had protected them by preserving their clothing and shoes[192] for decades.
- God had given them more than enough food and water on their journey. The food was manna, and later, quail as a source of meat.

What was Israel's response to these amazing provisions and outright miracles from a loving God? They were impatient. They expressed a hate for the food that God had provided. They accused Moses of leading them into the desert to die.

God is slow to become angry[193], but on this occasion, it seems like quite a reasonable response. It also shows how He feels about our tendencies to complain and question His intentions. We are free to approach God with doubts, fears, and anger at what has transpired, but it is still wise to remember that God's intentions are ALWAYS good. He loves us and wants us to experience the true joy that life brings when we are walking in step with Him. Sometimes, that walk is through a desert, or on the slopes of a treacherous mountain, but He is there with us. When we speak about our lives, including our struggles, it should be with words of utmost gratitude.

Set yourself one resolve: to joy-up the words you speak, whether in crushing times or the foreshadowing of tribulations that descend on Christians globally.

Of course, we find a great example of this resolve in the life of Job. After Satan accused him of weak faith, he lost his children, livelihood, and spousal support. He also suffered through sickness and ridicule from people he thought were his friends. Job's words reveal the depth of his

---

[192] Deuteronomy 29:5 ESV
[193] Psalm 145:8 ESV

faith. In Job 19:25, he says, *"For I know that my Redeemer lives, and that at last he will stand upon the earth.[194]"* Isn't that incredible? Job had lost everything, and his words still spoke of life abundant. His thoughts dwelled on redemption, wholeness, and hope.

Bringing joy to our conversations requires being in agreement with God[195]. He offers us peace and we would do well to accept it. If our words honor God, good will come to us. If we receive instruction from His Word, laying it up in our hearts, we will be able to draw on encouraging promises and truth when the going gets rough. Job was an amazing inspiration in this area of developing a golden tongue that speaks life and joy, even amid trials:

- Job 27:3-4 speaks of being alive as enough reason to rejoice saying, *"as long as breath is in"* him, his words would seek to utter truth. *Say, "I will praise God and speak the truth of His Word as long as I have breath!"*
- Job 1:21 continues with a revelation of being 'naked' as we arrive on earth and as we leave it, with the famous exhortation that God gives and takes away and we are still to bless His name! *Say, "I will bless the LORD whether he gives or takes away because He is worthy of praise and honor!"*
- Job 5:17-18 embraces the discipline of the Almighty as healing not hurtful. *Say, "I will trust in the LORD's timing and reproof for He cares! He binds my wounds and heals my hurts!"*
- Job 13:15 encourages us to trust in God, "though he slays" us. That's a big ask, but it is at the heart of faith. *Say, "LORD, I trust you with everything. Even if you tell me, it is time to join you in heaven, I will walk in your ways."*
- Job 19:25-27 implores us to remember that our redeemer lives! Victory is already won, and He shall stand as King before all

---

[194] Job 19:25 ESV
[195] Job 21:22 ESV

one day. *Say, "LORD, My Redeemer, I believe that you are victorious over sin and death and that you have triumphed over evil. Help me to hold onto the promises you have given that I shall see you one day in all your glory!"*

Job's words send chills up and down the spine, especially considering the start of his story. The first verse of the book sums up his character, *"There was a man in the land of Uz whose name was Job, and that man was blameless and upright, one who feared God and turned away from evil.*[196]*"* The man was blameless, absolutely free of any guilt, and still God allowed him to go through suffering, persecution from close friends, and deep loss. Yet, the upright man's words reveal his unrelenting admiration for God. He had a soul-deep knowledge of the greatness of his Heavenly Father that would remain, even if worms corrupted his flesh. There was a resounding joy in his words. *"I know my redeemer lives.*[197]*"*

If we consider uttering these words with faith and humility, joy will flood our souls! Our Redeemer lives, and, like Job, we can say that is true in any circumstance. Job acknowledged this joyful truth aloud, even after experiencing betrayal from those he trusted. He praised God, even as he watched his entire life crumble into the dust. When all he was left with was the sores covering his body, Job's humility demanded that God still be glorified and enjoyed. He had nothing left, yet he still had everything he needed.

Our words carry a greater power than we can imagine, as the Holy Spirit's power filters through us. He helps us speak life and brings joy to our souls as we grow in the knowledge of the Mighty God we serve. How can we not aim to be the most positive joy-speaking, joy-spreading people on earth?

---

[196] Job 1:1 ESV
[197] Job 19:25 ESV

#2 Speaking Joy and Life to Others Is Why We Are Here

If you're wondering how we know that God expects us to 'speak life,' consider the story of Ezekiel. God drew him into a valley filled with dry bones[198], showing him the valley's contents in great detail. There were dead, dry remnants of people who had lived long before; essentially, an area filled with very old bones. As Ezekiel walked around, God told him to 'prophesy' to these bones. He was to tell them that God would raise them and 'put breath' in them so that they could return to the land of the living. It probably seemed ludicrous to him, but Ezekiel obeyed. He started to speak to the bones as requested, telling them that God would bring them to life.

The rest is part of the long and fascinating history of miracles we see happening when God is near. Ezekiel saw the power of speaking life into dry bones that day because he was not just putting empty words into the air and hoping they would achieve some purpose. No, the words that Ezekiel spoke were Spirit-filled missiles of hope and life that came as a direct act of obedience to the Word of God. God spoke; Ezekiel listened. Ezekiel moved to speak life as directed, and God worked miracles to honor that obedience.

Without God's mighty power directing his efforts, Ezekiel's words would have fallen on dry bones, as ours do when we throw careless words into the world around us. Instead, Ezekiel's words brought amazing life as far as the eye could see, bones rattling and growing sinews, a literal life-giving transformation that resulted in both awe and rejoicing.

God already knew what He wanted to do in the situation, but He still asked Ezekiel to speak. When our Heavenly Father asks us to speak with joy and gratitude, He already knows the outcome. Our words have

---

[198] Ezekiel 37 ESV

the power of the Holy Spirit to guide their course, but He requires obedience of us to speak to them. If we do, we can experience the joy of seeing that power in action from our very lips. It seems that God wants us to participate in His miracle-making, not just stand as a witness. Why? So that we can testify passionately about all He has done and remember these demonstrations of His love as long as we live (that's forever!). He requires faith and fortitude from us, and all He needs is our mouths as an instrument to bring forth fruit. Your words can bring God glory--use them well!

Sometimes, there is no choice but for us to speak life over ourselves and others, even when it seems like a crazy or impossible situation. We must remind ourselves to hear the words and promises of God clearly and confidently, focusing on what He is telling us to do as we shut out the noise of the day. When we pray over others and speak joy into all kinds of situations, God hears, and brings forth abundant life where there were dry bones. When we speak life, the rumblings of good things come forth and we see dead hearts raised to a place of everlasting joy and hope in Jesus Christ. It was the same way when God created the earth and all that was in it.

"In the beginning God created the heaven and the earth. 2 And the earth was without form, and void; and darkness was upon the face of the deep. And the Spirit of God moved upon the face of the waters. 3 And God said, Let there be light: and there was light. 4 And God saw the light, that it was good: and God divided the light from the darkness.

-Genesis 1:1-4 KJV

When God spoke the earth into being, it was an entire universe that came from His lips. The galaxies, planets, and everything else began as a dark void until the Word who was with God and was God spoke. The Spirit of God moved, and He spoke life into the dark, letting light reveal the goodness of His commands. He told the universe He created, 'Let there be light[199]' and there was nothing then or now that could have stopped the light from obeying its Creator. God is sovereign over all things, and that is the power behind our words of life.

#3 A Heart's Treasure Overflows from the Lips

Job's example of curating God-glorifying words despite desperate uncertainty is captivating and inspiring. In Job 23:12, the man is replying to his three friends who are all accusing him of wickedness. They believe his misfortune is of his own making, punishment from God. However, Job withstands the temptation to delve in self-pity, anger, or complaints. Instead, He defends his faith and obedience to the LORD, saying to the doubtful friends, *"I have not departed from the commandment of his lips; I have treasured the words of his mouth more than my portion of food.*[200]*"*

Job's treasure was not in the children, possessions, spouse, or health that he had just lost; rather, he treasured his relationship with God above all things. His heart was steeped in faith, love, and hope in God. That is where his source of joy lay, even as the last of his friends abandoned him and unjustly accused him of treachery or sin as the only 'logical' explanation for his suffering. They were wrong; Job's suffering was a test of his resolve, a litmus test to see what his heart valued most in life. Job passed. Would you and me?

Our mouths should be a reflection of the joy of our salvation. If we have the living and active Word of God[201] penetrating our hearts, then the words that we speak will show this purity, gratitude, and unending joy as we treasure the connection with our Redeemer. Hearts are cleansed through Jesus, and when He becomes what we treasure most[202], what comes out of our mouths will show a faith like Job's that does not bend or

---

[199] Genesis 1:3 KJV
[200] Job 23:12 ESV
[201] Hebrews 4:12 ESV
[202] Matthew 6:21 ESV

break under pressure. If you want to joy-up your conversation, you need to realign with God's Word. A heart focused on God produces joy-filled words as a result of this treasure[203], and that is how we begin to glorify God whenever we speak. God's Word helps us to engage with others in more encouraging or edifying discourse.

Why is our salvation the greatest source of joy? Because it brings us into precious intimacy with the Person our soul was created to love Jesus Christ. If our hearts grow more and more confident in His love, our speech will be filled with grace and joy that shows others how much our Savior means to us. A grateful heart is a humble heart, and this is the stance we need to adopt before we open our mouths in any situation. Be slow to speak, and weigh what you are about to say with these checkpoints:

- Will my words bring joy to this situation?
- Will the other person see grace in what I have to say, or will it offend them?
- Do these words carry life or the power to destroy?
- Am I speaking from a place of humility or defending self-righteous indignation?
- Am I speaking in obedience to God's Word or reacting from human emotion?
- Do these words show that I treasure Jesus above all else?
- Do these words offer encouragement and godly solutions to a problem or add fuel to the fire?
- Would it be kinder to remain quiet and look to the Holy Spirit for guidance on what to say?
- Would I say the same thing if Jesus was standing right beside me? (He is!)

---

[203] Luke 6:45 ESV

#4 There Can Be Joy in Abundance Within Our Hearts of Flesh

Words are tricky, and most of us could probably give at least ten examples of how we have seen words destroy relationships or escalate trouble. It seems clear that God wants us to have joy in abundance, which is why He gives us His Living Water to overflowing. We should not be taking a defensive posture when our words could show humility and grace instead. We should not boast or take credit for the gifts and talents God has given us to steward when words of gratitude could bring Him the glory He deserves.

The Holy God expects His People's words to be honest and upright. It is not in line with His character to permit words that are 'not technically' telling lies or that create confusion. Circumventing issues while deceiving others is Satan's forte, and that is not an appropriate timbre for the children of God. Rather, our words should be a tree of life, building a space for others to rest and admire God's amazing provision. We should use every word for the glory of God because each of us will have to give an account of how we used these opportunities, or why we failed. If we are not consciously preparing ourselves for the final day when all will kneel before the King, that might be a good place to begin as we curate God-honoring conversations. Think about intentional, joy-filled words and pray about ways to practice using them--those are the words that we will be pleased to showcase before the LORD one day.

We also need to recognize the sheer power of words for death and life. Words can kill and they can bring about everything from nothing. God spoke and there was light; Jesus spoke, and Lazarus walked out of the tomb. The Creator could just as easily destroy what He has made with one word, but instead, He chooses to continue using words for life. The Word was there in the beginning, long before He dwelt among us. When we hear the Good News about this incarnation and resurrection, the

Word transforms us, once again using His words to grant us life. God made us in His image, which means that we, too, have the power to give life or destroy it by what comes out of our mouths. It should never be something we take lightly; Spirit-filled words are meant for life and joy, but they also carry the power to end that in an instant.

That's why hurting someone with our words is an act of great audacity in the face of a loving God. A person could be scarred forever by the words we speak with shameless abandon, and there is no undo button. Once the heart receives a word, it penetrates bone and marrow[204] to the deepest recesses of the soul. There's no going back. Words shape us, define our stories, and search out the truth of what our hearts believe. Our words could destroy others in the way that repeating gossip ruins families, friends, and churches. If we let rumors circulate, our words could be responsible for cancerous divides and gaping wounds in the communities God has called us to serve. So, how can we be part of the healing and speak life more consistently? Sometimes, it requires our silence. Do not let gossip destroy joy or ruin a life-giving mission; rather, be quiet before the LORD.

If we must speak, we should do so with great care. Purify the source of the words and use these words to give life to others for the glory of God. If it isn't something we would say to Jesus' face, we should hold our tongues. Take note of how the Pharisees did not understand why Jesus disregarded the importance of washing rituals around eating. They thought the non-Jewish believers were impure because they did not follow the Jewish law in this way, yet Jesus' reply was direct and easy to understand it is not what goes into the mouth that's dirty but what comes out of it! Our words reveal our hearts, and it is our hearts that need cleansing by the Word Himself.

---

[204] Proverbs 12:18 ESV

Seeking a joy-up experience requires a close examination of what truly lies in our hearts. Why did we say that? What are the deeper issues that need cleansing before these words can come out in a more joyful, God-honoring way? The only way to do that is to go to God and ask, like the repentant King David did, *"Create in me a clean heart, O God.*[205]*"* Only the gospel can penetrate our hearts deeply enough to transform our words for good. God already knows what we think and feel when nobody else is looking, including the lies, slander, and secret sins that we are yet to bring before Him in repentance. Christians are not complainers by nature; our nature has been renewed. If we find our words are made up of endless complaints, we should ask ourselves whether we have understood that the gift of salvation is truly sufficient. Is there something we are missing? Take the time to connect with the Savior and ask Him to show it to you.

It is not enough to learn how to filter our words; there has to be a real, heartfelt change in the way we think and feel about our salvation. The joy of our salvation is ever-present, even when life's challenges seem to suppress it. When we picture a life of joy, we typically think of it being filled with celebration, connection, worship, and an active working of the Holy Spirit. In Psalm 43:4, David wrote *"Then I will go to the altar of God, to God my exceeding joy,*[206]*"* which is the kind of image we could easily associate with David's joy-filled way of life. He praised God with music and words alike, and he achieved great feats for the sake of glorifying God and enjoying Him outwardly. David was a man who knew the power of a word and wielded it mightily, and it is a natural extension to imagine his conversations brimming with the joy of salvation; he so frequently referenced it. He sang, danced, built, feasted, and inspired others as the man after God's own heart, and we see clearly how David embraced joy even as his life took twists and turns that tested him.

---

[205] Psalm 51:10 ESV
[206] Psalm 43:4 ESV

If we want to joy-up the conversation, we need to bring that real, lasting joy to the surface and let it bubble right over into our speech. The joy of our LORD is in the river of newness--we are a new creation--and it can bring such glory to God if we use it in good measure.

#5 Do We Speak Blessings Upon Others or Invite the Joy Thief in With a Curse?

In the same breath that we summon joy and life to our conversations, we also need to recognize the potential for sin to taint those intentions. Satan waits expectantly for us to open our mouths so that he can reach in and help us blurt out the curses that linger among the seeds of blessing. Likewise, there are no gray areas with God when it comes to our hearts. We are either dead or alive; born of the spirit or born of the flesh. If words define who we are, then children of God should speak blessing and words of joy; those who are still dead in their trespasses would be more likely to lean more toward evil, unrighteous words that cause death. If our words do not reflect this renewal, it would be wise to examine whether we have truly embraced salvation's fresh start, or perhaps, missed the point.

God's people are alive in Christ and overflowing with blessings. As an extension, our words should be wise, like the sweet honeycomb that brings healing to the bones[207]. When we give in to the tongue that cannot be tamed, we confirm that our sin evokes words full of deadly poison. James speaks of how we bless and curse with the same mouth[208] and that this is not the way it should be in God's Kingdom. It is a great reminder of the freedom of choice God includes as part of our sanctification package--we can choose to speak blessings and summon a fountain of sweet water in our conversations, or we can choose to let lies, envy, and bitterness steal our joy.

---

[207] Proverbs 16:23-25 ESV
[208] James 3:8-14 ESV

If we want to joy-up our conversations, we need to remember that we are eternally connected to the Vine, even when we are speaking to a friend about trivial or mundane aspects of life. The fruit we produce is a gift from the Spirit, and our purpose is to bring forth love, joy, peace, patience, kindness, goodness, gentleness, faithfulness, and self-control in abundance. We do this in our meditation on Scripture as we fortify our hearts for action. We also see these fruits manifesting in our choice of words as we draw strength and sustenance from the Vine Himself. If we are producing other sorts of fruit, the products of sin and death, we need to reexamine our heart-mouth connections more diligently in the light of God's Word.

For example, James 3:13 reminds us that wisdom and knowledge lead to '*good conversation*[209].' Some Bible translations frame this conversational tone as '*meek*,' which implies a quiet, gentle, or submissive way of engaging with others. Cursing and shouting do nothing for our connections with others; it only reviles people and loses us opportunities to be salt and light to the world. If we commit to sharing only truth with others and doing so with a gentle spirit and loving intentions, miracles may happen in our conversations. Gentle discourse involves making our points with meekness, which will lead to engagement with others and plenty of room for joy. If we can put our point across calmly, people are more likely to listen, even when they aren't in agreement. It is the kind of connection that Jesus made with everyone He met, whether He was issuing encouragement or admonishment. Our Savior used gentle but firm words that pointed others to God. In doing so, the LORD dispelled the darkness around Him with an overflow of love, joy, and peace to all who heard Him speak.

The idea of control in 2 Corinthians 5:14 is also something we need to address when we start thinking about ways to speak life to others more consistently. The verse describes Christ's love that '*controls us*[210]' but this is

---

[209] James 3:13 ESV

not forced coercion; it is submission. Love exerts control on us because we submit to its power. When we see what Jesus has done for us--that Christ died for MY sin--the revelation changes how we see ourselves in relation to Him. It opens our eyes to His immense love for us, and that makes us want to hand over perceived control to Him (He is already in full control, we only have to acknowledge it).

God's love is honey to our lips, dripping with a sweetness that brings joy to the fore. The love of Christ takes us to new heights of joy because our sins are forgiven, and our debt is paid. We can celebrate, guilt-free. We can bask in gratitude for the blessings that we receive daily in knowing Jesus Christ, debt-free. Ceding 'control' to our Savior is not relinquishing our power, it is multiplying it! So, if we imply that God controls our lives, what we mean is that His love and joy become pivotal to our success; we cannot do without them once we *'taste and see that the LORD is good!*[211]'

Jesus asks us to take up our cross daily, to die to ourselves and live with Him at the helm, but this is not because He wants to enforce His rule. He already rules, with or without our acknowledgement or approval. Rather, taking up our cross is how we allow Christ to demonstrate His unfathomable love for us. He does not whip us as we stumble; our Friend and Savior walks beside us. He supports and encourages us so that we might see just how capable we are in Christ. He does not ridicule our desperate cries for help or ignore us; He answers our call. Jesus Christ is generous with His love and power, giving us even more light when the night seems darkest so that we may understand where to go.

God is most glorified by our conversations when we speak words that He places within us--His Word. That's what makes Him joyful, and that's where our joy is to be found. Nobody can bring us joy and hope like Jesus Christ. Sometimes, He asks us to move in mercy and grace, to keep going, keep planning, or keep speaking. Other times, He may ask us to be quiet

---

[210] 2 Corinthians 5:14 ESV
[211] Psalm 34:8 ESV

and stand our ground. When our faith is flailing and our words are deteriorating in quality or joy-up potential, we can be still and know that His strength is enough for us. Denying ourselves is sometimes the only way to find out who we can be, to fully immerse ourselves in that connection with Christ. I AM is in control, and He can direct our conversations as intricately as He directs our lives for our good.

#6 Speaking Joy Sometimes Requires the Art of Silence

Joy is in that active outworking of faith, a gift and a realization as we grow closer to the LORD. However, it is also worth meditating on joy as a kind of permission to hold our tongues when we risk going off track. Our greatest example of this is Jesus Himself, as He responded to questions from his accusers in Luke 22 and 23.

For instance, when Jesus responded to Pilate's questions, He was intentionally vague and unfathomably calm. He did not put His joy on the line by getting worked up as His accusers tried to sling mud and hoped it would stick. Jesus also declined to provide extra words to Herod's inquiries[212], remaining silent. Words would probably have inflamed the tension already present in that moment, and chaos has proven itself an efficient thief of joy if we let it in. Jesus wielded the art of silence, but it did not rob Him of His power or influence in those conversations. We do not have the same power as the Son of God on our own merit, and we have to be even more vigilant about wielding our words to safeguard our joy in Christ.

Thankfully, God is with us, as He was with Jesus that day during an unjust trial by popular opinion. We serve a God that is always present, not a God unconcerned about our well-being. Our loving Heavenly Father enjoys seeing us speaking life to others--it is how we pass the 'test' of what

---

[212] Luke 23:9 ESV

is truly within our hearts. Jesus' words confirm that He wants us to share in His joy forever, so when we open our mouths to speak, this should be the aim.

Will the words we are about to speak aloud show that we value God above all else? Joy-filled conversations do this by:

- providing biblically sound reasons for the hope we carry
- sharing the Good News explicitly or through our personal testimony of God's grace and favor
- grounding our approach on a measure of how well we exhibit the fruit of the Spirit (we might come away from the conversation and say things like, "Those words showed my faith (or love, kindness, gentleness, or joy)"

The Matthew 12:37 reminder is also a valid reason to practice the art of silence whenever we are about fling idle words into fertile soil. We will be condemned by our words and justified by them. We need a continuous resolve to put joy on our lips and only speak life. That may mean committing to choosing silence as a more loving, joyful, and peaceful alternative. The same idea applies to our relationships, which are complex and cumbersome to maneuver where words flow unchecked. In many instances, the Holy Spirit is the only one who knows the perfect words for bringing about a joyful, life-amplifying conversation. If we ask for it, the Holy Spirit will come into our conversations and show us how to find the joy, step by step.

So, when it seems that our words are making joy-up conversations elusive, the best approach is to press into the Vine for a fresh infusion of joy:

- In our quietness, we possess strength. (Isaiah 30:15)
- The fruit of the Spirit is love, joy, peace, and more. (Galatians 5:22)

- The joy of the Lord becomes our personal joy and strength. (Nehemiah 8:10)
- For everything there is a season, including joy-preserving silence. (Ecclesiastes 3)
- We can tell our enemies to be still and know that our resulting joy is a gift readily available from Jesus Christ. (John 16:33)

It isn't easy for us to be silent when words want to explode like hot lava at the first rumble of impatience, indignation, or indignity. However, it is an important skill for Christ-followers to master if we are to trust God's plans. He has promised that every situation will play out for our good and His glory.

Our connection to the Vine is the only way to grasp real and lasting joy. This is the relationship that we cannot live without; in Him we live, and move, and have our being[213]. Heaven rejoices when we use our words to bring healing to others and honor to the LORD; and the same applies to our thoughtful periods of silence and self-control. When we reside (abide) in the presence of God, the joy of our salvation brings forth fruit at the right time and in the right way. We can think of a joyful life as a tree, planted by rivers of Living Water. This tree can bring forth fruit in season, since our God assures us that there is a time and a season for everything under the sun. There is a time to speak and a time to refrain from speaking. If we are tapped into the LORD and open to all He is doing in our hearts, we can learn to appreciate His presence more and more each day. In God's presence there is fullness of joy, and the more cognizant we are of His presence, the more we magnify and glorify Him in our minds. God is near, so when we focus on that nearness diligently, we are less inclined to limit Him in our minds. The same idea applies to our spoken words; if we invite God into our conversations, there will be

---

[213] Acts 17:28 ESV

fullness of joy at hand for every word we speak (or choose not to say aloud).

People know that a negative tongue is a terrible stumbling block, but even more so for a believer's faithful witness to the lost. As Christ's chosen people, must resolve to become heavy hitters of joy, bent on presenting uplifting, God-honoring words in each and every conversation. The Mighty One is always with us, listening, watching, and ready to help. When we are drowning in temptation to sin by lying or being unkind, or anything else that detracts from joy, all we have to do is close our mouths and open our eyes. God is here, and He is good, all the time. Giving in to negative words clouds that closeness and tricks us into thinking God has retreated into some other place; He has not. We can turn around, redirect our steps, and find Him in the same place, faithful and true.

When we let God-dishonoring words drip from our ungrateful and self-possessed lips, we sin. Why? Because we go against what Jesus has asked of believers. God asks us to spread Good News, not hate, judgment, or chaos. If we choose to obey Him by making joy a priority in our conversations, we honor Him, and experience even more joy as He is glorified by our words. When we speak joy and blessing on others, God chimes in with granting us the same in abundance. So, God's love for us is the most compelling force behind our role as a joy spreader. Yet, we cannot forget that we love because He first loved us[214]. Knowing how merciful He is ensuring we enter these conversations with the right perspective and attitude. We can then more readily rejoice in our salvation, finding fullness of joy in the presence of God; our conversations will be better for it.

Why not let joyful conversations become the audible sound of your love for God? Bless the Lord at all times. Allow His praise to continually be in your mouth and boast in the LORD because He is worthy.

---

[214] 1 John 4: 19 ESV

Of course, we are not only called to have joyful conversations with other people; speaking to the LORD in this same attitude is also desirable. Joyful conversations with the LORD show that we find Him more precious to us than silver and gold. If this is truly what our hearts believe, the reward will be an ever-greater knowledge and understanding of Him, the God of grace and glory. What a precious gift it is to know Him! The sweetness of the relationship He offers us should make us want to be in constant conversation with Him. Prayer should be continuously on our lips, speaking to our Heavenly Father as His beloved child. Sometimes, this looks like child-like conversations, short and sincere snippets of praise, petition, supplication, and thanksgiving. Other times, it might be more earnest discourse that takes us long into the morning hours as we turn to the LORD for comfort, strength, guidance, and vindication. The more we connect with Him, the more of Him we will be allowed to see; love grows, peace reigns, and joy overflows. In the same vein, the more we study and memorize God's Word, the more resources we will have to draw upon when we need to curate joyful conversations that bring God glory. The Word of God sinks into our souls as nourishment for life; only once we are saturated with spirit and truth can we speak it.

We should also remember that it is best to be silent when joyful words do not come naturally. We need time to rehearse our responses, replaying the speech in our minds so that it will be edifying when we are ready to express it. If it seems like the opposite of joy is about to escape from our lips, we should stay silent and seek God's guidance. The LORD can heal our scars and deep wounds so that we can let painful experiences go. Our past should not define our future--God already knows the joy that's coming for us if we choose to follow Him.

So, let offense die before you speak. Proverbs 17:9 puts it this way, "*Whoever covers an offense seeks love, but he who repeats a matter separates close friends*[215]." Practically, this may look like us saying, 'Sorry, I do not

---

[215] Proverbs 17:9 ESV

want to comment on that right now. Let me think about it and get back to you.' Or it might be that we leave the room without saying one word. Love is a good reason for silence and saves us from lighting fires we cannot control in our relationships, communities, and churches. A God-honoring mouth covers offenses with love, which also means that we should not bring up old matters once the conversation ends. Repeating wrongs and showering others with guilt is not loving; and it does not reflect the forgiveness that Christ has afforded to those He saves. Jesus has forgiven us and covered our sin with love; we must do the same for others. Love keeps no records of wrongs! If a situation will embitter or cast offense, refrain from the temptation to speak.

Joy-filled Speech is a Picture of How Much Jesus is Worth to Us

Silence can be golden, but if we are prepared to speak, God will send opportunities our way. We can express joy in every circumstance by capitalizing on the chances that Jesus gives to us each day. Knowing when to speak and when to be silent is not always clear, but we have the power of the Holy Spirit to lead us. All we have to do is ask Him for clarity, as we wait patiently for His reply. We can rest assured that God is unquestionably pleased when He receives our undivided attention and hears us speak His Word with conviction. It may be through taking opportunities to worship, pray, or minister to others; or it may be clinging onto the love of Jesus when we are uttering our last breath.

A bridled tongue has the power to change lives. With a few choice words, we can cut right to the heart of the matter and heap joy onto the heads of those who hear us speak. There is perhaps no greater example of this Spirit-enabled self-control than that of Stephen. His story leaves no room for doubt that he loved Jesus deeply and was willing to suffer for his faith. However, those beautiful qualities were not even the most remarkable part of Stephen's life. In Acts 7:55-60, we read of Stephen's final prayer and God's reaction to that desperate plea.

> *"But he, full of the Holy Spirit, gazed into heaven and saw the glory of God, and Jesus standing at the right hand of God. 56 And he said, "Behold, I see the heavens opened, and the Son of Man standing at the right hand of God." 57 But they cried out with a loud voice and stopped their ears and rushed together at him. 58 Then they cast him out of the city and stoned him. And the witnesses laid down their garments at the feet of a young man named Saul. 59 And as they were stoning Stephen, he called out, "Lord Jesus, receive my spirit." 60 And falling to his knees he cried out with a loud voice, "Lord, do not hold this sin against them." And when he had said this, he fell asleep.*

-Acts 7:55-60 ESV

Stephen seems to have had a deep and abiding joy that restrained him under the most terrible circumstances. He was a man that had the Holy Spirit firmly entrenched in his life, and He preached the Word of God with boldness. In fact, it was his fervent passion for the Word of God that drove people to stone him, a painful and terrifying way to die. Yet, Stephen used his last breath as an opportunity to show love to the very men that were putting an end to his ability to speak.

Let's look at his final words again as they stoned him: *"Lord, do not hold this sin against them.*[216]*"* A dying man is an honest one. All he has is stripped away and laid bare at the feet of his Maker. Yet, Stephen did not cry out for deliverance or heap curses upon the heads of those who were in the process of murdering him. Instead, he called out to God for mercy and forgiveness for his killers. Instead of indignation, anger, and judgment, Stephen reacted in the same way to his enemies that Jesus did in His final moments, *"Father, forgive them for they know not what they do*[217]*."* Stephen's situation, like Jesus' crucifixion, was the most humiliating and

---

[216] Acts 7:60 ESV
[217] Luke 23:34 ESV

excruciating pain had experienced on earth. The words they chose to bring to that moment were filled with love and peace in abundance. They didn't ask God to avenge them; they asked God to forgive people and let them discover the joy in salvation. How many of us in the same situation would probably have asked God to pour suffering upon those who were in the process of hurting us or killing us in slow, painful ways? Both Stephen and Jesus uttered destiny with their last breath and the Spirit responded by honoring those requests.

Stephen's connection with the LORD gave him a clear joy-based perspective. We see it in the earlier verses, as he gazes into heaven and realizes afresh who holds the power over his life. Instead of seeing a bloody battle and his battered body fading into death, Stephen used his eyes to see heaven open. He did not focus on pain or the fact that his earthly walk was at an end; he only saw Jesus, standing there with him in solidarity. The King of the Universe was there, the Son of Man who had been through the very same humiliation, suffering, and death that Stephen was experiencing. *"Behold, I see the heavens opened, and the Son of Man standing at the right hand of God.[218]"* Jesus Christ was right there with Stephen, alive and well, in all glory and honor at the right hand of God. Ordinarily, we read of Jesus being seated at the right hand of God (Matthew 26:64, Hebrews 1:3, Hebrews 12:2, 1 Peter 3:22). However, this case accounts for Him standing up. There must have been a surge of joy that brought Jesus to a stand as He revealed Himself to Stephen. If you ever find yourself losing your joyful tone, the thought of Jesus standing right there beside you in anticipation may be enough to remind you to focus on the good.

The LORD is with us, guiding and affirming us. He is praying on our behalf for everything in our human experience that we do not have words to express[219]. God is love and, in His faithfulness, we can rejoice,

---

[218] Acts 7:56 ESV
[219] Romans 8:26 ESV

even when we are drawing our final breath at the hands of angry, misguided, or evil men and women.

Jesus urged his followers to count the cost of following Him[220], and Stephen had done this to the greatest degree. He did not stop sharing the message of love God had placed on his heart. Could we resolve to be equally determined to go 'all in' on our journey with Jesus Christ? We do not know where God will send us or what He might require from us during our lives on earth, but we do know that heaven is near. When we are tempted to let our words wound, we must be mindful that an outburst is preventable. Someone greater holds our soul in His hands.

We might also have to be willing to pay the price of silence in exchange for finding the joy we so desperately seek. God said, "*Vengeance is mine*[221];" and that means letting go and letting God. Our words can bring joy, mercy, and grace to others, no matter the other person's intentions toward us. All we need to do is focus on God's intentions, and that is always to give us an outpouring of love, joy, and a peace that surpasses understanding[222].

Stephen seemed to understand that the chief end of our lives is to love God and find joy through fellowship with Him. We must love God with all our heart, soul, mind, and strength, guarding ourselves against the fiery darts. Nothing can destroy God's gift of joy. If we are knocked down and feeling spent, this connection with God will bring fullness of joy amid any outward circumstance or inward struggle. Stephen spoke life to others as rocks pummeled his lifeblood into the soil. Jesus spoke love and mercy to others as He sank into darkness for three days before His resurrection. No matter what you are going through, joy is possible.

We must be determined to speak words of positive encouragement, godly conviction, and joyful celebration so that we can stay in the light

---

[220] Luke 14:28 ESV
[221] Deuteronomy 32:35 ESV
[222] Philippians 4:6 ESV

and bring others into it. If winning the argument is more important to us than producing the Spirit's fruit, there is work to be done and a golden tongue to mold. These are unprecedented times, and with uncertainties come great opportunities to lift our conversations and saturate them with joy. Some of us are spending more time in conversation with close family units than ever before, but does the conversation offer joy-sharing? Is there love where we open our mouths or do our words cut with the ability to kill relationships and decimate joy for ourselves and others?

In the same way, uplifting our social dialogue is far easier when we have curated a more loving and joyful inner dialogue. We need to clean up the words we speak to ourselves, filling them with Biblical truth and laying up God's Word in our hearts like treasure. The Holy Spirit does His work through God's Word, so if we have not memorized Scripture or meditated on its meaning, we are missing valuable resources in our Christian walk. These times require us to have a golden tongue, full of life, love, joy, mercy, and grace. 1 Peter 4:11 says, *"If anyone speaks, they should do so as one who speaks the very words of God*[223]*."* We are vessels of Christ, and even though we may never go through the terrible physical suffering that Stephen and Jesus endured, mental suffering can still be a fiery trial. To pass the test, we must stymie the temptation to speak negatively about what's happening to us. We may also need the wisdom to remain silent in the face of pain, lest we say something dishonorable to or about God as Israel did in the desert.

The heart drives the quality of our speech, as Jesus completes[224] His work within us. If we are joy-filled, we will speak joy. However, the only way to ensure that we don't find ourselves speaking sinfully instead is with active and frequent repentance. We need to 'handle' our sin by laying it at the feet of Jesus in repentance; we cannot do it alone. Daily confession to our LORD and Savior is part of this relationship we are building with

---

[223] 1 Peter 4:11 ESV
[224] Philippians 1:6 ESV

Him eternally. He already knows our hearts, but there is something profoundly special that happens when we utter aloud to Him all that we are too ashamed or weak to take to anybody else. The Shunammite woman bore her burden only so far as the person who could help her carry it, and that is what we need to do with our LORD Jesus Christ who anchors our souls. When we lay down hopeless, negative thoughts and words for 'handling' by Jesus, amazing things start to happen, and that golden tongue is one step closer.

How can we keep our tongue from spreading poison while we are disillusioned or downcast? By anchoring our souls to the love of God. Trust that in silence, God has our backs. Let Him fight the battle before we utter regrettable words that take the spark out of life. The result of repentance and continued relationship with our LORD is joy in freedom and forgiveness. Our position of hope opens our eyes to God's glory and helps us filter joy into every conversation and every situation. James describes the tongue like a rudder, powerful enough to move a huge vessel one way or the other. If our hearts are trained on Jesus, they will more easily learn to rein in the tongue and redirect our conversations for good. The Holy Spirit is on hand to help us in this quest, as verses like John 15:26 call us to 'bear witness[225]' about God's gift of love and righteousness. We testify to God's offer of salvation by speaking joy and life to others at every opportunity.

Allow the love of God to take you to heights you have never known in your relationships with your spouse, children, family, friends, neighbors, and whomever else God places in your path. Forget religion; embrace intimacy with God and the joy that percolates in the pursuit of Him and He of you. Words determine whether we win or lose, and The Word Himself has already secured a victory for us when the story ends.

---

[225] John 15:26 ESV

A plan to joy-up conversation shows that we love Jesus beyond anything else in life. Investing in this relationship is the key to binding and loosing blessing and favor on everyone we talk to so that they may know our God of joy through good tidings. For now, Christians need to start winning again so that others can see our good words and glorify the King. We need a golden tongue of biblical proportions to speak the fruit of joy.

Joy Up with Jesus

> *"Until now you have asked nothing in my name. Ask, and you will receive, that your joy may be full."*
>
> *-John 16:24 ESV*

Joy is a fruit of the Spirit, which is gifted to us so that we can bring glory to the LORD and enjoy Him forever. If we want to know more about who Jesus is, we need to take time to cultivate the fruit of the Spirit, including bringing these qualities to the words we speak to ourselves and others. As a start, John 16:24[226] reminds us that we only need to do one thing if we want joy: ask for it. We need to open our mouths and ask for a revelation of who God is and who we are in relation to Him.

We have seen how Jesus grants us a share of His joy so that our joy can be full to overflowing. Once we start to read God's Word to understand this gift better, we notice the trend of how joy manifests first in the heart, then on the lips. From the heart springs forth the words, we speak (see Matthew 12:34, Romans 10:10, James 1:6). Our thoughts and ideas of righteousness also dominate our inner dialogue, working and moving as they build momentum. Finally, this joy or lack thereof becomes evident in the quality and tone of our conversations.

---

[226] John 16:24 ESV

What does joy sound like? It sounds like words of righteousness, love, and integrity. When we think of joy, we think of good pleasure, rejoicing in what's happening all around us as we move and have our being in the presence of God. Likewise, our speech should have a tone of excitement and anticipation as we approach all kinds of situations. Our words should cause everyone around us to sense and feel joy, almost by a spiritual form of "osmosis."

How can we find encouragement to produce godly speech that exhibits joy at all times? By remembering the promises of God:

- Let the weak say I am strong, and the poor say I am rich (Joel 3:10)
- This is a mouth of wonders (Psalm 89:5)
- This is a mouth that waters (Isaiah 12:3)
- This is a mouth of joyful anointed words (Psalm 45:7)
- This is a mouth that declares it is never defeated (Isaiah 61:3)
- This mouth will make a joyful noise! (Psalm 100)
- This mouth will speak the Word of the Lord, (John 6:63)
- This mouth declares God's splendor (Psalm 71:8)
- This is a mouth that professes Jesus in boldness (Romans 10:9)
- This mouth will lift the anxiety of others (Proverbs 12:25)

Words begin in the heart, so one way to build a golden tongue mentality is to memorize Scripture as often and as thoroughly as possible. We need to mold our words, and to do that we need to have materials at the ready. We cannot speak life to others when there is life-crushing material taking root in our hearts and minds. We need the Spirit's power to be rid of this negative, God-dishonoring sin as we let the Word of God be our inspiration.

By grace, the Word of God teaches us sound doctrine so that we can internalize this message of love. The Spirit moves, letting God's message penetrate each and every bit of darkness trying to uproot our joy. It illuminates the way forward, giving us a genuine, heartfelt joy that others can experience at face value. Make no mistake, people understand when joyful conversation feels 'forced,' and this is not the purpose of connecting with others in this way. We do not want to offer a fake optimism, but a true transformation and awakening to Jesus-sourced joy! It will be life-giving poetry to the ears of all who hear us speak, and nobody will be able to resist looking up to see if the One we bear witness to is as beautiful as He sounds.

CHAPTER 7
Joy-Up: For the Fight!

For some, it has been a long while since stadiums were filled to capacity with adoring, competitive fans. The visible anticipation of the crowds makes the excitement palpable, a feeling that gets in under our skin and seems to draw us into some other-worldly place. It smells like fast food, spilled soda, turf, and imminent victory. At first, people seem to whisper in unison, a deafening buzz like the gathering of a million bees. The atmosphere builds until about a minute before the game, and then suddenly, there is nothing; only a collective intake of breath as everyone waits for it to begin. The beating wings of a pigeon overhead might draw a gaze from someone, as small children are quickly hushed and the pre-game countdown ticks down to zero. In that moment, the only sound is of thousands of lungs holding air, and thousands shifting on the edges of their seats. It is a slice of eternity caught up in wide eyes and bodies braced for action as the battleground emerges far below.

Stadiums are not for everyone; the level of noise as the game kicks off is nothing like we experience in other modern settings. Our rushed lives do not allow for most of us to show up to the town square as important news announcements or political statements are broadcast. Instead, we listen to these events on our smartphones, alone, or with earphones at the preferred volume. We read the summary so that we do not have to listen to an hour of rhetoric on crackling speakers or engage with messages we don't really have time to hear.

The only other comparison that might resemble the tension at the start of a stadium game is the start of a battle. Not a surprise attack that comes out of nowhere for one of the sides, but the kind of fight where enemies are poised on opposite sides of an open field, brandishing weapons. The troops are in position, knowing that the clash is unavoidable, yet wishing peace was not on the other side of violence, death, and fear. They wait, silently, almost reverently, wondering when they will see or hear the dreaded signal to move. Some rile up comrades, pumping the adrenaline as they prepare to defend their cause. Others groan inwardly and resign themselves to fate, a numbness that often lingers long after the battlefield is behind them. In the moments before the battle call sounds, there is no certainty of victory, no indication of how long it will go on, and no help coming. There is the same moment as in the stadium, lungs holding air, wide open eyes, and a bracing for the fight that is sure to come.

In a stadium, the feeling is excitement and even hope. But the battlefield's cries are steeped in fear and doubt. There is courage, but also immense trepidation. There is hope for a win, but also a palpable uncertainty about whether the enemy will uncover some advantage and end it all. Half of the stadium's crowds might rejoice as the final whistle blows, but for the battle, joy is not so easily found. Celebration is fleeting as the body count becomes evident, injuries start to hurt with waning adrenaline, and the cost of life is counted. Can there be joy on the battlefield? What about after it? How do we head into the fight with joy in our hearts when we know that suffering awaits?

Some of us are feeling the 'light affliction[227]' that the Bible promises to Christ's followers deeply. It might be that we have faced the reality of a

---

[227] 2 Corinthians 4:17 ESV

pandemic's widespread deaths or that there are other stress factors at play. We might be enduring political upheaval or new and varying challenges and feeling like we are on the losing side. Whatever the struggle, many Christians appear to be losing their grip on joy, drifting into disillusionment or fear as life takes a turn that none of us could have reasonably expected. It might be just a moment in the eyes of an eternal, all-powerful God, but for those of us standing in the midst of a storm, it feels like an eternity. We feel the weight of that suffering in every bone, bearing down on us, and testing our will to live. It's a battle to keep our head above the waves as the trouble keeps coming, like heavy rains; it buckles courage and drenches self-motivation.

The Biblical mandate to 'rejoice always[228]' might be the last thing on our minds as we contemplate all that is happening around us. That kind of human reaction is understandable as we face a universal testing of our faith in times of trouble, and time will tell whether we have passed the trial with flying colors or failed to leave the ground. The global upheaval since COVID-19's emergence was particularly challenging for those who lost loved ones or colleagues, saw government restrictions limit former freedoms, or felt fear rising. Believers and non-believers alike experienced sickness, job loss, grief, aggressive mandates, and financial pressures. Inflation threatened livelihoods and social issues reared their heads. Churches could not meet freely in fellowship, and ministries stagnated under contact restrictions, financial strain, and fewer hands and feet to help.

When we think about joy amid suffering, we have to allow ourselves to recognize the fight that we will face. We have to look honestly at the commitment it will require to take hold of and cling to joy when the storm rages and our lives feel in jeopardy. Those who profess to be the hands and feet of Jesus in the world also have to realize the scale of the attack on the church's joy from every side. The Enemy looks to exploit all

---

[228] 1 Thessalonians 5:16 ESV

angles in a bid to dislodge our grip on joy. He wants to sever us from the source of that joy. The Bible uses wartime language to describe the life of a Christian, and that is no mistake. These words are divine-inspired truths about how life will look on earth as we wait for the LORD's return, and it looks more like a battlefield than an airport waiting lounge.

While we know that the Bible's focus is on the fight that is not how it ends. Rather, God's story ends with victory--already won by Christ on the cross--and those who believe in the Son of God are on the right side. All that comes with this promise is only a reminder of how to walk toward peace with a joyful disposition while we are not yet at the point of fulfillment. We are walking through the battle now, one fight at a time, but on the other side there is peace everlasting. That's the only reason we strive forward into each moment of the fight with joy in our hearts. However, it is undeniable that we often simultaneously feel many other emotions while we also feel joy; emotional rollercoasters pervade our experience. Yet, joy is an ever-present help when less helpful feelings arise. It is something we can cling to *while* we feel scared or anxious or confused. A solid grip on joy brings us back to Jesus, reminding us of the anchor for our hope. We wouldn't need to look for peace if there wasn't conflict first, and we wouldn't need to treasure joy if there were no opportunities for the enemy to extinguish it while our focus languished elsewhere.

Why did Jesus emphasize so many verses of encouragement to stand fast, gird up, trust, and anchor our hope on God's promises? The answer lies in what He knew was coming for those who took up His call. When we take up our crosses, we have to understand the burdens that may come with the gnarled, sacred wood rubbing against our shoulders. What we choose to carry may feel like it is making it harder to breathe at the moments when we are not feeling our best, but Jesus is with us. The Holy Spirit gives us a spirit of power, not timidity. We are strong in the LORD and His love never fails.

'In this world (we) will have trouble,' and that means we will have to keep facing tough situations and heartbreaking decisions, even when we are feeling a little tired of all the drama. This is not the kind of self-inflicted drama that seems to follow so many people around, but rather, a directed, strategic attack on our wellbeing for the purpose of distraction, disillusionment, and doubt. It is relentless, an evil source of constant tension in our lives. We want peace, and we were made for peace, but there is work to do first as we fight for what is ours to keep. The day is coming when Jesus will give us a crown of glory as a reward for our willingness to fight. Indeed, the joy that we fight to preserve in this life is an eternal treasure that nobody will ever be able to steal from us. The joy we find now will be within our souls forever and ever, and it is worth the fight.

Unsurprisingly, finding and holding onto the kingly treasure is challenging work that tests our spiritual muscles. It is especially difficult to joy-up and launch ourselves into the fight for God's Kingdom when we do not feel happy with our circumstances or certain about our campaign. How do we know that we are fighting for the right things? How do we avoid pitfalls and sideshows that keep us from progressing in our sanctification? Satan is a master at distraction, typically sending us on only a slight deviation from our original course. Sometimes, we do not even notice the ploy until we are far from the intended rendezvous.

The fruit of the Spirit is literally a list of ingredients that help us prepare for our task ahead. These qualities secure a victory in the battles we face daily, a holy gift that comes with our salvation in Jesus Christ. We have full access to these spiritual gifts at all times, but it still takes a concerted effort on our part to grab hold of what's available. We have to move as the Spirit does, obeying His call to fight, and accepting the weapons, strategies, and courage He wills for us. When we fight for joy, we are effectively saying that we are willing to make room for joy in our hearts as we enter challenges, temptation, and even terror. When we take hold of love, joy, peace, and other resources for spiritual warfare, we are agreeing to let the Holy Spirit fill us with these good things while we fight. At the same time, we focus on letting go of sin that binds, including the fear, doubt, and disillusionment that one might reasonably expect to find in the middle of a war.

And, we are in the middle of a war between good and evil.

War is a strong term, but it rightly describes the state of the world as it moves ever closer to that glorious day when Christ will return. There is a continuous tussle for souls between the two forces, even though we know that Christ's death and resurrection has already secured our victory. Jesus is already King over all. He has the authority to put evil in its final resting place, but it is not quite time yet. There are still people who need to believe in Jesus to be saved, our children, great grandchildren, neighbors, and friends. The timeframe is closing for humanity, but the eternal God does not have the same temporal limitations as all of us. He sees past, present, and future as one, and He does not change. He remains our ever-faithful, ever-joyful LORD.

The joy of the LORD is our strength because it is permanently part of who He is and impenetrable by dark or opposing forces. On earth, time is a factor. We live second by second, and year by year. We watch our bodies grow old and our progeny grow up, and then we leave it all behind. That is how God has made us, with a cycle to teach us many lessons about Himself. He gifts us with seasons, an allotted time, and one window of opportunity to invite Him into our existence as our LORD. That's it. The Enemy understands this concept better than any of us, and he works and weaves to ensure that we miss that opportunity by any means possible. He might use pride, distraction, lust for money or power, envy, selfish ambition, greed, or complacency. It is a bitter fight for souls, and joy is a huge part of that endeavor. If Satan can quench our joy or keep our eyes from seeing the good, he might crush one more soul for eternity. It is that serious, and that makes finding and holding onto joy a genuine battle for our souls. God takes the fight just as seriously, even though He knows who wins. As we walk with Him in our time-bound life, the Savior gives us the tools we need to joy-up for the fight. These resources include grace that is sufficient to redeem us and encourage us after of any skirmish we lose along the way. The battle is the LORD's, and He is on our side.

In Ephesians 6:10-17, we see a powerful description of the Armor of God. This protective gear is gifted to those who are in God's 'army,' as the fight rages for the redemption of souls. Yes, victory is assured, but each moment on earth presents one more opportunity for evil to try again.

Before we move into the armor of God in more detail, it would be wise to remember why joy requires a fight at all. After the directive to press into the Vine--to abide on the Vine that is Jesus Christ--the passage in John 15 goes on to state the reason that God wanted us to stay so closely connected to Him. It says, "*These things I have spoken to you, that my joy may be in you, and that your joy may be full.*[229]" God seemed well-aware that we would need to fill up our joy tanks, so to speak, while we went about life on earth amid struggles and temptations. The Word is a clear reminder to God's people that His eternal and complete joy is available to us when we pursue a deeper relationship with Christ Jesus, the Vine. It also states the reason that God wants us to live this way--so that our joy may be full. Isn't that an amazing picture of Fatherly love?

Our Heavenly Father wants to see His children so saturated in joy that they can face anything with complete assurance of who they are and where they are going. Surely, that is what we want for our own children, and even more so when we look toward heaven. Full joy means that no more filling is possible and that our hearts will be entirely able to rejoice with the joy of Jesus Himself for all eternity, no matter how life looks or feels. When we joy-up for the fighting that is ahead of us in life, that is the

---

[229] John 15:11 ESV

goal. We want to receive the joy of the Father to our full capacity, to the point where we are absolutely satisfied in Him and Him alone.

To get us to the point of fighting for joy on a daily basis, the LORD has graciously given us The Ephesians 6 armor[230]. This kit consists of six pieces, as follows:

- v17 the helmet of salvation
- v14 the breastplate of righteousness
- v14 the belt of truth
- v17 the sword of the Spirit
- v16 the shield of faith
- v15 the shoes that carry the gospel of peace

The seventh component of this set of armor appears in verse 18, which puts out a call for us to keep alert and persevere in prayer; specifically, in supplications for fellow believers. Exploring each layer of this beautiful analogy would take a tome on its own, but for now, we will look at how each of these seven ideas helps to get us battle-ready under the banner of God. We will also discuss how we know whether it is time to defend our position, stand our ground, or go out on the offensive.

Fighting for the Joy That is Ours Forever in Christ Jesus

Pandemic-induced afflictions are heavy for many of us in this modern, disconnected world. The church has faced challenges, like not being able to meet freely under law due to government restrictions. Of course, this a trial already felt by thousands of believers in countries where Christianity is equal to a punishable offense under the law. Even still, online meetings have become the norm in many 'free' countries since the start of the global pandemic and it feels like there has been a shift in how

---

[230] Ephesians 6:10-17 ESV

the church operates. However, the head of the Church has not changed the mission nor revoked the calling. Trials come and go, but the Word of the LORD stands forever[231].

Even as life and the way we do church have changed for a time, it is difficult to dwell in self-pity when we look at the suffering that Jesus and other believers have faced before us. For example, we might take a few moments to dwell on the church at Smyrna (modern-day Izmir, Turkey), mentioned in Revelation 19. This church was mentioned fleetingly in the Bible, and we do not know much about how it started. However, we do know a lot about its apparent suffering as we delve into the text and historical context (you might want to sit down for this one).

Revelation 19:8-11 tells us the following about the church in Smyrna as the Apostle John passes along the message of Jesus to these faithful Christ-followers:

"8 And to the angel of the church in Smyrna write: 'The words of the first and the last, who died and came to life. 9 "'I know your tribulation and your poverty (but you are rich) and the slander of those who say that they are Jews and are not, but are a synagogue of Satan. 10 Do not fear what you are about to suffer. Behold, the devil is about to throw some of you into prison, that you may be tested, and for ten days you will have tribulation. Be faithful unto death, and I will give you the crown of life. 11 He who has an ear, let him hear what the Spirit says to the churches. The one who conquers will not be hurt by the second death.'"

-Revelation 19:8-11 ESV

The text is clear about a few facts:

- The church was suffering under persecution from Jewish non-believers (v9).

---

[231] 1 Peter 1:25 ESV

- The church was poor (v9). Some commentaries mention it being 'dirt poor' (Keeth, 2008) as their social and economic standing in society plummeted with the rise of their faith.
- The church was going through a lot of trouble and would continue to face slander, suffering, imprisonment, testing, and even death (v10).
- The church had a reason to be afraid in earthly terms (v10).
- The church was faithful and was under the protection of God (v10-11).

If any people had a reason to abandon joy under suffering, it was Smyrna's believers. Everything seemed to be against them in their hometown, with a prosperous port city bustling around them and nothing they could do to cash in on that success. They were sidelined, slandered, and set to suffer for the name they chose to carry, yet Jesus' words (He is the "first and last" mentioned in verse 8) show such compassion and offer strength. He says to the church, "*I know your...poverty (but you are rich)*[232]." Jesus had walked that road of owning nothing, relying on the hospitality and kindness of others. He understood how persecution extended not only to words and emotions but to basic human rights. The poor do not have the food, shelter, or love that every human deserves. We can argue over these 'rights' but in our hearts, we know that this is the truth. Every person deserves love. Every person deserves to be able to nourish their body and find a safe place to rest their head each night. Anything else feels wrong; intuitively, we know that it is wrong to lack these basic life-giving necessities. Body, mind, soul, and strength is commanded to love God, but that seems a lot harder to do when the stomach is grumbling, and the mind is racing at a hundred miles per hour in fear or worry. Smyrna had challenges in all these areas, and Jesus wanted them to know that everything was going to be okay.

---

[232] Revelation 19:9 ESV

Interestingly, the text does not say that their suffering would end or that they would be able to get back to prosperous, happy lives once the trial was over. On the contrary, verse 10 calls for these believers to be 'faithful unto death.' Jesus seems to be reiterating the call to find and hold onto joy *because* death is indeed coming for all of us. This phrase refers to the time when our bodies on earth will die and our souls will be taken up to Heaven; the first death is our soul's separation from the body but the second death (in Revelation 20:14, 21:8) refers to the separation of our souls from the presence of God. These images are the stuff of nightmares, but Jesus' follow-up reminder quells that fear. He promises that faithfulness begets eternal rewards. So, what should faithfulness 'unto death' bring for Smyrna's church and for us? A crown of life that will always glitter as it reflects the radiance of our King before us.

The language in these verses reiterates the battle talk we mentioned with a call to 'conquer' in verse 11 (or 'overcome' in other translations). What do we conquer or overcome to not pass into a place of eternal separation from God? Perhaps, we start by conquering the enemy's strategic decimation of our joy. We find joy in Jesus, commit to the relationship, and hold onto that joy day in and day out, even unto death. That's the way we conquer the enemy and find ourselves with a crown of life bestowed upon our heads by Jesus Christ our LORD.

Of course, that joy might be all we have in times of suffering, persecution, poverty, or prison-like experiences. But Jesus has promised that He is all we need. The enemy comes to steal, kill, and destroy anything that resembles God, and this includes our joy. Smyrna was a good and faithful church that will receive great reward for its conquering of the enemy's designs, but it still suffered tremendously here on earth. The joy that we have access to today is the very same joy that Smyrna's believers had access to while they were hungry, imprisoned, misaligned, and watching their brethren die horrible deaths; it is the joy of Jesus, and He has not changed in the few thousand years that have passed since this passage was written. He is the same, yesterday, today, and tomorrow, the first and the last, the beginning of time and the end of our fight. His Faithfulness is why we can draw such strength and comfort from Him in times of trouble--the joy of the LORD is our strength. Amen.

When the enemies of God threaten our joy, it is time to rise up and do battle. We must joy-up for the fight, preparing our heart, mind, soul, and strength for all that is to come, even unto death. How can we do that with joy instead of fear? By believing the promises of God and staying in proximity to the One who holds our joy steady. The roar of the enemy tries to make us tremble, but we will not quake at the sound of swords clashing or blood awash with tears. The people of God will stand and fight, joyful and ready to serve under the banner of love that Jesus offers to all who believe in Him.

Joy is the right weapon to bring to the battle, and we cannot allow circumstances or fear to overtake us. We must conquer all that hinders us from taking up the call to arms, including pride, doubt, and personal areas of distraction. The enemy sneaks in wherever he can find a foothold, which is why God has given us such a full set of armor to cover every eventuality. Head to toe, heart and soul, God's protection and love cover every mark of sin or death lingering in us. When, not if, adversity pounces, we must fight for joy and pay careful attention to the Holy Spirit's lead through the fray. Fighting for joy represents a crucial turning point in our lives, the moment where we finally understand why we are here and the extent of the commitment we make as we take up the call of our LORD. This is counting the cost and finding it of no value compared to the surpassing worth of knowing Christ[233].

How can we find that kind of renewal and readiness when we see the battle right in front of us? How can we fight for joy when the oncologist confirms our worst fears, or the eyes of our children remain closed despite

---

[233] Philippians 3:8 ESV

our desperate cries for help? Is there joy to be found in the desert, where poison, thirst, and devastation are indiscriminate. Yes, there is still joy to be found there, even as the tears fall and the last drops of blood run dry. Even unto death...because death is not the end for those who walk with Jesus, it is only a doorway. For what can a powerless enemy do to us if death is his only threat? Where is the sting if opening the door is simply walking through to eternity in the presence of the King[234]?

What joy we can find in our relationship with Jesus while we dwell where moth and rust and disease and disillusionment destroy! How much fuller our joy will be as we finally see Him face to face and watch as the last remnants of darkness disappear forever behind that doorway of 'death.' There is no sting in that; only joy is the surpassing worth of our Savior. No power or circumstance will change a full joy; there is no room for anything but pure and lasting joy. That's the level of joy that we are fighting for when we go out in the full armor of God. We need weapons like the sword as we internalize Bible verses, and we need stamina to continue for as long as the LORD's call sounds. We also need patience or perseverance to know that sometimes, the night is long, but joy comes in the morning. If we hold onto the fruit of the Spirit and dress daily in the armor of God, we will be able to prepare ourselves for the tribulation to come.

So, put on the whole armor of God and get ready to find out just how powerful it is to have the victorious King's joy as a constant source of strength during the fight.

Follow Jesus and Fight for Joy

As we take up the call of the LORD and agree to journey with Him on the mission ahead, there are two aspects we need to consider. The first is that we are called to fight for joy against an enemy that would try to

---

[234] 1 Corinthians 15:55 ESV

take it from us in any way that He can. Our joy is found in a relationship with Jesus, so the enemy destroying that joy is effectively a blow to our intimacy with Christ. We make progress as we dwell on the Word of God and then we fall back a few steps as the enemy targets our joy with distraction or despair. It's a game to him, watching us stumble forward and find a grip. The enemy's scouts watch closely as we finally regain our momentum and forge ahead in our relationship with Jesus, and when we seem to be winning the race, they throw another pebble (or boulder) into our path so that we stumble or deviate or break a limb. Our LORD graciously warns us of these tactics and stays right by our side as we pick ourselves back up and keep going.

One thing that we cannot do is faint at the first sign of attack. The LORD God is strong and mighty, and He gives us fortitude. The Holy Spirit gives us a spirit of power and endurance to overcome the advances of the enemy, and that means we do not have the 'small' strength of Proverbs 24:10 or the bone-deep anguish of Psalm 6:2. And boy, do we need the strength of the joy of the LORD and the armor, weapons, and strongholds He provides to get through what lies ahead of us.

When David found himself under attack, the man after God's own heart asked the LORD for help and guidance. "Shall I pursue[235]?" In that case, God gave David permission to pursue the enemy and overtake them by force, but there are many other instances where God commanded people to stand their ground and watch Him do the work. In the amazing battle of 2 Chronicles 20, King Jehoshaphat inquired of the LORD about their approaching enemies. God's response was that Israel should stand firm that day and watch. God then proceeded to raise up other nations to destroy the enemy of Israel, and then caused those nations to destroy themselves. When Israel arrived at the place God told them to go the next day, all they saw were the dead bodies of a vast army--none of them had to lift a finger in that fight.

---

[235] 1 Samuel 30:8 ESV

When Jesus asks us to be of 'good cheer' in our time of tribulation, He is gently reminding us that He is the giver of that cheerful disposition. If we are at a place where we can put our trust in His power, our reward will be an unquenchable joy, whether we are fighting, standing, or dying. We can have soul-deep peace while war breaks our bodies and disease penetrates our earthly defenses. We can have soul-deep joy while the enemy plays tricks on us and tempts us to despair because Jesus has overcome and invites us to join Him in victory.

The Word of God is described as a sword because life is a fight--a struggle against dark forces that want to prevail over the light of Love Himself. We struggle against our own sin, too. God has given us protection and retaliation tools, including the powerful fruit of the Spirit and the impenetrable armor of God. Why? Because we cannot expect Christians to be exempt from the experiences and heartbreak that will require us to use that wartime grit. We have it because we are going to need it; frequently. Sometimes, the battle will require us to stand and fight, and other times we will be able to watch the LORD scatter the enemy before us as we hold our ground and worship. For both situations, we need training, weapons, and courage.

For fighting, we need arrows. These might be internalized Bible verses, continuous prayer, or a gratitude that the world will never be able to explain. We also need stamina, which might be to realize the depths of ideas like "the joy of the Lord" as our strength. It is also necessary to realize that we are fighting a war, not one battle. It may come in the form of one battle after another, a daily fight, but the bigger picture of our Christian walk is that joy comes in the morning. We need patience to overcome the world as Jesus did, and for that we need hope. Do we trust our LORD to lead us through danger or even death's door? Do we fully believe that rest will come, even when we are exhausted by our physical, emotional, and spiritual trials? It will. Joy is always at hand in our relationship with Jesus, even when we are tired or heartbroken or wounded.

So, when we fight for joy, we must also fight with joy. Jesus wins: death has lost its sting. We know that the path of life is leading us to the fullness of joy, no matter the obstacles we may face on the journey. How do we fight with joy as we fight for joy? With the armor of God. It provides us with adequate defenses against the rulers of darkness and spiritual wickedness in high places[236]. God has given us all we need to stand up to these attacks because His return draws nearer, and He has already seen that we will experience many such trials. The armor is for defense purposes in the evil day[237] but it is also to help us stand and withstand. If God asks us to fight, are we ready? Are we fully dressed for the occasion that might determine whether we receive a crown of glory or only a pat on the back?

Jesus' words in the Gospel of John confirm that the fight is coming for all of us who profess to follow the LORD, our God and King. His wish is that we take comfort during the battle in knowing how it ends. It is true; we know who holds the key to continuous, unshakeable, battle-winning joy. Jesus wants our joy to be full enough to carry us through any trial, temptation, or attack, and He gives that joy to us straight from His own heart; that His 'joy may be in you[238]' and that we 'might have peace.[239]' What a gift!

Let's start with how we can prepare ourselves for the fight ahead by putting on the full armor of God:

- the belt of truth
- the breastplate of righteousness
- the shoes of the gospel of peace

---

[236] Ephesians 6:12 ESV
[237] Ephesians 6:13 ESV
[238] John 15:11 ESV
[239] John 16:33 ESV

- the shield of faith
- the helmet of salvation,
- the sword of the Word of God

We also discuss how to cling to joy with perseverance, make supplications for our fellow soldiers, be constant in prayer, and take strength from the joy of the LORD.

Joy-up with the Belt of Truth and Breastplate of Righteousness

The first two pieces of armor are the belt of truth to hold our weapon in place and the breastplate of righteousness to protect our hearts from all that comes at us during the battle.

On the offensive, a soldier's weapon should be at hand so that they can access it quickly and wield it as needed. Having the belt there to hold up the weapon is crucial to surviving the clash of swords and also having a hand free while the other holds the shield. In this case, the Bible speaks about our weapon of choice being the Word of God (the Sword of the Spirit), and the belt of truth is what holds this weapon in place and ready for us to use at will. The truth is not a version of something that's real; the truth of God's Word is the only thing that is real. It never changes and it 'stands forever.[240]' When we wear truth around us, joy can flourish amid the battle cries because we know how it ends. If we die, we gain a reunited life with Christ in heaven. If we live, we carry God's name as we continue to serve His purposes on earth and bring others to know Him. Both are beautiful outcomes, and both are the only outcomes possible when we are girded up with truth and invested in an eternal relationship with our LORD and King, the One to whom the battle belongs.

---

[240] 1 Peter 1:25 ESV

The enemy comes with lies, treachery, distraction, and guilt tripping, but the truth sets us free from all those attacks. As we fight for joy in Christ, we can also fight with joy because Jesus has already overcome the enemy and lives victorious. He extends that victory to us, even when it feels like we are still picking our way over the battlefield.

We mentioned the subtleties that Satan favors in his attack on God's people, but the Bible also describes his attacks as 'flaming arrows[241]' and a 'roaring lion[242]' waiting to devour the vulnerable. When the battle feels stifling and our hearts are tempted to fall into fear, that breastplate of righteousness is the protection we need to keep going with confidence. Even if there are flaming arrows and roaring lions up ahead, righteousness--a right standing before the Living God--is our full protection and strength. It wraps itself around our fragile hearts and makes us brave enough to keep following Christ into the thick of the fighting. Our clean slate before God is how we revel in that relationship while still grappling with some lingering sin in our lives--He already sees us as acceptable by the blood of the Lamb. Righteousness comes the moment we confess with our mouths and believe with our hearts that Jesus is LORD and that God raised Him from the dead[243]. Our hearts are secure because they belong to the victor, and it is the LORD's joy that sustains us as we walk with him through the fight. He may not ask us to spectate from afar, and our joy is not dependent on circumstances being peaceful, comfortable, or safe. But, where Jesus is, there is joy. And sometimes, that is right in the middle of a war.

There are times when our fight is against our own desires, too. We might have to fight to deny ourselves; that is, to focus on following the will of God rather than our selfish ambitions. If we do take up the cross of Christ, there is great reward in that, including eternal joy as He

---

[241] Ephesians 6:16 ESV
[242] 1 Peter 5:8 ESV
[243] Romans 10:9-10 ESV

strengthens our souls and affirms our path. In this pursuit of truth and righteousness, it is also vital that we remember that we follow a good, good God who wants to show us how much He loves us at every turn. If we make an effort to realign our walk with where He is headed, we get to walk each moment in life in step with a friend, father, and King. He is good, and He takes joy in knowing that we are enjoying His company and upholding His truth. He enjoys seeing us happy in our relationship with Him, which is why it sometimes feels like He lavishes blessings upon us in the same way that an earthly Father dotes on his own children. God's love abounds, and He delights in His children.

If this is our focus, the raging battles around us dim in comparison. The noise of war becomes a background feature of our safe, happy place in the company of the LORD. Joy bubbles up as we walk in His footsteps, the way a small child jumps into His father's footprints on the beach and tries to imagine what it might be like to fill them one day. It is a beautiful truth to know that we are righteous in the eyes of our Father, and the more our hearts understand what they are worth to God, the greater our joy is in Him.

Joy-up with The Feet of Peace for the Race to The Finish

The third piece of armor is technically a shoe, but a special one. Verse 15 of Ephesians 6 talks about walking in the gospel of peace, like having our feet comfortably protected in it. As we walk with Jesus from battle to battle, it is easy to see why shoes of peace might become something we rely on to keep us grounded. Battle is hard, and we have to continue to pass through trouble spots if we are to reach our destination (eternal life in heaven).

Have you ever felt a blister rising while you are on a long hike or a jog, and still very far away from the comfort of your home? It is cringeworthy knowing the pain that is sure to come as we feel the skin rubbing and our steps faltering. In battle, shoes wear out quickly with all the marching, running to or from the battlefield, and carrying us to the next task. We need feet that take us forward with peace in our hearts--no blisters or sprains. We need shoes that are tough and offer protection while things look bleak on the battlefield; shoes that we know will take us a hundred miles if we have to turn on our heel and run back to the stronghold of our LORD.

Peace in our hearts cannot fail if it comes from the Holy Spirit. He has not given us a spirit of timidity, and He gives us peace that surpasses human understanding. It is those moments when we become aware of the Holy Spirit's whisper that this peace becomes evident. We would be justified in feeling confused by the fight around us because the natural response to this kind of situation is terror or a desire to flee. However, Christians have the resources to feel completely at ease with our circumstances and ready to walk through to the other side of the fight. What gives us that peace when every human body and mind feature is shouting 'RUN!'? Surely, it is only the supernatural power granted to us by the Holy Spirit. It takes our feet and plants them in the peace of God, no matter the direction our steps take us. Peace rises as we follow the footprints in the sand made by our LORD. It blooms in knowing that we are going the right way, even when our path is uncertain beyond the next step.

When we look at those who die because of their faith in Jesus and their profession of His Word, we see people whose feet are shod in the gospel of peace. They do not seek out conflict, but they can walk confidently with Christ's joy and peace into any circumstance. Feet of peace do not avoid conflict-ridden areas of the world because they know that, even in the middle of a fight, the peace of Christ will rule in the hearts of those who love Him and are called by His Name. The truth we find in God's Word, our right standing with Him through Christ, and our peace-filled hearts are all part of the arsenal God gives us to battle for His Kingdom. He also shares his joy with us because He knows that we are still only human and working on our stamina for the battleground.

We have discussed how strength comes from having an accessible joy in the LORD as we abide on the Vine. In that spirit, there is a wonderful passage in Zechariah 8-9 that speaks of the way that God will save His people and restore them after their time of suffering. In Zechariah 8:19, it describes Judah's *'seasons of joy and gladness and cheerful feasts. Therefore, love truth and peace.*[244] It then goes on to prophesy about the coming of Jesus, including verse 10 saying, *'and he shall speak peace to the nations; his rule shall be from sea to sea, and from the river to the ends of the earth.'*

Does the modern church 'love' truth and peace in this way? Do we seek it out and let it illuminate our path and sustain our very being? Do we walk through our days with the peace of God ruling our hearts or do we let circumstances dictate how we feel, what we say, and what we choose to do with our time? The enemy waits for us to kick off our shoes of peace and forget about the gospel for a few hours or days or weeks. He pours hot oil from the ramparts or cakes our path with thick sludge because our feet are unprotected. Even if we have that truth belt secure, and the breastplate of righteousness guarding our hearts from fear, forgetting about the peace we have in Christ is a sure way to find ourselves stuck out in the open. The Good News is like wearing joy as sandals, ones that can skate over the mire, dodge the hot oil attacks, and outrun any roaring lion that we find locking onto our scent. Nothing can quench that joy, not even a long, hard trek through a warzone.

We also know from the Word of God that we find joy in our salvation. God lifts our hearts from the mire with the unchangeable truth of His Word and the affirmation of His Holy Spirit. It is in this way that God honors our commitment to the fight, whispering to our hearts as we

---

[244] Zechariah 8:19 ESV

stand and face the many trials of Christian life. He exalts us, singing over us with gladness[245], so that when we are knee-deep in suffering, fear will not overcome our joy. He is our rock, our shield, and our provider.

Paul described Christ's lead in this fight for joy as a 'triumphal procession[246]' and a way for us to spread 'the aroma' of Christ and speak life into others' souls. When we are in the fight, fighting for joy and trying to remind ourselves to fight *with* joy, it is like we are testing out that stamina we have built up in our training sessions with Jesus. He is our leader in battle, but while there is peacetime, He gives us the opportunity to find joy in training, too. If we have to run the race to the end and kept fighting the good fight, we must have the stamina to face any eventuality. And, we do alongside Christ. Jesus fills our hearts with joy to give us strength for the battle ahead, as an athlete would carbo-load before a big race. We know that at the last stretch, Jesus always wins, but there is work to be done as we make our way to the finish line.

The joy of the LORD gives us the tenacity to continue to fight for what is good; to keep our heads up, our hope anchored in Jesus, and our hearts at peace with whatever is going to happen out there. We cling to the promises of God, knowing that He loves us and wants us to be overflowing with eternal joy! Whether we are racing to the finish line or palming our way through a battlefield, God is with us. Joy is accessible and encouraged. Jesus is the source of joy, hope, strength, and peace, and we know that this is true in every situation forever. The Word of the LORD stands forever, and that means our joy is unshakeable.

Psalm 27:6 says, *"Then my head will be exalted above the enemies who surround me; at his sacred tent I will sacrifice with shouts of joy; I will sing and make music to the LORD.*[247]*"* Isn't that a striking image of victory with Jesus Christ? We are so honored to be part of Christ's victory that we

---

[245] Zechariah 3:17 ESV
[246] 2 Corinthians 2:6 ESV
[247] Psalm 27:6 ESV

sacrifice any selfish plans we had with 'shouts' of joyful celebration and praise for our LORD. He exalts us for our part in the battle, our tenacity or obedience or perseverance, and we sing and make music to Him as we relax and enjoy His presence. Nobody can 'make music' when they have to focus on a battle in front of them; that comes afterward.

How do we fight for joy and with joy when the gospel of peace guides our steps?

- Ask and don't stop asking *Matthew 7:7*
- Pray and don't stop praying *1 Thessalonians 5:16*
- Seek and don't stop seeking *Luke 11:9*
- Read the Word of God and don't stop reading *Joshua 1:8*
- Pray without ceasing *1 Thessalonians 5:17*
- Worship in spirit and truth *John 4:24*
- Trust and don't stop trusting *Proverbs 3:5-6*
- Forgive and don't stop forgiving *Matthew 18:22*
- Love the Lord putting all your heart soul and mind into it. *Deuteronomy 6:5*

Do not grow weary of doing good[248] and hold fast to what is good[249] for the LORD is good[250], and we follow where He leads.

Joy-up and Take Up the Shield of Faith

As we journey on with Jesus and look to the Word of God for more and more knowledge about the one we follow, we need to keep a handle on that shield of faith Paul mentions in Ephesians 6:16. Joy is accessible at all times, and we can joy-up no matter our situation, but holding up the shield gives us those precious seconds to call out to God before the weapons of the enemy rain down on us. As the darts of the devil try to

---

[248] Galatians 6:9 ESV
[249] 1 Thessalonians 5:21 ESV
[250] Nahum 1:7 ESV

find their mark, faith is invaluable. When we can't see where the attack is coming from and it is testing our strength, holding up faith in the Son of God and His rule gives us time to regroup, stand firm, and regain our grip on joy.

For people in the midst of terrible upheaval, fighting, unrest, riots, or a direct attack, it is easy to understand how a shield of faith might be useful. Isn't it such a comfort to know that when the eyes are blind and the body is tired, we can still rejoice in our salvation? We can call out for the Spirit's power, guidance, and healing. We might have stumbled and looked behind us for too long, finding ourselves face to face with enemy forces as we turn back toward the battleground, but we are not alone. Christians can put up the shield of faith and sound our trumpets as we worship the Mighty One. The Holy Spirit comes when He is invited into the fray, and He comes in all power and authority. Do we believe that the same voice that told the storm to stop can tell the enemy to stop firing at us? Do we trust that Jesus is King of ALL, with complete jurisdiction over the enemy? Faith comes with hearing[251] and hearing by the Word of Christ. Yet, we cannot hear and understand unless Jesus has opened our ears and ignited something in our hearts. That gift of faith is what pushes us to call out to Him, to really listen for the sound of His rescue party coming to pick us up where we have fallen.

The Word of God entreats us to guard our hearts[252], and that is the purpose of our breastplate of righteousness. However, that piece of armor is also described as a breastplate of faith and love in 1 Thessalonians 5:8, where we are encouraged to seize the day, so to speak, and rely on the armor to get us through the trouble we face. Righteousness, a right relationship with God, is only possible through the blood of Jesus Christ shed for us on the cross. When we choose to put our faith in Jesus Christ (because of His enabling), we choose to protect our hearts with His

---

[251] Romans 10:17 ESV
[252] Proverbs 4:23 ESV

strength, love, and involvement in our lives. We can approach the throne of God unimpeded, and that is a great source of joy to us when it seems like the walls might be caving in or the enemy becomes relentless. God pours out His grace upon us so that we might place our faith in His Son, the Messiah. Why? Because God the Father knows that we need the power of the Almighty if we are to keep walking in joy from battle to battle until we are ready for our heavenly reward.

Our faith in the Faithful One is what keeps us grounded in love, joy, and peace when it seems the storm is going to throw us overboard. It is that decision to guard our hearts and fight for joy that causes us to lift our eyes above the waves and see Jesus standing there on the water, ready to see our faith in action as we step out of the boat like Peter did[253]. That's the key to fighting with joy, too; we have to exercise our shield of faith and move it into position. A shield is useless hanging by our sides when the arrows are coming for our heart of joy. We need to hold it up--faith in Christ--and put all our heart, mind, soul, and strength into making sure we do our part in that defense. If our arms grow tired, the Holy Spirit will be right there, encouraging us, guiding us, strengthening us, and reminding us of the joy we have in Christ's salvation.

Above all, Jesus understands our suffering. He understands what we go through each day on a very intimate level because the Son of God went through the same emotions, trials, and weakness as we face when He came to earth in human form. He faced death as we do, perhaps, more violently than many of us may have to suffer. Jesus faced disappointment in others when His disciples fell asleep instead of praying with Him or keeping watch. The Lamb of God also faced temptation in Matthew 4 as Satan tried to derail his faith through:

- physical hunger (flesh)
- the promise of success (pride or ambition)

---

[253] Matthew 14:22-33 ESV

- instant Kingship (a shortcut to His true purpose but not by the narrow way that God intended for it to happen)

All three temptations were like well-placed arrows to the heart of the Son of Man, exactly the right strategy from Satan. However, Jesus' humanity was not enough to derail His holy convictions. The Son of God met the lies of the enemy with an impenetrable shield of faith and the Sword of the Spirit as He held up the truth of God's Word. The truth stood firm against everything The Father of Lies tried to throw at Jesus in His weakest, hungriest state. For forty days, Jesus faced temptation, and for all that time He fought to uphold the truth and glory of God despite His suffering.

Jesus Christ was walking the same earth that you and I stand upon today, under the same sun, and in the company of the same Holy Spirit. He understands how we feel, what we face, and how easy it is for us to give up when life's challenges are insurmountable. That's why our Messiah was sure to leave us an explicit message of encouragement before He left to prepare a place for us in heaven. Jesus said, *"I have said these things to you, that in me you may have peace. In the world you will have tribulation. But take heart; I have overcome the world.*[254]*"* Make sure that verse sinks in; it is the cornerstone of our fight for joy.

Believers live here on earth, drifting in and out of the storms. Circumstances mold us and threaten to sink us, and attacks against our faith occur with alarming frequency. Are you tempted to equate a lack of joy with a lack of faith? Jesus said that faith the size of a mustard seed could move mountains, so perhaps, a lack of joy has nothing to do with how strongly we believe something; there must be more. Faith is defined as complete trust or conviction that we have or develop in something or someone. The crucial part of that idea is that we need to place our faith in the right Person because having faith in friends, family, political leaders,

---

[254] John 16:33 ESV

the universe, karma, or ourselves only leads down one path: disappointment.

The only way our faith leads to lasting joy and contentment is when we place our faith in the only Person who holds the power to bring us through any storm unscathed; that Person is Jesus Christ. Our faith in Him only happens when He calls us and opens our eyes to the truth. The Bible is clear on how we can be saved--by grace through faith--and that this is purely the work of the Holy Spirit. It makes sense that "faith" without the Spirit's work is not enough to turn our hearts to Jesus. There are many people in the world who place their faith in money or power or other people and find themselves adrift. It is only those who place their faith in Jesus who are never disappointed or alone. It is by faith through grace that we believe in Jesus, and the bonus for exercising that faith is an outpouring of the Holy Spirit's bounty. He gives us love, joy, peace, patience, kindness, goodness, gentleness, faithfulness, and self-control. Some of the fruit take time to grow, but we can thank the LORD often and loudly that grace is not an exhaustive resource. We serve a gracious God who wants to see us thrive, and that includes those times when we face the temptation to sin or place our faith in anything other than the LORD Jesus Christ.

We tend to think of joy as happiness, an emotional response, but biblical joy is both a physical and spiritual concept, even more than an emotion. Joy comes from a rational, non-emotional choice to align our spirits with the Holy Spirit who loves us. Our spiritual choice to be joyful is a deliberate step, not a knee-jerk reaction to something fleeting. It moves from a place of knowledge about who God is and who we are in him, taking us to a place of acceptance and appreciation. Yes, it can make us happy, but not in the Disney sense. Joy is true happiness that does not depend on circumstance or feeling or hormones; it is intricately linked to our faith in Jesus Christ and our pursuit of a relationship with Him. Choosing joy in Jesus is also the only way to make it through war, famine, and life's many other challenges with the right attitude and perspective. Thankfully, we have the joy of our salvation always at hand.

Joy-up with The Helmet of Salvation and The Sword of the Spirit

The fifth and sixth pieces of armor mentioned in Ephesians 6:17 are the helmet of salvation and the sword of the Spirit (the Word of God). The sword is the only weapon mentioned as we put on the various pieces, and it is the same weapon that Jesus Christ chose to wield when He faced temptation from Satan for forty days.

Paul was the writer in the letter to the Ephesians, and the sword was a very meaningful choice of weapon if you consider some of the options that were around then. It is a weapon with which you have to fight with courage and intention, up close and personal. To cause harm with a sword, you have to be within reach of the target and on point with your aim. It is heavy and it takes skill to hold it up and direct it where you need it to go. A sword is also a one-handed weapon and requires maneuverability to get into position ahead of the opportune moment.

As we think upon the sword of the Spirit, the Word of God, the comparison seems apt. The Word of God, the Holy Bible, is able to cut right to the heart of a matter with a few simple words. As we have seen, '*a word in season*[255]' is powerful, and even more so with the might of the LORD behind it in spirit and truth. The Word of God is also something we have to know intimately in order to use it correctly. It requires training, practiced moves and memorization, deep insight into its form and function, and continuous use to keep it sharp enough to do its work.

The Word of God also bestows life and death. It presents the law and the prophets, a story of love and redemption so that all may believe in

---

[255] Proverbs 15:23 ESV

Jesus. But it also acknowledges that not all will be saved from destruction when the Word comes forth on that final day. Some will die an eternal death, an eternity away from the presence of God. Surely, there can be no greater pain possible than to be unable to feel the love and acceptance of the One who made us because we chose unbelief when we had the chance. That is why the sword of the Spirit is such a huge asset on the battlefield; it is the kind of weapon that makes the enemy look twice before getting into the tussle. It invites hesitancy and reflection, and a choice to attack or to turn around with a repentant heart. The Word of God cuts, but it is this severity that makes its healing power even more glorious.

Those who believe in the Son of God have seen the power of the sword and know it's might. Instead of walking into its judgment and pain, believers have stopped in their tracks at the bidding of the Word that stands before them. Believers are sinners who have seen their standing in relation to the most powerful thing on earth and acknowledged the truth: they have been found wanting. Joy is a product of repentance and obedience to the word of God as our faith leads us into a renewed relationship with Jesus Christ. So, we could also say that the sword of the Spirit is a source of joy because of who powers it, as well as what it can achieve.

When we wield the Word of God, it does not give us free rein to use a weapon against those who would do us no harm; it is a defensive tool for if and when the fighting comes to us, or the LORD tells us to move. Then, the sword is lethal because the truth cannot be quenched or destroyed. The Word of God stands forever, and it divides truth from lies, sheep from goats, as it makes its way to each nation, tongue, and tribe.

But how does knowing the power of the Word of God make us more aware of joy in daily life? For one thing, the truth reveals more about the source of joy, Jesus Christ. He is The Word, and it is His story we are playing out on earth. When we memorize Scripture and have it ready for action on the tips of our tongues, joy comes whether we are watching a sunset or kneeling beside a dying loved one. We can declare with all confidence the victory of Christ and rejoice in our place as co-heirs to the Kingdom. We can bury the promises of God in our hearts for those awful times when grief seems to penetrate even our happiest experiences. God comforts those who mourn, and He is close to the broken-hearted.

When we hear the Word of God, we need to take it to heart. There will come a time where suddenly the words we have treasured for 'such a time as this' will suddenly spring to life. We will find ourselves in a situation where the Word of God lights up some truth we need right in that moment, even from a Sunday School song or memory verse we learned decades before. It will rise up from within, girding up our armor, and preparing us for action. As we step into the will of God for that moment, leaning on God's Word for strength and guidance, the result will almost certainly be a joyful outburst of praise and gratitude.

When sickness looms large, we can joy-up for the fight and fight with joy because we know that death has lost its sting. We are going to receive new, perfect bodies when the Messiah ushers in our eternity in His presence. Joy can follow lamentation as light dispels darkness; it can also accompany it, as we feel pain while holding onto joy as a comfort and product of gratitude. One preacher describes it as the difference between "tearful joy and tearless joy" (Piper, 2021). Joy remains, whether we are sad or not. If we are connected to the Vine, thriving in our relationship with Jesus Christ, then joy is always going to be a part of our lives, whether we are grieving, sick, healthy, or confused.

The Bible is clear that we have to joy-up for the fight because there will be pain coming while we live here in an imperfect world. Passages like Isaiah 35:10 is a great comfort for believers who are eagerly waiting for the LORD's return. It describes that final day as a time of singing, everlasting joy, and gladness. It speaks of sorrow and sighing that will 'flee[256]' while

---

[256] Isaiah 35:10 ESV

joy overtakes them. When Satan throws lies at us about what life should 'feel' like or 'look' like for success or happiness, these are the verses we have to defend our joy. Promises of hope and gladness and beauty fill our hearts, even as the enemy tries to pierce it with his arrows of untruth or distraction. The presence of joy is also girded by hope, as we intentionally anchor that hope on our Savior's gift of life. In 1 Thessalonians 5:8, Paul also refers to the helmet as one of 'hope' in salvation[257], a great source of joy as we fix our eyes on our Savior. As salvation gives hope, it also gives joy, especially as we seek to be more intentional about loving God with heart, soul, mind, and strength.

Hope is rooted in Jesus' return for His people, as He has promised. While we are still here, fighting the good fight alongside our brethren, our sixth piece of armor is that helmet of salvation. The function of a helmet is to protect the mind because the brain tells all other parts what to do, where to go, and how to do it. Salvation is a sturdy defense as the mind processes the stresses and strains of battle; it gives us time to take our thoughts captive and submit to the process of sanctification, a renewal of our minds. The truth and hope found in salvation also help us to refocus our thought life on a more joyful walk with Christ, even in the midst of a fight to hold onto that joy. When it seems like our joy is under attack, and we have lost that initial spark we felt when our salvation was at its freshest, we can remind ourselves of David's cry to the LORD, "*Restore to me the joy of your salvation!*[258]" The LORD will help us put on that helmet so that our vulnerable minds can find comfort and a source of security in the truth; we are forgiven, we are blameless before God, and we are dearly loved. What a joy it is to serve the one who upholds us with His willing Spirit in this way!

It is also worth noting that the helmet would have protected the brain, the rational part of us, but it leaves the senses open to the elements.

---

[257] 1 Thessalonians 5:8 ESV
[258] Psalm 51:12 ESV

With salvation, our saving faith in Jesus serves this function as it frames our beliefs and gives us a safe place to explore those thoughts and ideas. We can still use our eyes, ears, and other senses to send messages to the brain about our circumstances, but under the amazing protection of our salvation, the brain will process these sensory inputs differently from when it was exposed to danger at all turns. When God switches on the light and allows us insight into His Word, our helmet of salvation gives us this safe place to take that knowledge and ask questions, make observations, or analyze its validity. We can take anything to God, any question or doubt or worry, and it will not change the way that He looks at us or dim His love for us. If we keep our eyes and ears open and remember that our minds are a safe space to interact with the Living God, we can grow in our knowledge of who He is and where He is leading us.

Joy stems from a greater knowledge of God because we realize more about where it comes from, the PERSON it comes from. Be encouraged by the hope of salvation as God helps you figure out the chaos racing through your mind, especially during intense fighting or scary situations. To know God is to know the source of all wonder, and we can rejoice as we stand in that place of awe. It doesn't matter what the world around us looks like in that precious moment of truth; our eyes can remain fixed on God's glory and marvel at the one who lavishes such blessing and joy on us as His children.

Watch the LORD Preserve Your Joy While the Fight Rages on and Thank Him

The final piece of armor we explore is a prayer life that includes perseverance and supplication for the saints. Unlike the other physical pieces of armor mentioned prior to verse 18, Paul now moves into the attitude with which we should approach the battle for our joy. Where the belt of truth holds up the Word of God so that we can fight as needed, the attitude that goes with that weapon is one of humility and dependence. Where the shield of faith and the breastplate of righteousness guard our hearts and remind us to trust the LORD, the attitude with which we do this is one of love and care for those fighting alongside us, not indignation or fear for our own safety. Even as we shod our feet in the gospel of peace, listening carefully to God's voice as He leads us on to the next mission field, our journey requires a prayer life that is constant, passionate, and a first option rather than a last resort.

As we put on the armor of God, the attitude that comes after it is one of watchful perseverance. We need to obey God when He commands us to move or stand, and we need to be in constant communication with Him as we see the battles unfolding. Being alert is a challenge with so many distractions in life, yet God asks that of us as His 'soldiers' on a mission for good. The LORD asks us to zone in on His Word, and to ask Him about it as we think through the strategies, cautionary tales, and heroic deeds of the Bible. He encourages us to not be afraid of what is to come but to embrace His lead and trust Him to turn it all for our good as we exercise faith. As we fight for joy and fight with joy, He also asks us to extend ourselves beyond the scope of our personal space bubble on the battlefield; other lives matter to God and they should matter to us.

Verse 18 ends with a call to present "supplication for all saints[259]," which refers to a specific and fervent request to God on behalf of those who fight beside us. Believers are 'the saints,' the redeemed of the LORD. The gospel is for every heart, and only an individual can make that choice of submission for themselves. However, once you are part of the Kingdom, you are part of the family of God, and there are other members to consider as you figure out your place in the tapestry.

The enemy likes to lie to us about the role of unity in the body of Christ, mostly showing us clear instances of how diversity leads to disunity

---

[259] Ephesians 6:18 ESV

or dissent when Jesus is not at the heart of the church. Why do we have thousands of denominations if we are meant to unify as Christ's bride? Because as humans, we are still working out our sinful natures. That is a challenge that each of us needs to pray fervently about at every opportunity.

In contrast, the Bible talks of unity in Christ as being an additional source of strength and joy when we are under attack. For example, Philippians 2:1-2 says, *"So if there is any encouragement in Christ, any comfort from love, any participation in the Spirit, any affection and sympathy, 2 complete my joy by being of the same mind, having the same love, being in full accord and of one mind.*[260]*"* Well-trained troops move together as one, and Christian unity can bring an additional layer of protection as we each face down the enemy as a united force of love. When we trust God to be with us in the battle, there is no stopping the power at our disposal. He is sovereign and putting our hope in His victory is always a sure thing. The work of Jesus on the cross preserves our joy while the fight rages on, and we must be patient in our obedience to His call. The battle might be a long one, requiring us to rest between phases. We need to revere the King we follow if we want to stay motivated when we are growing weary. We are patient because He is unfailingly patient with us in our stumbling and gives us the means to overcome, hope, joy, peace, and love in His gift of eternal life.

The Son of God understands how our courage can fail when we are uncertain about the timeline of our suffering. He gives us so many verses of encouragement to fill our tanks for the journey; He doesn't want us to run on empty or risk a breakdown at a crucial moment in our fight for joy. Our LORD and Savior exhorts us to:

"Rejoice always, pray without ceasing, give thanks in all circumstances; for this is the will of God in Christ Jesus for you."

---

[260] Philippians 2:1-2 ESV

-1 Thessalonians 5:16-18

We need to keep going in our fight for joy, and we need to do it with joy in our hearts instead of fear or doubt. How? By keeping our eyes fixed on Jesus, the author and perfecter of our faith. We anchor our hope to Jesus, trusting in His unfailing love, knowing that He will work all things together for our good and that we are safe under His banner.

One of the benefits of being in constant prayer and striving to make supplications on behalf of those who fight beside us, is a constant flow of joy that revitalizes the soul and body. As we hear God speak or see Him move, our hearts leap with joy at the work of His hands. As we realize that the LORD has answered a prayer we prayed for a fellow believer, we rejoice at His graciousness and faithfulness to His church. Whether it is our blessing or another's, there is much joy to be found in seeing God's handiwork come to life.

What is the result when we live a life of prayer and supplication, honoring God and loving others as He does? The God of hope fills us with all joy and peace as we put our trust in Him, and we overflow[261] with the power of His Holy Spirit! The mark of trust in God is hope, joy, and peace, and those are vital components of any battle endeavor.

Standing alone is a sure way to fall, but with Christ at the helm and our fellow believers on each side, there can only be victory. If we close our eyes to the needs of our church and fellow believers, we are losing a powerful ally in the fight for our joy. Others need prayer, and so do we, so encourage one another and build one another up[262]. Even Jesus intercedes[263] for us to the Father and secures our citizenship in heaven[264]. We are not destined for wrath but for salvation through our LORD Jesus Christ[265]

---

[261] Romans 5:13 ESV
[262] 1 Thessalonians 5:11 ESV
[263] Romans 8:34 ESV
[264] Philippians 3:20 ESV
[265] 1 Thessalonians 5:9 ESV

and the joy we find in that truth is a treasure trove that will hold its value for eternity.

Joy-up and Remember Who Wins the Fight

There is no denying that fighting for joy and with joy is an intense way to live, but it is helpful to remember that it is not an ongoing or uncertain war. It ends with Jesus Christ as the King of all, every knee bowed, and every tongue confessing His supreme worth. Trials and temptations come to us daily, but there is always an opportunity to joy-up for the fight.

God has graciously given us the armor for strength, protection, and motivation to keep running our race. There is strength in joy, no matter what we face, because Jesus has overcome the world. In the sacrifice of Jesus, sin and death and darkness lost their power over us and that is why we can rejoice always[266], even when it doesn't feel like the day has put us on the winning side. Likewise, if life feels a little jaded and we are struggling to hold on to joy, it is helpful to meditate on the Word of God, press into Jesus, and ask the Holy Spirit for a power boost to get us back on track. May we have the sincerity of David as he danced before the LORD[267] and shook off his title. He forsook the royal robes that day, choosing instead to wear the humble clothing of the priests and musicians who were worshiping the LORD. The mighty King David did not seek one ounce of glory for himself on the battlefield; he put his focus fully on the LORD and gave Him full credit for the victory. Even as David's wife, Michal, looked down on his actions[268] and accused him of acting beneath his station, the LORD took notice of the humble king's intentions.

---

[266] Philippians 4:4 ESV
[267] 2 Samuel 6:14 ESV
[268] 2 Samuel 6:20 ESV

We do not always do the right thing when we fight, but if we can train ourselves to cling to joy and humility in our walk with Christ, we will always find ourselves moving in the right direction. God sees our hearts, and He wants us to enjoy His good gifts, even amid a fight. Like the church at Smyrna, we can rejoice because we are rich in Christ Jesus. We have the truth and righteousness of our Savior, peace for the journey, a helmet of hope, a shield against the fiery darts of the evil one, and the Word of God to cut through the darkness. We also have the might of a great army of God to keep us motivated as we forge ahead. We are rich, indeed!

Are you fighting for joy right now? Remember, Jesus Christ is already triumphant, and it is His joy with which you are filled. The joy of the LORD brings strength for the journey ahead, and the particular opponent we are fighting doesn't matter because God is on our side. Be constant in prayer and don't ever stop receiving joy--you are going to need it.

Joy Up with Jesus

As we joy-up for the fight before us, it is easy to find ourselves at a point of indecision. Do we stand or do we defend? Do we speak out or stay silent and watch God work? Is the fight ours or should we step away from the battlefield for a moment and kneel down in prayer?

As we learn how God wants us to fight for joy and fight with joy, taking up the cross of Jesus seems a little less daunting. We have the Holy Spirit right here, in our hearts, speaking words of life and love to us in the darkest places and the lowest valleys. We have Jesus Christ, our King, our LORD, standing beside us with all power and authority over whatever it is we see in front of us. He is a Faithful friend, but He is also the leader of our troops and commands respect and obedience. God the Father sees all, and as such, He has gifted us with the armor we need to get through the journey. He has set our feet upon a path, and He is waiting at the finish line as the Holy Spirit cheers us on and

Jesus leads the way. It's a coordinated effort to help us win our part in the fight, with support and a fresh injection of joy from the ultimate victor Himself whenever we need it.

Remember, "My God will supply every need of yours according to his riches in glory in Christ Jesus.[269]" Like Smyrna, we are rich beyond measure because of the blessings and joy that Jesus Christ pours out upon His beloved bride, the church. We are well-equipped to overcome what the world throws at us, because Jesus has already overcome all our most powerful enemies. Now, there is only perseverance, and a conscious attitude of gratitude for the joy that fills us to overflowing.

If the full stadium fills us with such a deep excitement for what is to come as we stand shoulder to shoulder with perfect strangers, just imagine how joyful it will be to stand on the battlefield as the victorious King reveals His might and glory in all its fullness. We stand with brothers and sisters in Christ, with our family that will live with us forever in the presence of the LORD. There is no greater joy than to see the fruits of labor ripen; shared joy is always sweeter.

John 17:3 is a powerful reminder of what truly matters in the face of trials or temptation; it says, "This is eternal life, that they know you, the only true God, and Jesus Christ whom you have sent.[270]" What matters is that we know God, and that we know His Son, our Redeemer, Savior, Friend, Ruler, and LORD of all. Fighting for joy means fighting to know Jesus better as we share in His suffering for the sake of His glory and our good. Joy is worth the fight!

Friend, may God strengthen you today with "all power, according to his glorious might, for all endurance and patience with joy.[271]"

---

[269] Philippians 4:19 ESV
[270] John 17:3 ESV
[271] Colossians 1:11 ESV

CHAPTER 8
Joy-Up: on Your Resilience!

In today's throw-away culture, the concept of steadfastness is not something we hold on to too tightly. We tend to let go when we see chinks in the armor or stains on what was once a sparkly new ·ior. Instead of working out the cracks or fixing the problem with a spirit of joy and thankfulness for what we possess, many of us would rather throw it away or buy another one. We might replace it and forget about it, rather like an old set of sneakers we used to love.

It might have been a brand-new trendy pair at the beginning, and the shoes may have carried us many miles through countless adventures. But all that is left are a few tears in the fabric, a smoother tread, and quite a lot of history that has worn away those shiny new kicks and given them a 'vintage' look. They are comfortable, but they have lost the strength they once had. The shoes no longer provide the cushioning we need for hard runs, challenging hikes, or long days on our feet.

Sometimes, we let our relationship with God dwindle like a pair of sneakers. It sinks into comfortable routines instead of exciting possibilities. At first, we embrace the joy of our salvation and draw strength from it as often and as passionately as we can. We read our Bible and pray and give thanks. We worship the LORD and seek Him with our whole being, heart, mind, soul, and strength. As we know more of who He is, we start to feel our place in His family more securely. We follow Him fervently, sharing His gospel message with others, and rejoicing in all that He is and all that He has done for us. It's a beautiful fit, with so many miles to hope for together and so much energy to get going as the road up ahead starts to reveal its twists and turns.

As we press into the love of the Father, share in the joy of Jesus Christ, and listen to the power-filled whispers of the Holy Spirit, we let joy fill us to overflowing in the most precious life-giving way. With many miles, though, comes a test of that joy. There might be a bump in the road or a crossroads where we need to make seemingly impossible decisions. Slowly, we may realize that the fit we thought was so perfect is beginning to chaff a little. It might start with an almost undetectable discomfort, or it might blow up into a blister that lasts for weeks, but it is there; a doubt, a questioning, a brake pedal on the joy we once felt so strongly as Jesus called our hearts home.

Why does momentum slow when we were once so excited to take up our cross and walk the narrow path? Why does energy wane when those shoes still have so many miles planned for us?

Resilience.

For many, there is a little voice that calls from somewhere in the depths of our minds. It says, *'This is beginning to feel uncomfortable. Where are we going? Pull back.'* When our faith in Jesus is new and untainted by trials or temptations, it feels so fresh. It fills us with amazing peace, inexplicable joy, and the desire to know Jesus more and more in every way possible. It's like a 'high' of salvation, a 'first love[272],' as the warning in Revelation 2:4 so aptly puts it. However, adversity is a powerful deterrent of that first love because it tests how deeply our roots are secured in the Savior. If we are still exploring our transformative gift of faith, those roots are yet to go deep enough to push through the rocks and forge lasting foundations. The resilience will come by the grace and favor of Christ, but

---

[272] Revelation 2:4 ESV

it takes some time to let those roots grow with our knowledge and experience of God's love for us.

Resilience is our inner joy kicking in, the joy that we receive from Jesus Christ as we tap into His fountain of life. As we abide on the Vine[273], we learn that there is an endless source of joy in Jesus, the True Vine, but it takes some practice and much perseverance to keep returning to the source of joy to drink our fill. Indeed, learning to joy-up for a resilient approach to life when we are tested is the only way to prepare to embrace uncertainty with the humility it requires. We are not in control, but we have a God who is nearby. Our God has all power and authority to grant us joy when we need it, and somehow, there's a determination to keep the forward motion alive as we live off this 'joy fuel.' We take supernatural strength from our connection with Christ, and it grows stronger as we deepen our relationship with Him and start to discover where He is leading us. The joy of our salvation does not need to fade like an old pair of sneakers that has walked us through amazing experiences. Just the opposite, our salvation grows stronger, and more able to grant us contentment in all situations[274] as we understand more about the God who walks beside us.

We must not lose our first love. If we seek to work on that relationship with Christ daily, through His Word, prayer, and humble service, our joy will not fade.

The 'DO NOTS' of Learning to Joy-up with Resilience

We've seen how fighting for joy is worth it, and that fighting with joy is the only real way to get through the battles we face. However, it is important to remember that we are not expected to be resilient on our

---

[273] John 15:4 ESV
[274] Philippians 4:11-13 ESV

own strength. The Holy Spirit is with us in power and love, in Spirit and truth. There is nothing that can stand against us when our God is for us[275]. How do we joy-up and embrace resilience in our Christian walk with Jesus Christ? By understanding that our strength lies in Him alone.

Let's look at a few 'do nots' that we need to remember when we want to hold on to that first love and maintain open access to the joy of the LORD that is our strength.

DO NOT Grow Weary of Doing Good

When we look at verses like Galatians 6:9, it is easy to see that the Bible is aimed at human hearts, not perfect souls. God's message to us is that we keep going, no matter how we feel or what we see before us. If He calls us, we need to put one foot in front of the other and keep on moving in the direction He illuminates for us. The verse mentions not growing weary of '*doing good, for in due season we will reap*[276]' the rewards of this resilience. It ends with a motivational phrase: "*if we do not give up.*" If we do not give up or grow tired of doing the work that God places before us, we shall reap the crown of life in due season.

Take careful note that this is not a gospel of works--we are not earning our salvation by doing good works. Rather, doing good is a response to our salvation, a desire to share the love of Christ with the world as He has revealed it to us. We do good because God loves us and makes us want to spread that love around. We do good with joy because each time we show compassion, kindness, and gentleness, especially to those who don't 'deserve' it, we see a little more of who God is and how we can be more like Him. Resilience is a wonderful gift to a Christian because each barb, each fall, each knee scrape or broken bone is another growth point for us. It is another opportunity for us to press harder into

---

[275] Romans 8:31 ESV
[276] Galatians 6:9 ESV

the Vine and declare the goodness of all that pours from His heart straight into ours.

If we keep on doing good, being kind, learning to act compassionately, caring for others, and showing God's love to the unlovable, we will reap the unending joy of communion with Christ. We are His hands and feet, and our hearts were made to find joy in the things that He finds joy in, like seeing others coming to a knowledge of the truth and realizing how much God loves them. That is the "how and why" of persevering with joy and seeking to glorify God in all that we do, say, think, and share.

DO NOT Lean on the Wisdom of Men

Passages like Jeremiah 17:5 make no bones about what it means to rely on God's strength ahead of our own self-serving solutions. The prophet's chilling admonishment calls out hearts that are not aligned with their Creator's, saying *"Cursed is the man who trusts in a man and makes flesh his strength.*[277]*"* If we lean on human strength and determination, we may be able to move forward or win one of the smaller battles we face, but it won't be sustainable or optimal. We were meant to rely on God, to submit to His power and authority and might. That humble dependence is the place where our hearts feel most empowered. Our strength is an illusion compared to the might of the LORD who is not bound by time, circumstance, age, or experience. His strength does not fail, and if we ask it, He will bless us with what we need to endure.

Do you believe what the Word of God says about what you are capable of achieving in conjunction with the Spirit? Do you believe with your whole being that Jesus is the Way, the Truth, and the Life, as He claimed? If so, then trusting in Him will be your first priority, in good times or bad times, in sickness or health.

---

[277] Jeremiah 17:5 ESV

We share in the joy of the LORD because He has saved us from our own stubborn sin. Jesus has drawn us to a place of freedom where we can submit to Him joyfully, and He did it by allowing the spilling of His own blood on our behalf. Giving up our own ambitions is no burden within the embrace of Jesus Christ, and following Him produces far greater joy, an everlasting joy, than following our own path would ever be able to muster.

DO NOT Faint in the Day of Adversity

In the Old Testament, there are 11 mentions of the command to 'be strong.' Reminders like Proverbs 24:10 put it more bluntly, saying that anyone who faints when things are going wrong for them is someone with only a small amount of strength[278]. In other words, Christians who faint are not tapping into the fullness of the strength we could find in our salvation. The joy of the LORD is our strength, and we should be prepared to tap into the joy on offer whenever God asks us to stand firm, fight, move, take a risk, or face heartbreak. Joy is there within our grasp; all we need to do is look up and grab hold of it. There is nothing that can remove that strength from us once God has poured out His blessing upon us, no matter what we face in the moment. If we joy-up and embrace resilience, we conquer in the Name of the Lord Jesus Christ who rules heaven and earth.

Instead of giving up, leaning on human strength, or letting adversity overwhelm us, we need to prepare to 'bounce back' with a joyful and tenacious spirit. Proverbs 24:16 reminds us of that righteous men and women fall seven times but always get back on their feet. The key here is to realize that it is 'when' not 'if' we fall. We will fall, and we will have the opportunity to show resilience by getting back up again and returning to a full, beautiful place of joy in the company of our LORD.

---

[278] Proverbs 24:10 ESV

How to Joy-up on Resilience Amid Challenges

How do we rebound in a biblical sense when we face challenges, pain, or grief in our daily walk? If we consider that the Word of God asks us to be resilient, to get back up, we also need to consider some of the tools He might have blessed us with to achieve that task. In Chapter 7, we looked at the armor of God, a kit we do to help us fight for joy and with joy until we receive our crown. God makes these qualities available to us as we press into the Vine and seek to exhibit the fruit of the Spirit, including our joy in Christ.

What should that look like in a resilient Christian walk? We should be:

- showing off the faithfulness of our Creator,
- thanking God for His gracious gift of righteousness, and
- stepping into His will with an enduring sense of peace.

We should also be guarding our minds and taking our thoughts captive, strengthening our resolve against trials or temptations. We do this by cultivating a deeper knowledge and appreciation for the Word of God, and that takes patience.

Isaiah 54:17 is a powerful reminder of who we serve--no weapon can succeed against Him[279]. This is our Redeemer, the One above all other things on earth and across the heavens. He is the one who holds our heritage in His hands and vindicates our faith with everlasting access to joy and unconditional love. When we love Jesus' back, this victorious approach to life becomes part of who we are. Joy remains accessible, even as we understand that many challenges will arise before the final trumpet sounds.

---

[279] Isaiah 54:17 ESV

The resilience of our joy is a telling indicator of how well we are dressing ourselves in God's armor. It also reveals our core beliefs about who Jesus is, what He has done, and who we are as His Redeemed people.

Let's explore five tips on how to joy-up and embrace resilience so that we can keep moving forward in our walk with Jesus Christ.

1 Empty Out

The first step in developing a resilience of joy is to follow Jesus' suggestion and die to self[280]. The process is like an emptying out of the heart and mind because all the sin that entangles has been loosed, but we still need to sweep it out one meaningful stroke at a time. It might mean rejecting our former opinions or analyzing various situations under the lens of the Bible instead of worldly wisdom. It also means rejecting and resisting the urge to feel like a victim when trouble comes; we are victorious in Christ in every situation. Christians rest in the knowledge that God can turn each moment for His glory and our good, and those are the promises that we use to fill up our transformed, 'emptied out' minds.

Emptying out our souls before our loving Heavenly Father provides room for Him to share what we need to thrive. If we deal with our sins, one by one, there is more room for joy, love, peace, and self-control as the Holy Spirit gives us these life-changing qualities directly from Himself. All have sinned and fallen short of the glory of God[281]. Yet, Jesus' gift to us on the cross was a way of pouring out grace upon us to start afresh. Now, we can live off the fuel of the supernatural, the joy that Jesus wants to give to us at every opportunity.

Remember, resilience only comes with victory over bad experiences. We must pass through those adverse situations or trials to see what we are made of and become more aware of the Holy Spirit's power within us.

---

[280] Luke 9:23 ESV
[281] Romans 3:23 ESV

Without a conscious effort to cast off sin and embrace holiness, there can be no lasting joy. It requires obedience to God's Word, and the same self-sacrifice that Jesus demonstrated at Calvary.

2 Go Through the Process

The second step is to let Jesus walk us through the process, step by step. James 1:4 explains it as letting 'steadfastness[282]' or resilience have its 'full effect.' We need to let our trials play out; indeed, we typically have no choice in this matter. But it is the way we act, speak, and think during that trial that shapes how we look as we emerge on the other side. God's role in our suffering is not one of perpetrator or audience; He is near to us at all times, creating a buffer between us and trouble so that we only experience the very little bits we can handle at that moment. Many times, we are not even aware of all that God is doing in the background to protect us, shelter us, nudge us in the right direction, and bolster our morale as things get messy.

Keep going.

The process may be long or hard or seem impossible, but God is near. We must let go of the disappointment surrounding what we face and let God give us exactly as much of it as we need to pass the test. Let go of the bitterness, pain, resentment, and memories that do not edify the soul, and place them at the foot of the cross.

Learning patience in suffering is never easy, but once we conquer it through Christ, joy awaits. It gets easier to harness that joy when we know who stands between us and the storm. That wind we feel on our cheeks, tousling our hair, is just a taste of what God holds back with His mighty arms surrounding us. Press into Him and agree to let Him show you what you need to learn from the experience. It might be simply learning to trust Him, or it might be that He has created you for such a time as this[283].

---

[282] James 1:4 ESV

Stand strong before the LORD, letting Him pour joy over you and quieting you with His love[284], and do not give up hope!

3 Remain Faithful

Another key to resilient joy is to understand the role of faith when things are looking ready to fall apart. We must remain bold for the gospel and its message, which means always being careful to place our faith in Jesus Christ, and Him alone. The LORD is so faithful to us, and He will put people in our paths to remind us of that love.

There's a reason that He has made humankind to enjoy relationships and rejoice in connection; it is who He is, and we are made in His image. Going to church is a great way to pick up on this joy on the best and worst days. When we worship and pray together and meditate on the Word of God with heaven-bound brothers and sisters in Christ, something powerful happens deep within us. There is meaning in these relationships and Christian practices that draw us closer to our Savior. There is a wholeness that is possible in a large group of believers that is entirely implausible on our own. Each one brings a measure of the fruit of the Spirit to that place, and joy rises up from those faithful souls who meet under the banner of the King.

Hebrews 10:25 encourages us to meet together frequently for this purpose, to worship God and encourage one another[285] to lead Christ-honoring lives. We are to remain faithful to the will of God, obeying His commands out of our love for Him. Remember, there is nothing that can separate us from the love of God[286], and it is our responsibility to put in the effort and pursue that love through an ever-deepening relationship with Jesus Christ. We must give permission to the Holy Spirit to enter

---

[283] Esther 4:14 ESV
[284] Zephaniah 3:17-19 ESV
[285] Hebrews 10:25 ESV
[286] Romans 8:35-39 ESV

and allow the joy of the Lord to be our strength if we are to emerge from life's troubles intact. Resilience is also something we earn through these kinds of interactions because God helps us to see that we *can* face adversity, and that we can bring others into the light with us. Christian relationships are not always easy as we work out our sanctification in unique ways and from our own perspectives, but unity is possible in Jesus Christ. We do not have to eat the same kinds of food or dress the same way to experience a shared and eternal joy in our salvation. What better location might there be to develop a resilient joy than in the context of a church striving to glorify God? Remain faithful and remember who it is that we serve.

4 Embrace the Strength

The Bible gives so many examples of how weak people achieved such mighty things for the sake of God's Kingdom, and each one shows the LORD's strength. When we look at ordinary, scared people who chose to obey God, the results we see are not a testament to secret superhero strength buried within that person's DNA. Rather, it is a clear picture of God working through people like you and me. It is His work, His power, that changes the world, but the gracious and loving God we serve has asked us to be in partnership with Him. He wants our participation, as we grow in the grace and knowledge of our LORD Jesus Christ.

It seems that God finds joy in giving us a task to achieve and watching us embrace those responsibilities. Perhaps, we can equate this to the same way an earthly Father watches his children and takes joy in seeing them achieve their given tasks. However, God does not expect us to do it alone. On the contrary, He hopes, He expects, that we will ask Him for help and accept the strength He gives us in return. The joy of the LORD is our strength, and part of that joy is in wielding the Spirit's power and achieving what God has asked of us. He loves to see us obeying His Word, forging ahead in faith, and believing that the outcome will be just as He intended. He rejoices in our achievements alongside us, a proud Father who delights in His child's development and unique contributions. The tools are available, but we have to bend down to pick them up and learn how to use them effectively.

Welcome yourself to the school of hard knocks; it is where God brings restoration to the soul. Adversity develops strength and confidence when faced with the great big God we serve standing right beside us. He does not ask us to joy-up because of our tribulation, but to worship Him in the midst of our tribulation. Pain is not something He made us to know--sin brought it into being. However, God uses any pain and suffering to our advantage so that He might be glorified in the way that we overcome it. When we consider it 'pure joy' to face a trial[287], it means knowing who is standing beside us as we fight our way through the battlefield. He is cheering us on and ready to listen. He offers rest, peace, and such strength in joy; we only need to accept it.

So, let the weak say I am strong[288], pray, rejoice, and be thankful[289]; no matter what you face.

5 Spruce Up Your Faith

The final step in learning to joy-up with resilience is to place an unquenchable expectancy within your heart. Spruce up your faith as Mary did when she was expecting her first child, while a virgin. Mary felt the need to meet with her cousin Elizabeth[290] who had her own miraculous story. As she neared Elizabeth and Zechariah's home, the baby in Elizabeth's womb leaped for joy! In fact, Elizabeth's reaction is incredible: she is filled with the Holy Spirit and blesses Mary, saying that she carries the LORD! Elizabeth's words to Mary were prophetic and have

---

[287] James 1:2 ESV
[288] Joel 3:10 ESV
[289] 1 Thessalonians 5:16-18 ESV
[290] Luke 1: 39-56 ESV

implications for all of us who now follow that same LORD and Savior almost two thousand years later. It came simply from seeing her dear cousin approach and being open to the prompting of the Holy Spirit who wanted to reveal the treasure of that moment to her.

Elizabeth was an ordinary woman of faith who had faced much heartache. She was receiving the miraculous blessing of a child from God in her old age, yet her expectancy of what God could do was quite evident as she embraced her younger cousin and sought to bless her. She might have had questions about how a virgin could be pregnant or what Mary's supportive fiancé thought, but this was not her first reaction. Rather, it was one of great joy and blessing that would have made young, overwhelmed Mary smile from ear to ear.

When we joy-up and allow the Holy Spirit to develop resilience in us, we emulate the journey of Mary, Elizabeth, and so many others to whom God gave hope, joy, and peace in believing[291]. He gives us power through the Holy Spirit so that this hope will abound and rub off on others as a testimony of God's love. The LORD wants us to know that we are resilient; it is the only way He can show our stubborn hearts how powerful they are in Christ. It might be that He lets us walk through something that requires us to reach out for joy or fix our eyes on the hope we have in Jesus Christ. Whatever it is, we must persevere.

Our faith in Jesus is on trial while we walk the earth that is bound in sin, but it is much more precious than gold[292] and needs our careful attention. We need to expect great things from God, as He expects the same of us. For that, He gives us the ability to joy-up and fuel our journey by His strength, hope, love, and peace. If we can press into joy and find strength that keeps us moving forward, we might just see that promised result: *"praise and honor and glory at the appearing of Jesus Christ*[293].*"* That

---

[291] Romans 15:13 ESV
[292] 1 Peter 1:7-9 ESV
[293] 1 Peter 1:7 ESV

is the reward for fueling our resilience with everlasting joy in the Almighty. Nothing can take us out of the place where we meet with Jesus Christ face to face; He is ours, and we are His forever!

The Joy Set Before Us is Where Resilience Grows

When the baby came from Mary's womb into the darkness, He brought such light with Him that He changed the entire world. Jesus lived on earth with joy in His relationship with God the Father, as He had before His incarnation. Just look at how He sat in the temple as a young boy to study the Word of God while His parents searched everywhere. Jesus understood how joy fueled the work that God had for Him to do, and He went ahead with the work that would require everything from Him. He kept going, even when He knew the outcome. He was well-aware that the end of His ministry would be the most difficult thing He would have to face while on earth. The manner and circumstances surrounding His death was something He talked about, telling the disciples about the suffering to come, the three days, and the resurrection. Yet, the Son of Man went ahead with the mission anyway.

Jesus' resilience is a perfect example for us of how to live. However, the most critical point is how Jesus held onto the joy set before Him[294] while He entered and then moved through that pain. He did not stop moving, even when He prayed and asked for the cup to be removed. When the cup remained, He drank from it and did so with a joyful heart for all that would come afterward. You and I were the joy set before Jesus Christ on the cross because it was through His selfless act of love that our souls could be redeemed in preparation for a right relationship with the LORD. It was a joy to Jesus to save us and see us flourish as He created us to do. It was His greatest labor of love, even though it wasn't a joy to

---

[294] Hebrews 12:2 ESV

experience that pain. Rather, Jesus rested in the knowledge of what that pain would be achieving for all who are called by His name[295].

Can we find the same resilience as we face whatever challenges are around the corner? The joy set before us is an eternity with Christ Jesus, at complete peace with the same God who made us and loves us so dearly. Jesus' love enables us to keep moving forward; He is the author and finisher of our faith[296], the Savior who fills us with His own joy so that we might be complete[297]. We can do all things through Christ who strengthens us[298], and that includes leaning in with expectancy and letting the joy of our LORD fill our hearts.

Joy UP with Jesus

As we choose resilience, we choose the same path that Jesus modeled for us during His time on earth. Paul understood this kind of life, one of complete dedication to God with a laser focus on enjoying our relationship with Jesus and seeking to bring Him glory. In Philippians 4:11-13, Paul talks of contentment in Christ, no matter how the situation looks from the outside. Whether in poverty or abundance, pain or good health, under persecution or enjoying freedom, we can be content in who we are as beloved children of God. The joy of the LORD is our strength[299] for every situation, and that gives us the resilience we need to face absolutely anything with a sense of peace and hope.

Rejoice always, be watchful in prayer, and give thanks to Jesus Christ for all He has done for us.[300]

---

[295] 2 Chronicles 7:14 ESV
[296] Hebrews 12:2 ESV
[297] John 15:11 ESV
[298] Philippians 4:13 ESV
[299] Nehemiah 8:10 ESV
[300] 1 Thessalonians 5:16-18 ESV

CHAPTER 9
Joy-Up: Fulfill Your Fruit-bearing Calling!

Have you ever rushed into a busy store with a list in mind as you prepare for the year-end festivities? Perhaps, it is shopping for presents, decorations, treats for the family, or the roast dinner around which the gathering will revolve. As you tick off items, navigate aisles, and try to guess which will be the shortest checkout line, you may just hear a tinkling in the background as the joy ringers try to get your attention. These smiling, joyful folk ring their bells to remind shoppers of why they are here at Christmas time. They ring to caution busy, distracted shoppers to stop and think about others in the mad rush of another festive season. The sound of the bells is a beautiful and often jolting interruption to our busiest moments. *Stop. Look up. Remember why Jesus came. Tell someone.*

Christians carry a bell of joy, too. As witnesses of God's love, it is Christ followers who carry the power to interrupt the lives of others and pour joy, love, and peace into their hearts. We have the boldness of the Holy Spirit to tell others about the joy they are missing as they rush to and from in no particular direction. Like the joy ringers of Christmas, believers in Christ can point the way to the source of all joy with words and songs that lift eyes and hearts toward the King. We can sing of His love, and we can tell of His wondrous works. We can spread joy to all who happen to come within hearing range.

What a privilege it is to carry that joy, even when we are busy ourselves. We can stop and listen to the prompting of the Holy Spirit as He calls on us to bless those we happen to meet. We can look up from our lists and expectations and remember that Jesus is the focus, always. Remember why Jesus came to earth and tell someone of His love. Joy-up and tell someone how much the God of heaven has done for the people of earth that He loves so dearly and share the joy of the Good News.

Joy ringers are people just like Christ followers, and there are sure to be days where both feel profaned, exhausted from prolonged periods of work with minimal to no pay, and ready to wish the hours away. But the rewards of ringing that bell come from the moments in between, where the joy ringer sees the child's face light up or a tired grandmother smile as she realizes that her gift list doesn't matter as much as her hugs. Like joy ringers, Christians need to hold onto those joy-up moments to keep up with the task.

Real joy means anchoring ourselves in internal contentment while life's external factors are out of control; it is only possible with supernatural strength. Joy comes from living a life that honors God and loving Him with all our hearts, souls, minds, and everything between. God is a God of hope who can fill us with joy and peace if we truly believe in Him[301]. He grants us contentment by the power of the Holy Spirit because it is this connection that shows us the extent of our hope in the Savior. The LORD opens our ears to the message of love, peace, and joy that we so often set aside during the festivities at the end of the year. Yet, this is why we are here; we live because of Jesus, and we live for Him. Joy is not a part of Christmas cheer, it is the entire reason for life, in and out of season.

Joy is why we were made and forgetting to ring the bell is neglecting the very core of what it means to be a human being. Spread the message of

---

[301] Romans 15:13 ESV

joy because we are made in the image of the Living God and loved beyond measure.

Sunshine, Daisies, and the Mercies of God

Just as the sun rises, Christians should endeavor to emerge in joy every morning. Getting up on the wrong side of the bed isn't an option with a wholehearted commitment to glorifying God and enjoying Him forever. When the day seems like a challenge, our first step should be to fall to our knees in prayer and worship. We need to joy-up and prepare Him room because how can we hide the joy that lights the very day that we are about to walk into?

When the sun awakens, it sees the darkness and thinks about the brightness that sustains it, the heart of God. It does not hide its light or lament its position. Rather, the sun rises as joyfully every morning as it has since the beginning of creation. It demonstrates a full commitment to bringing life and light to the world as it fulfills its calling. That's the reason that darkness dissipates, every single day. So, too, Christians have a unique calling from the One who created us to be a light in the darkness. We have been called to glorify God and enjoy Him, to spread His love, to take every opportunity to be joyful, and to present ourselves as holy before Him. Why would we hide our joy? Why deny that which makes us dance, sing, or laugh in abandon? Joy is ours for the taking so that it may be ours for the sharing. Everyone needs more light in their lives.

Christ's followers are called to light up the world with the love of Jesus, whose birth encompasses the greatest joy that has ever come to earth or ever will. Unto us, a Savior was given, a Son was born. He has made us glad by giving us new hearts, alive in Him. We are being filled with everlasting joy. We must rejoice because He has made us glad, and that includes on mornings where we don't 'feel' joyful. The wonders of His love are always there for us, all we need to do is joy-up and listen out for the angels' voices. If we have to repeat the sounding joy a few times to feel ready for the day, we might better appreciate our role as instruments that need to practice serving joy to the world before we can excel at this in any circumstance. God has given us talents to steward; now, we need to make music.

It is such an honor to let our light shine before men and bring glory to God through our actions and words. One way to do that is by making joy the low-hanging fruit that anyone can witness and reach for in our lives. Salvation has come through the birth of the Savior, and joy resides with each of us who profess to believe in Him and love Him. Like the sun rises to its calling each day and brings joy and life to the entire world, we need to remember our place as joy-filled, eternal souls. We aren't daisies that look good for a few weeks and fade away at the first sign of bad weather. We are more resilient than that because we have full access to the Holy Spirit's power. We do not need the sun to make us thrive; even dark days can be filled with inexplicable joy as we joy-up for each moment under the mighty hand of God. Nothing can separate us from His love, not even a sun that fails to rise. We have the Son Himself, where there is life, love, joy, and peace in abundance for all.

Catering joy as the joy ringers do is a task that we are called to perform every day of our lives on earth. Jesus told us to love and obey God, and love others as ourselves, but catering joy to others might need to start at home. First, we connect with Jesus in a joy-filled one-on-one relationship, and then we see how He creates opportunities for us to branch out. The first task is to minister to ourselves, to grow joy-producing seeds and work out the sin that entangles. But a garden is also something that can bring great joy to those who see it in full bloom. We need to keep moving in this quest to share joy, ministering to our children, spouse, and family members as we remain faithful to Christ's call. If this goes well, God may ask us to branch out even further into our communities and church families, producing more and more joy in us as circumstances test our resolve and improve our depth.

It is a joy and a privilege to follow Christ's call to love others, particularly those of the younger generation who are yet to discover the grace and mercy of the Living God. What a joy to see souls alight with the knowledge and love of Jesus, as angels rejoice over the returning of each blessed soul to the fold[302]. Can you remember what it was like to be young enough to question everything? How frustrating it could be to go through testing without a full picture of God's plans or purposes. Doubt crept in when things got complicated, or expectations found disappointment and empty ideals. Help others; help young and old see the beauty that waits for them in trusting God's timing and provision. Spread joy into the conversations and other interactions you have with people because God may have put them into our paths so that we could light up their darkest moments. Tell them of God's love and joy so that they can understand that they are not alone in the struggle.

You and I may be the only 'Jesus' a person sees, the only victory cry they hear on the battlefield, and the only hands and feet that come to help them out of the pit of despair. If we share our joy at every opportunity, there can only be more. Joy will overflow as we see souls come alive in Christ and realize the privilege of being asked to make a contribution to the Kingdom. Our God is merciful, and He loves us so!

Joy-up and Trust in the Purposes of God

Part of our calling as Christ followers is to put our faith in the One who leads us, even when the outcome is unclear, or the way ahead seems dark. If we face temptation and do nothing to propel ourselves through it, we open the way for distraction and disobedience. Jesus allowed Himself to be tempted on the mountain to create an opportunity. How could He

---

[302] Luke 15:7 ESV

show us that He was our Savior if we couldn't see His power, resilience, authority, or unconditional love displayed at His weakest physical point? We saw Him suffer, and we saw Him overcome, and that sparked something in us. It evokes joy to see Jesus conquer temptation in this way because it gives us hope that we might be able to do the same.

What if Pilate had let Jesus off the hook at that unjust trial? Peter expressed his wish that this would happen, yet it pleased God to allow a different outcome. His purposes were unclear to those watching events unfold, but each action or inaction in the life of Jesus was filled with the joy set before Him[303]--our salvation! For God so loved the world that He gave His only Son[304]. Why? To achieve His overall purpose of reuniting us to Himself in perfect peace.

Suffering created a contrast in this image God wanted to paint for those of us who learn lessons the hard way. Without darkness, we could not see the magnificence of the light breaking forth, as the dawn of salvation brought everlasting joy to the world. Without pain, we could not appreciate the fullness of the life that God has prepared for us free of pain. Sorrow and grief and heartbreak are not what God intended for us, yet He has used these consequences of sin to bring forth a joy that cannot be shaken. We serve a glorious and gracious God, indeed.

When we look at stories like Joseph's brothers selling him[305] to slave traders, the purposes of God seem even more difficult to grasp. Thankfully, we do not need to understand the purposes of God to benefit from them. His intention is always to turn our situations for good[306], whatever that may look like in the end. Joseph's journey was a tumultuous one, from beloved and favorite son to banished and rejected family member by ten angry brothers who were meant to protect him. Yet, God

---

[303] Hebrews 12:2 ESV
[304] John 3:16 ESV
[305] Genesis 37:12-36 ESV
[306] Romans 8:28 ESV

used that darkness to remind Joseph of how much God loved Him through a long, and sometimes, confusing journey. He kept going and ended up in a powerful position in the country to which he was taken. And what was the result of all this pain, betrayal, fear, and heartbreak? The opportunity to experience the joy of providing for his family, the very same people that had thought him unworthy so many years before. Joy never left when Joseph was thrown into pits, accused of heinous acts, falsely imprisoned, or threatened with death. The sun continued to rise on Joseph, reminding him that God's mercies are new every morning[307].

Imagine that family reunion. Would it have been joyful if we were in Joseph's shoes? Would we have reacted with the same loving acceptance and forgiveness as Joseph showed to the family members who betrayed him? It's a convicting notion for most of us. Family is sometimes the hardest trial when it comes to our joy-up abilities because we are so invested in those relationships. The deepest ties hurt the most when damaged, but Joseph's story is one of many that prove joy is still possible, even after we are wronged.

Likewise, David understood that the trials initiated by King Saul toward him were necessary for his journey. He trusted God to help him continue his ministry, leadership, and long-suffering with joy. He did not fight the flow of events, though he openly expressed trepidation before God and asked for help. Trials were the catalyst God ordained to birth purpose, destiny, and progress into the life of David, and it might be the same for us. Don't give up; be on high alert. When others hurt us, we must overcome the evil with good[308], humbly allowing God to work His purposes through it. God is faithful to show us how to joy-up for the moments where we feel like we don't have what it takes to keep moving forward; we simply need to ask Him.

---

[307] Lamentations 3:23 ESV
[308] Romans 12:21 ESV

For all have wronged the LORD with sinful hearts[309], yet He has forgiven us[310]. He has embraced us joyfully as we have returned to Him, like the prodigal's father. Our Savior has waited from far off to see us return home, and there is unbridled joy when that moment finally arrives. God's purposes are often not within our reach, but joy is still fully available to keep us moving forward in the calling He has bestowed upon us. Joy-up and trust Him; that's how we were meant to live!

Repeat the Sounding Joy Again and Again

As producers of joy, we may not always feel up to the task. However, we must prepare ourselves to rejoice, again, and again. We must joy-up and abide in Jesus Christ until we feel refreshed, refilled, and ready to percolate joy for all who cross our paths. Today's sorrow is tomorrow's joy, and the pain we feel today is temporary.

Pain is temporary[311]. Joy is permanent[312].

Psalm 30:5 reminds us of two vital facts about our merciful God. The first is that His favor lasts for a lifetime, not His anger. The second is that even when weeping endures for a night, we can look forward to the joy that comes each morning. God's favor on us includes our God-given ability to joy-up when there is a night of weeping. We have a full and glorious hope that what comes after pain will be worth holding on to, because in the end, only love, joy, and peace remain.

Part of the problem with enduring suffering is the uncertainty involved; we do not see what lies ahead until the time has arrived for us to know these details. Yet, God's purpose will be revealed, and it will always be for the good of those who love Him[313]. The challenges of today may be

---

[309] Romans 3:23 ESV
[310] 1 John 1:9 ESV
[311] 2 Corinthians 4:16-18 ESV
[312] Isaiah 51:11 ESV
[313] Romans 8:28 ESV

part of the intentional plan of God to take you closer toward your destiny. Without these challenges, you may not reach your greater purpose in the way that God knows is best. Joy comes in trusting this process and enjoying the journey with Jesus Christ, wherever He may lead.

If we can learn to 'trust in the LORD with all (our) heart(s)[314]' we will find that our confidence grows with each new revelation of His grace. He is always there, even when we are looking into a mistiness of the unknown. He is always working things out for our good and His glory, even when we cannot understand where the path is going to lead us. Do you have confidence in God's timing, provision, and power? If so, take joy in His presence as He begins to demystify the pending triumphal joy of His complete, holy purposes for you.

The joy set before Jesus Christ spurred Him on, but it came with difficulties. The expectation of victory helps us to endure as Jesus did, but we would be unwise to forget that Jesus knew the nails would hurt. Jesus knew His suffering would be a bloody and awful experience; that those who claimed to love Him would betray Him. Yet, He held onto the joy set before Him: our salvation. His greatest desire was to see us whole and happy, and He deemed His suffering worth that outcome. You and I were worth it to Jesus!

As Joseph held onto God's promises, his faith and hope culminated in a healed relationship with treacherous brothers. He also received the ability to save his family from certain death by starvation. The foreshadowing of Jesus' story is powerful; Jesus focused on overcoming suffering with that same joy set before Him, a healing reunion that brought life to His family (us). The adopted sons and daughters of God, children of the promise, had betrayed and rejected Jesus in much the same way as Joseph's family, yet unblemished hope stood firm in the joy of

---

[314] Proverbs 3:5 ESV

salvation. Joseph believed in God's deliverance; Jesus was the instrument by which our ultimate deliverance would come to fruition.

Let's not forget that God used Joseph as a catalyst in pivoting a messed-up family's complex dynamics. But Joseph still had to choose whether to be bitter or "better." It is not difficult to surmise that he must have maintained a relationship with God during that time of suffering. How else could he have produced such a phenomenal capacity for joy through pain? However, there was still work needed, and Joseph had to show faithfulness in how he chose to live under despair. God did not forget him in that place, blessing Joseph with the ability to interpret dreams and hold steadfastly to the love he knew God still had for him. Joseph produced joy because he was willing to carry on, in hope. He was willing to forego past hurts and joy-up for what God had planned for him, even when the situation was unclear.

Again and again, God's Word relates examples of how this happens for those who love God and are called according to His purposes. He is faithful. He is trustworthy. And He safeguards the joy set before us no matter what life looks like or feels like in those hard moments. Joy-up and know that God has called you for His purposes and that He will ensure the ending is a great one.

The Jars of Clay That Serve Joy Always

God gives us the treasure of joy to fill us, and it is even better when we receive this gift in the spirit of earthen vessels[315]. The joy we carry in our fragile hearts is enough to overpower the circumstances that shake us out of our comfort zones. The Potter Himself holds that clay in His hand, keeping it intact so that His power may be known through us. We are not durable metal or stone, we are carefully formed, well-loved jars of clay that should not put any confidence in their own strength or purposes. God's

---

[315] 2 Corinthians 4:7-9 ESV

strength sustains us, and God's joy fills us abundantly. When we share that joy with others, even those who mistreat us, we become part of a full and blessed demonstration of God's glory to those who are yet to witness it.

This is why we are here; to serve joy to others at every opportunity. The more we share, the more Jesus refills our earthen vessel and encourages us to keep loving those around us. We are to serve joy even to those who persecute us[316] because God does not withhold His sun from those who do not love Him; everyone greets the morning under the same heavenly gaze, and everyone has the opportunity to give thanks for the rain. Our job does not involve rationing sunshine, rain, or joy to a deserving few, for all have fallen short of the glory of God[317] and nobody 'deserves' His favor. Yet, He continues to pour it upon us, the saved and the unsaved, and waits patiently for us to acknowledge the source of every blessing. We can serve joy to others just by walking in joy before them, by displaying a lasting, unrelenting gratitude for blessings big and small. However, serving joy does not need us to serve up a superficial smile or empty platitudes; it needs humility and a deep knowledge of who holds our joy intact.

We may be the only Bible that others will ever read, the only visible outworking of the power of God in their lives. If we allow ourselves to be filled with joy, and overflow into the lives of others with humble adoration for Christ, the power of God will be on display through us. Can there be any greater privilege? Others need to witness the power within us that overpowers and overshadows the attacks launched against us, but humility is the key ingredient in that recipe for joy. Jesus had the power to call down legions of angels to rescue Him. He could have answered Pilate who accused Him falsely or proven His innocence with one simple demonstration of power. Yet, He chose to remain faithful to the greater

---

[316] Matthew 5:44-45 ESV
[317] Romans 3:23 ESV

good--our good--and let God's glory work out its fullness through suffering.

Humility like Jesus' radiates joy because it understands the temporal nature of suffering and the danger of pride, stubbornness, and carnal desires. As vessels of clay, we can humbly let God fill us with His joy and faithfully undergo the kiln's fire. The outcome of our perseverance will be perfection in the hands of the Potter. Joy endures, and it is worth the wait.

The Joy of the Spirit Might Take Time to Cultivate

As believers, we are called upon to provoke one another to good works[318] and this is part of our journey. We are not alone, nor can we thrive alone. We are called into a relationship with Jesus Christ, and the outworking of that is to connect with others in the same way. Once we grasp that we are loved, covered by grace, and fully acceptable to God, we will be compelled to let others know about this amazing news for every soul. The gift of joy is open to everyone, and the only reason any of us is able to accept it is through the calling of God. John 15:16 describes being '*chosen to bear fruit*[319]' and this had nothing to do with our own power. Rather, we were chosen, and we are expected to cultivate fruit as we abide in the love and joy of our Savior.

Are you intentional about bringing hope to others with a spirit of joy? This kind of fruit often starts with our family at home as we tackle the most vulnerable (and ugliest) parts of ourselves through the work of the Holy Spirit. Spirit-produced joy is the way that we can start to be more mindful of our family members, however those relationships look at the start of the journey. Joy will always make things better because bringing a joyous celebration of eternal life into a relationship is the

---

[318] Hebrews 10:24 ESV
[319] John 15:16 ESV

equivalent of bringing Jesus into the midst of that interaction. Jesus is the secret to restoring estranged, broken, or complicated relationships, but it takes humility to hand over all that emotion and pain to Him on such an intimate level. The love of a family is complex, but Jesus' power can make it as simple and beautiful as it was meant to be.

"He has told you, O man, what is good; and what does the Lord require of you but to do justice, and to love kindness, and to walk humbly with your God?

-Micah 6:8 ESV

God has shown us what is good, and we radiate with the joy of Christ when we appreciate His goodness. In God's presence is fullness of joy because of the sheer gratitude that erupts as we taste and see that the LORD is good. It's an uncontainable surge from the depths of our hearts, spilling over to all who see us experiencing joy in its supernatural state. When we feel that joy in abundance, as we will when the Spirit pours it into our hearts, we need to joy-up and ship out. We must ride that wave to do justice, love mercy, and be willing to hand out second, third, and three-hundredth chances to those who look the least deserving in our eyes. It is this joyous approach to life and relationships that can keep us humbly serving the LORD and enjoying Him each day.

Pride distorts God's glory, but a humble answer to His call brings such joy in life. It accompanies meekness and humility that mirrors Jesus' character, and there is no greater example to us of how to live rightly and at peace with our God. When we share the joy of the LORD with the world and help others understand the great joy-up supply for those who abide on the Vine, we confirm the call of God on those who love Him. He has chosen us, and we are to bear fruit as we press into that Vine connection until our last breath and then beyond. Joy doesn't end; our call to love and worship Jesus is an eternal one. We will be with the family that God has chosen and called for eternity, rejoicing in all that He has in store for us. Is that reward not worth taking up God's burden for the souls of men and women?

The joy that the Spirit inspires in our hearts may take time and trials to cultivate in the way that best serves God's purposes. But, when it is ready, we must be prepared to act. This one life we have on earth calls for radical obedience to God's call, even when we feel doubt, fear, or pride rising up to quench the Holy Spirit's bold directives. Take the thought captive[320], hold onto what is good[321], and let the Spirit move! There can be no greater joy than surrendering to the purposes of God and seeing Him work through us for the good of others and ourselves. Will we answer His call? Will we do it with great joy, as the voices of heaven raise their Hallelujahs at the returning of even one soul?

A Soft Heart Can Joy-up and Follow the Savior's Call

In John 4:4, Jesus felt the need to go through Samaria, even though it was out of the way and a hostile area for Him and His Jewish comrades. However, He listened to the prompting of the Holy Spirit, allowing Himself to be moved by an occasion that was birthed deep within His soul. His receptive response to this call brought joy for hundreds of people who met with the Living God that day, including the woman at the well. If we respond in the same way to the Holy Spirit's prompting to various opportunities, we can spread joy with the same intentionality as our Savior did. We can change hearts for good, as Jesus did, by the power of the Holy Spirit. We can see young and old come to an understanding of who created them and how much that Creator loves them and wants a relationship with them.

---

[320] 2 Corinthians 10:5 ESV
[321] 1 Thessalonians 5:21 ESV

We need to joy-up and sow the seeds of joy in the hearts of everyone we meet, for what greater joy can there be than knowing Christ? Nothing intensifies our joy like taking time to cultivate a deeper love for Christ and feeling His reciprocity as He opens our eyes to His love. He loves us, and joy abounds more and more as we seek to strengthen our relationship with Him and present the same truth to others.

Why not ask God for the precious opportunities to share joy with others in unique and wonderful ways? The downtrodden, the poor, the young, the imprisoned, and the destitute can know Jesus through your joy. And that may be the greatest privilege we have while on this earth.

Joy UP with Jesus

The fruit of joy that Jesus is cultivating in our lives may be the salve that He uses to change the world for better. If we are responsive to Him within our family units, places of worship, communities, and those He puts into our paths, who knows what wondrous joy awaits? Think of the lives we might help to save.

Yes, it is true that hurting people hurt people, and this is a particularly difficult area for many of us who want to joy-up and answer God's calling on our lives. How can we be joyful when the person in front of us is displaying outbursts, relentless anger, destructive bitterness, and animosity to anything we have to say? There is no easy answer to that question, but God still calls us to obey and love them anyway. Those who hurt us are most in need of the fruit of our joy, and while we serve them joy in greater abundance, we will need to stay firmly connected to the Vine to refill our joy tanks as needed. There's no other way to approach an enemy of Christ but with a willingness to share supernatural joy with them; that is what Jesus did for us while we were still sinners, and it is the only reason we responded to His call. To serve joy to our enemies, we must leave our egos at the foot of the cross and inflate only the desire to be more Christlike in our actions and countenance.

Joy-up and serve joy to others, sunny side up. Smile while appreciating that the pain on the inside is a catalyst to more abundant, lasting good. Joy becomes a ministry when we let our lights shine in every circumstance, including in those places where we aren't sure about what to do or how to respond to the threats in front of us. Obey the call and surrender the outcomes to God; He already has everything we need to get through this life with joy in abundance.

The only true hope is found in Christ Jesus. Abide on the Vine and let Christ serve as the inspiration and source of joy in and out of season. Joseph served many years in prison and under threat before his joyful faithfulness was rewarded with greater authority and responsibility under the call of God. David, too, suffered many things before He ascended to the throne of Israel and was able to execute that role with true humility and joy in His Savior. We were made to glorify God and enjoy Him forever, and part of that call is to joy-up and keep ringing the bell. We are loved beyond measure and spreading that message with joy is the right way to respond to such undeserved favor from our merciful, wonderful LORD.

CHAPTER 10
Joy-Up! Take the High Road!

"...but they who wait for the Lord shall renew their strength; they shall mount up with wings like eagles;"

-Isaiah 40:31 ESV

    Most people are familiar with the well-known fable about an eagle that grew up in a chicken coop. The eagle believed it was a chicken, acting and eating in the same way that the other birds did, even though it was created for so much more. When a naturalist came to the cage to see this phenomenon, he was amazed. He was also indignant that the eagle could not possibly have forgotten its natural abilities, believing the bird would still take to the sky if prompted or shown the way. He tried to coax it into flight with several failed attempts that saw the bird simply hopping back down into the coop. So, the naturalist decided to take the eagle up into the mountains to the precipice of a cliff, knowing that it was a choice to fly or fall from that height.

    We can all imagine how the fable ended, with the eagle stretching out its great wings for the first time and leaping into the open air with the grace it was born to wield. It soared, honoring it's given purpose, and understanding how much it had missed in the wasted years scratching in the mud. The story is reminiscent of C.S. Lewis' analogy of children being happy to stay in the yard making mud pies because they cannot possibly imagine what their parents mean by going to the beach! What a waste of an opportunity; what a waste of the joy that awaits if we forego the adventures that Christ Jesus wants us to experience with Him.

The LORD has prepared a way for us, where we are meant to *"mount up with wings like eagles[322]"* and find the strength we need in the joy of the LORD. He is that naturalist who shows us how we were meant to live but, more importantly, He is our Creator who desires to see us free and fulfilled. God surely enjoys seeing us soaring and stretching those wings He has given us so that we may see the world through His eyes. If we take the leap, we can experience our destiny of pure joy, no matter the turmoil far below.

Followers of Christ are not directionless chickens pecking at the fringes of real life beyond the coop; we are eagles made to soar where the Spirit leads us. Joy is there for us, but sometimes, that means allowing our loving Heavenly Father to carry us along the high road into the mountains so that we can see more. It might feel treacherous at times, requiring faith in His intentions for us, but the rewards will be great. We can joy-up and take the high road knowing that we are equipped, loved, and made for the gift of joy that will follow our trust in the LORD. All we need to do is follow His call.

What to Do When God Calls

Joy is indeed a high calling. The principalities of this world would prefer to keep us trapped in a cage rather than see us ascend where they cannot follow. Satan's forces do not want to see people thriving within the purposes of God; they want to see misery, suffering, brokenness, and disillusionment. But the people of God were made for more than this, for a life that is full, beautiful, and marked by imperishable joy. If we want to find that joy, part of our journey is to accept the gift of salvation and press

---

[322] Isaiah 40:31 ESV

into the relationship that Jesus Christ now offers to us. We can acknowledge that He is the LORD, and that we are saved, forgiven souls. And we can revel in the joy of our salvation.

The second leg of that journey requires more from us than just belief and acknowledgement, though. The next step is to obey the call we hear Him speak over our lives and allow Him to lead us ever higher. Once we have the gift of salvation, our eyes are opened to the truth of God's Word and His story. We can use that new vision to delve deeper and deeper into the Scriptures as the Holy Spirit lights up each part of it for us. He brings us into a greater understanding of the God who loved us enough to send His son, Jesus Christ.

Taking up the call also requires following our LORD's footsteps carefully as He shows us the way. Our focus on Him allows us to find safe passage along the rocky ground, with the final destination a joy set before us, always a source of hope and motivation.

Joy is a high calling and an act of courage in a world that threatens to clip our wings. Like the Prodigal Son who made his way back home, we have to fix our eyes on our Heavenly Father's call, knowing that it will all be worth it when we reach that place of love. We anticipate the celebration by celebrating each step, and that is where joy becomes a part of each moment in life. Joy starts now on the high road we are walking to the place of wholeness. But it doesn't stop once we leap up into the arms of our Savior, face to face. The moment we see Jesus in His glory is the moment our joy will be at its fullest. Yet, we have been blessed with a taste of that same full and perfect joy whenever we need it in the relationship, we have with Jesus Christ right now. Joy is here, and it will be here forever because Jesus is where it resides.

When Jesus gives us encouragement in verses like John 16:33, we can have absolute confidence that these things are said from a place of power, omniscience, and love. He knows that there is peace for us in Him, and He knows that we will need it at certain times of life more than at others.

He reminds us that He has *'overcome the world'* because He understands how difficult it is for us to still be here, in a place where muddy stomping grounds are the norm. But take heart, our LORD has given us wings.

When God calls, we are to move forward, stepping out in faith and knowing that He is near. We are to be of good cheer because Jesus has already overcome all that would hold us back. Now, there is nothing more to keep us on the ground--we can soar with the joy of the LORD as our strength and leave all the petty nonsense of the world far behind us. Rising up and taking the high road is not easy, nor is it popular. However, every step we take in following God's call takes us further in the right direction, and the reward for our tenacity, courage, and obedience will be immense.

The Challenges of Taking a Road Less Traveled

Keeping all of this in mind as we walk on the high road, we are also to remember that making progress is easier when we lay aside every weight, every chain that still hangs on us like a bad odor. Sin and death have lost their sting, but when we joy-up and refuse to be bound, walking in the way of the LORD is more productive. Sustainability in important life decisions ensures that we can keep going, and the kind of life that Jesus wants us to have is one that enjoys continuous momentum. For us, there can be an ever-flowing source of joy from the God who gave the Samaritan woman Living Water.

Let nothing separate us from the love of Christ; not petty nonsense, self-defeating thoughts, unsupportive spouses, grumbling neighbors, needy loved ones, or malicious coworkers. Nothing is more important than our continuous connection with Christ, the source of all hope, love, and joy as we follow God's call to be light and salt to the world. Sin is missing the mark, and that is not an acceptable way to live if we want to experience a full anointing of Christ-centered joy. Perhaps, we can look at ourselves as archers, making sure that we do not miss the mark (which is

Christ) by giving ourselves fully to the discipline of getting it right. It might take time, but we must 'win' Christ by getting ourselves back onto the high road and staying the course when challenges arise. The Christian life does need discipline, but this is a slightly different idea to forming good habits or entrenching healthier thoughts; this is supernatural. Yes, we must form good habits and entrench healthier thoughts that focus on Jesus, but the power by which we do this is directly from the Holy Spirit. God fuels our discipline, makes it effective, and keeps it sustainable for a lifetime. Without His help, our mark will fall short again and again.

As we joy-up and walk the high road, we must also press into the grace that Jesus Christ extends to us. His grace is sufficient for each moment of each day. Sometimes, we need more of it to propel ourselves forward or overcome fear. Other times, we have enough to extend to others as their paths intersect with ours.

How do we know that we have the joy we were created to experience? We will mount up as eagles, soaring and sweeping away doubt without the useless flapping of wings that keep chickens on the ground. Chickens walk low to the ground and make a noise when danger forces them to flap furiously away to a safer location. Eagles do not need that kind of empty drama; they simply open their great wings, point their gaze heavenward, and let the thermals take them beyond into a joyous adventure. We are eagles, living in a world where chickens walk in disillusionment, fear, and the muck of sin. It is our God-given ability to soar that brings continuous hope to each of those fellow earth dwellers that they could one day reach those same heights. With Jesus, all things are possible[323].

---

[323] Matthew 19:26 ESV

The High Ground Is No Place for a Proud Heart

It is wise for us to remember that joy takes us to the highest places without one ounce of our own strength in the mix. Humility is all we need to bring to the table, and pride in our own abilities will only bring with it disastrous consequences for the flight ahead.

Icarus was a great example in Greek mythology of how pride can derail free flight. The son of a master craftsman, Icarus decided to create a pair of wings so that he could escape his circumstances. Unfortunately, Icarus used wax in his construction and then flew too close to the sun, melting his fake wings to drop himself into the sea below. Philosophy puts his fatal mistake as one of arrogance or pride, but most of us could relate to this situation when we reach for quick solutions as trouble arises or we find ourselves in seemingly inescapable circumstances. Our first reaction is often one of complaining or expressing the 'unfairness' of what is happening to or around us; yet, joy in every circumstance is possible, and preferable in our walk with God. We cannot aim too high on our own merit (pride) or too low (complacency or lack of trust in God's miraculous work). We must aim at the heart of God, pressing into His strength for joy that takes us forward.

In the story of Icarus, some versions put his father as issuing him with a warning about the upcoming flight because of the volatile nature of the wax wings under heat. Icarus still ignored that warning and let pride make decisions. What could have been a joy-filled, amazing adventure to relate to wide-eyed grandchildren became his downfall, thanks to blatant disregard for a loving father's concern. God's love for us sometimes gives us warnings and guidelines about how to live (like the Ten Commandments) and ignoring such valuable advice certainly has the potential to take us out of that place of joy. Ignoring God's Word, leaving Him out of decisions, and not paying attention to the prompting of the Holy Spirit are sure ways to kill joy as we fall into the abyss.

Ill-fated Icarus also made the flight over water and flying too low would have been just as dangerous as his proximity to the sun. When we have low ambitions for what God can do in our lives, we deceive ourselves that the path we have chosen is a safe one. Yet, the high road is also not one of secure, comfort-zone living that avoids risk. On the contrary, God often requires us to take steps of faith, which can look like risk-taking from our point of view. However, the outcome of our obedience is not death but life abundant. If we let God serve as the wind beneath our wings and the guiding force that points us onward, we thrive. We humbly allow Him to strengthen our wings, push us off into the adventure, and fuel us with joy as we feel His presence for the duration of the thrilling flight. It's how we were meant to live, and it is the most freeing way to see the world from a higher, holier place.

What a privilege it is to serve a God who would bless us with these kinds of experiences as often as we are willing to follow Him up the mountain. The rich place their trust in money or power, but Christ's people place their trust in the One who richly provides everything they need[324]. Tragedy occurs when we try to be too safe and avoid dangerous signs that our trajectory might be misplaced. Step out of the comfort zone; God wants us to expect great things. Indeed, He applauds those who have the faith to move mountains. Yet, it takes courage and commitment to leap when He asks us to trust Him. The eagle must soar high above the sea, not just above the currents, but it also needs to take care to stay low enough to avoid the thin air and the heat of pride far above it. We must be energetic about the work that God would have us do, yet we need humility enough to realize that the strength, talent, and effectiveness to these things comes solely from our LORD.

Press into the presence of God, take note of His Word, and get ready.

---

[324] 1 Timothy 6:17 ESV

It's Time to Mount Up and Soar

How can we 'mount up' spiritually to rise above our spiritual challenges with the supernatural power that God has placed within our reach?

Spiritually, we face an actual enemy, Satan, and a remnant of our old lives, sin. How do we fight for joy and with joy when spiritual battles threaten to destroy our motivation or the work we are doing for God? First, we take up the Armor of God, bulk up on the Fruit of the Spirit, and call upon the name of the LORD for a mighty work of upliftment. He may ask us to stand, as Moses had to hold up his arms and watch the LORD's power prevail. Or He may ask us to fight, as David stood before the terrifying giant that mocked His God. He may ask us to focus more closely on planting joy-producing seeds in gardens of our minds as He helps us clear away the rot. Whatever the call, answer it with boldness and tap into the joy of knowing that Jesus is right there with you. The joy of the LORD will continue to be your strength as you diligently pursue the fight for your joy.

The second commitment to joy-up on the high road is to 'mount up' personally, to reach our God-given potential and soar where He would have us go. We need to pay attention to the dreams that God has placed within us. Is there something that really makes your heartbeat faster and your imagination run wild? It might be that this is part of the purpose that God has created for you, a way for you to serve Him and achieve His kingdom-based tasks through something you were made to do. Look at your interests and pray about how you might be able to use those talents to the glory of God. Choosing to follow God is not giving up that which makes you feel happy but knowing how to wield and steward those passions to help you enjoy God more, spread His Word, and glorify Him in every thought, deed, and word.

Joy-up and go for your goals in boldness, honing the Fruit of the Spirit, donning the Armor of God in case of attack, and learning daily how to commit all that you do and say to Christ. Joy is found in this kind of walk with Jesus, a close and personal connection that sees you grow, learn, and lean into God each moment of each day. We are to share our hearts with Jesus, open and true. Allow the Holy Spirit to reveal more about us, our Savior, and how we are to relate all of this to those we come across in our families, churches, communities, and workplaces. If our will aligns with God's, achieving our goals will be a most gratifying experience that is sure to bring even more joy to life.

Pleasure in the will of God is healthy and God-honoring, and the more we pay attention to aligning with God's Word, the more we will look like Jesus. The changes in us might be small at first, but these transformations will filter into our prayers, our choices, and our expressions of genuine love toward others. When we love God with all our heart, soul, and mind, and learn more about what that looks like, we will understand how to better love our neighbors as much as we value ourselves.

Four Ways to Walk Christ's High Road

The Father is pleased with us when He sees us living righteously[325] and part of making wise choices is to follow His lead. We can study the life of Jesus closely and follow His example. We can read the Word of God and ask the Holy Spirit to reveal its truth and help us apply these ideas to our thoughts, actions, and words. Jesus explicitly said that one way to glorify the Father is to 'bear much fruit[326]' because it shows that we are truly following Jesus and learning to love Him as we should. It's a dance of two hearts--yours and His--and it exudes a beauty and depth that

---

[325] Proverbs 23:24 ESV
[326] John 15:8 ESV

cannot be hidden from the world once the soul starts to glow with the joy of the LORD.

Let's look at four ways to ensure there is joy on the high road as we soar with purpose.

1. Understand that what is happening in you is more important than what is happening around you

When we take the high road, it is not easy. Jesus makes reassurances like, '*I have overcome the world*[327],' because life will test us in many ways. When trouble seems to be all around us, we need to joy-up and refuse to be bound, and joy-up for the fight. We have the power of Jesus Christ within our grasp, and there is no greater authority in heaven or earth. Nothing can control us but the love of God, and even that is a constraint that we gladly take on as we see the heights and depths[328] of the love the Savior has for us. Christians are not enslaved[329], nor are they subjected to doing what they do not want to do. We are free by the blood of the Lamb, and the changes within our own hearts are of eternal value compared to the temporary suffering we may face on the high road.

We mentioned the 'light affliction[330]' that many people are feeling deeply in these uncertain times, but not even a global pandemic has any power against the One we serve. It is not appropriate to linger in anger over situations that make us uncomfortable because the love of God 'constrains' us and fills us with peace that surpasses understanding, no matter what we face. Joy-up and spread love, even to those who are lost in their sin. That's what Jesus did for us!

---

[327] John 16:33 ESV
[328] Ephesians 3:18 ESV
[329] Galatians 4:7 ESV
[330] 2 Corinthians 4:17 ESV

2. Stay focused on Jesus and tap into grace

Grace is often described as undeserved favor, and Jesus makes these blessings available to us for each moment. His grace is sufficient[331] and it never runs out. If the high road is taking you to places that are making it harder to breathe, grace can carry you through it. Tapping into grace is not a last resort, it is a free, first-choice element of salvation that is a cornerstone of our faith. We are saved by grace because faith was only possible through the Spirit's awakening in us. Our faith in Jesus is only possible because of God's grace that opened our eyes to all that He means to us and to the riches of His glory[332].

It shouldn't be a surprise for those who witness Christ's generosity that God also extends an extra supply of grace to us at certain pivotal moments on the high road. It is this bounty that we can draw upon to get us moving into acts of good, like walking justly, kindly, and humbly[333] with God as we become His hands and feet to the world. So, joy-up and take the high road, but remember that you are called to do so with humility and full trust in the purposes of God.

3. Embrace your status as a blood-washed child of God

It is never appropriate to respond in anger to suffering for Christ's sake, just as it is never appropriate to see ourselves as a victim. We are not victims of circumstance; we are eagles surrounded by chickens. The Word came down to show us the way, but it is still up to us to get on the path and make our way to the peak in anticipation of God's call to take a leap.

---

[331] 2 Corinthians 12:9 ESV
[332] Philippians 4:19 ESV
[333] Micah 6:8 ESV

All have sinned[334] and life is challenging in so many ways, but there is more for us than sinking into despair or letting situations determine our grasp on joy. The wicked are always here, and they have no joy or peace to offer. Still, God wants to finetune our attitudes so that we can receive and give joy in every circumstance, giving light and love to the world that so desperately needs these good things. Sometimes, it requires us to rise above petty arrows and the snares of the devil with a humble, Christ-powered joy. It requires us to understand ever more fully the strength of the LORD that is in us, and that is there for us through thick and thin. When we humble ourselves in this way, God has an opportunity to exalt us, to lift us up and help us rise above these unpalatable life experiences to a higher, better place of joy, peace, love, and assurance. There, God *"adorns the humble with salvation*[335]*"* and lifts them to a higher calling. He is with us through the winepress, the fire, and the valley, encouraging us as we take up our crosses. Why not allow Him to get the glory from what we say and do along the way?

We joy-up on the high road by knowing the greatness of the One within us. At the end of the path, He will be the wind beneath our wings that takes us beyond all we could ask or imagine[336].

4. Recognize the joy set before you and fix your eyes on Him

The final way to joy-up on the high road is to hold fast to the One who leads us through it all. Our joy comes from the LORD, the maker of heaven and earth[337]; it is fixed in Jesus. Christians should be motivated to stay on the high road by a desire to look like children of God (we are made in His image!). The joy set before Jesus[338] was you and I, His

---

[334] Romans 3:23 ESV
[335] Psalm 149:4 ESV
[336] Ephesians 3:20 ESV
[337] Psalm 121:2 ESV

church, and we were worth it to Him. Jesus said that those who want to be great should be humble like children[339], with a child-like faith in the greatness and purposes of God. He died for us so that we could be there with Him as the Kingdom comes into its fullness, but there is work to do here if we want to be 'great' in that Kingdom. Children of God need to possess the same character as the Father; one of love. What we do and say must be an extension of the love of God that rules our hearts.

Do our lives look like that? Humility, gratitude, and joy are part of that God-honoring character. Are we walking in love and acting out of love? Are we letting love replace fear and doubt or are we still running to hide as we hear the voice of our Maker searching for us? From the garden, God breathed His own breath into the man and the woman, and that was the beginning of our living souls made in God's image. It was perfect and whole, an unblemished picture of what love looked like on earth. We are not children of Satan, broken, marred, and representing the opposite of what God wanted to bring to the world. No, we are children of the Living God, and we carry His holy image in our flesh and spirit alike.

We need a strong resolve to joy-up and represent the Father in a way that brings Him glory and honor, and that is a high calling indeed. May we believe that Jesus is the Way, the Truth, and the Life[340] with a child-like faith, not the '*show us*[341]' mentality of so-called intelligent adults like Philip. We are part of the Kingdom and there is great joy awaiting those who walk humbly with their God on the high road.

Joy Up with Jesus

Jesus is the wind beneath our wings and the light before us, no matter the obstacles or detours we may face as follow Him with joy. The secret to thriving

---

[338] Hebrews 12:2 ESV
[339] Matthew 18:4 ESV
[340] John 14:6 ESV
[341] John 14:9 ESV

in this journey is to remain yielded vessels, jars of clay that God can fill with purpose and work with strength to achieve what must be done. It is God's nature, His image, that must be seen in us during the worst times in life, when the need to take the high road or get back on it is imminent. We need to stand fast in our relationship and dependence on Christ, in the same way that Jesus described being one with the Father[342] and wishing to see us be part of that union.

What would it look like for us to be so united with Christ that when people look at us, they see only Him? Imagine the beauty of that agreement, that holy connection, that shows others the complete, loving character of God. Love is the very essence of who He is. If we look at God's Word, displaying the character of God would look like joy in all circumstances, alongside humility, endless grace, child-like faith, and supernatural peace. It would be to pour out love on others, with patience, kindness, goodness, faithfulness, and gentleness. It would show up as inexplicable self-control in the midst of terrible suffering or injustice for the sake of Christ, because we understand that our suffering produces perseverance[343] and leads to hope.

Taking the high road with a singular focus on Jesus gives us a new understanding of what it means to have the joy of the LORD as our strength; it is an act of surrender that takes us right into the freedom that comes from unity with Christ Jesus. The LORD's will for us is to know that eternal connection and to take joy in it; there is no greater calling. Now, it is time to stretch your wings.

---

[342] John 17:21 ESV
[343] Romans 5:3-5 ESV

CHAPTER 11
Joy-Up: Repeat the Sounding Joy!

Joy to the world!

The Lord is come.

Let earth receive her King!

How wonderful it is to imagine that beautiful night when the Savior was born in Bethlehem. Heaven and nature literally sang out with a joyous song of praise that could not be silenced nor ignored. Jesus has come and it is time for every heart to prepare Him room, which means embracing all that He wants to do in our lives. God has gone out for the sake of His anointed ones, for the salvation of His people[344] who are called according to His purposes[345]. Like Habakkuk, we are seeing some of the destruction that must take place before Christ Jesus comes a second time to deliver our full inheritance as sons and daughters of God. We are seeing pain and testing in every part of the world. Yet, the promises of God are trustworthy, and our Savior is faithful to the very last moment when the fullness of time reveals His glorious might. This is why we can rejoice in the LORD and take joy in the God of our salvation[346] in every circumstance we face, no matter what.

---

[344] Habakkuk 3:13 ESV
[345] Romans 8:28 ESV
[346] Habakkuk 3:18 ESV

The joy-up power we can access in Christ is proof of His reign, which holds all power and authority in heaven and earth. Jesus is King, and our joy is secure in Him. Joy in Jesus does not run out. It does not fade, and it is never going to be in limited supply in this life or the next. The Scriptures resonate with that beautiful joy, with every written line drawing us toward God. We worship the one true God who is joyful, and generous in sharing that joy with those who ask for it. If the trees could clap their hands, they would, with fields, floods, rocks, hills, and plains repeating the sounding joy they take in their Creator. We can sing too; our King's ears are attentive to the praises of His people. *"For the eyes of the Lord are on the righteous, and his ears are open to their prayer.[347]"*

As we reflect on all that Jesus has done for us, it seems fitting that we should feel more and more joyful about Christ's victory over sin and death. We live in a time and place that does not yet recognize the fullness of that accomplishment, a world with scales on its eyes and a tongue that denies love. To its detriment, the world chooses to remain in darkness. As such, our directive from the LORD--to be a light to others--is entirely appropriate given the state of things. There is no joy in darkness, only lost people who have taken the wrong path and followed deception. How the heart of the Father must break for those who stumble around in darkness. Dead hearts refuse to acknowledge the beauty of light as it crests over the horizon each day. Eyes are blind and ears are deaf to the truth of God's Word, but mercy and grace follow those who are called by His Name.

Thankfully, the secret to a joyful life is only hidden until Jesus Christ opens our eyes to the truth. The Savior reveals the magnificent truth behind why we are here, and that changes everything. How can we forget that our Creator has formed us to thrive in a relationship with Him? Joy is an essential part of our DNA that we cannot live without; indeed, we were never meant to live without it. Joy is part of the very essence of who we are as Jesus invites us into a right relationship with Himself. We were

---

[347] 1 Peter 3:12 ESV

made for Jesus, and the product of that eternal relationship is joy everlasting that brightens how we see the world and gives us hope for the future.

A relationship with Jesus is such an essential part of life that the joy of being in His presence cannot be contained. Even at the start of the Messiah's arrival, the stars shone brighter, the angels sang in chorus, and the universe rejoiced at the amazing love of God. The King of Heaven had come to save us from darkness, to offer us a restored relationship with the One we were made to love! The Savior brought with Him immense, unshakeable joy as He gave us the ability to see the light clearly. Now, His Word shows us how to press into that unconditional love through our connection with the True Vine. It is this connection that brings joy to the fore when it seems that the chaos around us might quench our spirits.

Jesus' love for us penetrates every sliver of darkness, cleansing us of all unrighteousness. It brings us into a place of intimacy with Himself that is full of comfort. David understood that in God's presence was the place to find '*fullness of joy*[348]' and He continuously went back to that place, asking God to restore the joy of his salvation when he stumbled or found himself on the wrong path[349]. Like David, we can find that contentment by tapping into the electrifying joy that's available in knowing God on a personal level. It is a boost of energy, a thrill of hope, as we find ourselves face to face with our Maker. Sometimes, we need a reminder that we are building a relationship that will last for eternity; death has lost its sting. Thanks to Jesus Christ who endured the cross, we can approach the throne of grace with full confidence[350] and bask in the presence of the LORD all our days--there is no greater joy for a soul than knowing that kind of love!

---

[348] Psalm 16:11 ESV
[349] Psalm 51:12 ESV
[350] Hebrews 4:16 ESV

In Psalm 103, we saw the great love that God has for His children and some of the many ways in which He expresses that affection in our lives. Those whose eyes He opens will better understand the depths of this love, rejoicing in the forgiveness He offers, even when we were still sinners. Our LORD is slow to anger and steadfast in His love for us, even when it seems we are allowing darkness to creep back into our hearts and minds. Thankfully, His goodness and mercy follow us as we take step after step in the company of our King. Countless Christ-followers can attest to this comforting presence, even as they have found themselves under the discipline of the Holy Spirit or felt prompted to reexamine their own hearts. God's presence ensures peace, turning the intensity of our mourning into a catalyst for joy and intimacy. God spins and weaves situations into an anointed oil of joy and gladness[351] so that we can withstand the attacks of the enemy and the valleys that God may allow in our path.

As we joy-up in our relationship with Jesus, we can also learn how to focus on Him more effectively. We can embrace the work that the Holy Spirit is doing in our hearts and minds and refuse to be bound by the chains that once held us in sin. We can raise our hands, shake ourselves free of our shackles and step away from it all as we follow Jesus. Occasionally, we may notice the wile enemy trying to entangle us in old, broken chains, and it is then that we must joy-up in the hard-won freedom that Christ has given to us. Walk back toward the light. The freedom of our salvation intensifies any feelings of joy, hope, and contentment in Christ. It resets our focus to what is good so that we can bring glory to God and enjoy His presence in our lives for eternity. We are free people; let us use that freedom well and take joy in the One who secures it.

---

[351] Isaiah 61:3 ESV

Joy Deepens in Our Relationship with Jesus

Certainly, life presents us with many opportunities to pursue a deeper relationship with Jesus, whether through suffering or setback. As we seek to experience that fullness of joy in His presence, we may begin to realize that the process of sanctification is often longer than expected and a constant challenge. That's no surprise considering our old nature's prominence--our habits, our long-held incorrect beliefs, our physical tendencies or temptations, our biases. But the good news for all is that joy is not an end goal. Rather, it is available here and now, amidst the strife. When we are struggling to bring our sin before the LORD and tempted to run in the other direction like Jonah, we need only bow our heads and bend our knees. The Bible illuminates God's will for us, including the right way to approach life. The introspection that follows is not always easy to accept, yet when we see what God sees within our hearts, and act accordingly, we cannot help but rejoice. The blood of Jesus covers our transgressions, and it is more than sufficient, no matter our past or present.

Joy-up by coming into the presence of the LORD as you are, knowing that the Holy Spirit's conviction of our spiritual depravity is not an accusation but an invitation. The purpose of God's discipline, of the Father's discipline for His children, is to bring us closer to His Son. The attitude we meet is one of forgiveness, not contempt. The eyes we dare to look into as He lifts our chin are full of love and passionate about helping us make a fresh start. There is no shame here; only the joy of knowing that Love reigns. The woman at the well had that uplifting experience, meeting a Savior that showed her how to tap into the wells of joy that the Living Water provides. He pointed out her sin for the purpose of drawing her closer to Himself and giving her a fresh start at life. Nobody is beyond redemption, no matter how far-gone life seems to be. Come and drink of the Living Water and don't be afraid to gaze into the reflection of your redeemed, white-as-snow soul.

Remember, it isn't only a spiritual pursuit to know Jesus and live in step with Him: it is a total 'all-in' commitment to bring Him glory and enjoy the relationship. Faith in Jesus is a mind-engaged activity that requires us to read, understand, question, discuss, and apply truth to a life that does not always fit the mold. Believers need to be willing to engage with everything they have, heart, soul, mind, and strength. Sometimes, like David, we need to cry out for God's intervention in our spiraling, toxic thought life. We need to ask for that revelation, to *'hear joy and gladness*[352]*'* in the voice of the Holy Spirit as He encourages us. When we listen intently to the voice of our Good Shepherd, it becomes easier to cut through the noise and allow joy to grow in the garden of our minds. He helps us rip out the weeds, the lies that entangle, and sow joy-producing seeds that will bloom in the redeemed heart. This is the treasure that we seek to store up for ourselves in heaven, unending joy in our Savior who bestows holiness and honor on us as co-heirs.

Children of God can joy-up and stop negativity and sin-producing thoughts before these take hold because the Holy Spirit's power extends to every part of us. Our relationship status encourages us to bring these things before Jesus Christ daily, for instant relief. Joy-up and rejoice in Jesus' willingness to help us move beyond anything that holds us back, even in terms of what we think, imagine, and dream. Our hearts will always focus on where our treasure lies, and if that is Jesus Christ, we are on the right track. A mind steeped in the truth of Scripture and planting joy-producing seeds will always be the starting point from which the Holy Spirit works--first a new heart, then a mind transformation of biblical introspection and meditation on the truth, and then other changes, like the quality of our speech.

---

[352] Psalm 51:8 ESV

It is true that if our conversations do not carry much evidence of the joy of our salvation, we might have missed an opportunity. Have we taken the time to hide God's Word in our hearts and truly grapple with what He wants us to understand by it? Our relationship with Jesus, the Vine, is a top priority because He is our source of joy. And what we should be seeing on that journey is a full turnaround. Our Savior calls us, cleanses us, and sets our feet on the path that we must follow. He then gives us the Holy Spirit, a constant help in times of trouble or plenty. He probes our minds, illuminating what is true, good, and God-honoring against what is unhelpful, and then helps us shake off those chains. But that is not the end of the process. Sanctification also involves a physical outworking of these inward transformations. Godly conversations filled with words of joy are one of these expected outcomes, and often, the most challenging area for God's people to embrace.

How can we cultivate a golden tongue that brings glory to God? How can our speech be steeped in positive, Christ-honoring words that embody the fruit of the Spirit and lift hearts wherever possible? As the world descends even further into chaos, disillusionment, and mental illness as a norm, our words hold a supernatural power to change lives. With a secure connection to the Vine, we can ensure that we tap into joy when we need a boost. The Spirit helps our speech overflow with a word in season that 'speaks life' to all who hear it. If we want to produce a golden tongue that persuades others of the authenticity of our salvation, we have to let love and freedom in Christ inflame an earnest intention in us to glorify God with what we say. A golden tongue glorifies God and brings others before the throne of grace, and indeed, that is our chief purpose on earth. Where silence is beneficial, we need to listen carefully to the prompting of the Holy Spirit and bridle the torrent that could wound others irrevocably. Speak life, and watch God pour out joy in abundance in every situation.

Joy Fuels An 'All-in' Commitment to the Business of the Kingdom

Life with Christ is full of joy, but sometimes this rejoicing comes at a time that's entangled with trepidation, uncertainty, or doubt. Jesus encouraged us to take heart when we face these trying situations that are sure to be a part of our earthly experience. He asks us to fight for our joy because the victory is already secure, and we are to fight *with* joy as we realize whose banner rises above us. Jesus has overcome the world's hold on us, granting us freedom from fear, sin, and death if we accept the gift. Part of the invitation into a relationship with Jesus involves walking toward peace with a joyful disposition while we are not yet at the endpoint. The battle might be raging, and even in this, we can find joy in salvation and gird up the joy of the LORD as our strength. Jesus is the secret to our hopeful outlook during a particularly gruesome experience, an ever-present source of joy that we can cling to *while* we feel scared or anxious or confused. He covers us with His wings, anchoring our hope, and pouring everlasting joy into our humbled hearts. Nothing can separate us from the love of God, and that is well worth celebrating as we diligently seek to follow Jesus through the fight.

For this reason, the LORD has seen fit to provide us with an arsenal of joy-protecting, joy-spreading resources that can secure our victory battle after battle. We must train ourselves to cling to joy and humility in our walk with Christ, even in a fight. Rejoice! We are rich in Christ Jesus, with truth and righteousness. We have the Savior's peace, hope, a faithful God, and light for the dark nights. We are rich, we are loved, and joy is worth the fight. In fact, if there was ever doubt that joy is a secret ingredient in a fulfilled life, our dependence on resilience dispels that notion instantly. The armor of God gets us through the day's battles, but it is the joy of the LORD that is our strength. And we certainly need that strength to have a life of resilience while we meet each challenge head-on and head for the high road that God wants to show us ahead.

It is wise for us to regularly remind ourselves that a resilient joy only comes with the experience of overcoming hard things. Like a tree, we cannot test the depths of our roots or the value of our progress until we find ourselves in the middle of a storm. Only then will we see the mark of strength beneath the surface, as we call out to the One who can quiet that storm with one command or bring us safely through it without a scratch. The relationship we have with our Savior is the only source of joy, and we can tap into the Vine whenever we need a fresh injection of supernatural power, unwavering strength, and a drink from the wells of joy. We cannot give up or grow weary of advocating for what is good. We cannot let sin linger or lose our focus on the mission that Jesus has entrusted to us by his gift of salvation. We must keep our eyes on the joy set before us, as Jesus did, and we must always remember that no circumstance, trial, or attack will change the truth that the joy of the LORD is our strength, if we choose to accept it. Following Jesus is always a choice, so why not choose to go 'all-in' and reap every benefit of His grace, mercy, and love?

Once we understand that the freedom to choose Jesus belongs to us alone, we can begin to make better decisions about how we approach life and all the challenges that come with it. A transformed mind suddenly sees the goodness of God in startling clarity, as the Holy Spirit shows us the inexplicable love that has shaped the very essence of who we are in Christ Jesus. The one life we have will be our only opportunity to grasp the beauty of our God and to express praise, honor, and humble gratitude for all that He is and all that He has done. Give thanks, for the LORD is good! Surrender to His call and joy-up; the more joy He pours into our hearts, the more it will overflow to others at every opportunity.

God has called believers into the light, giving us the faith to believe and the grace to accept His gift of life. Now, He calls those same believers to surrender to the Holy Spirit's lead and soften their hearts toward others who may still be in darkness. We need to serve joy to others with intentionality, day in and day out. God gets the glory, and our reward for participating passionately is more than we could ask or imagine. There is so much in store for those who say 'Yes' to God's invitations to serve, and humility is one of the key ingredients in accessing the joy-up moments we need to keep moving forward. Look at what God has done for us and marvel! How can we not share the wonders of His love with every single soul He places in our paths? It is why we are here, and faithful obedience to this call brings even more joy, especially on days where we don't feel inspired to act like children of God. Joy-up and get ready for what God has in store for you; the high road awaits.

The Son is Coming

Practically, curating joy-filled days and interactions with people is one of the greatest challenges we may face as believers in a broken world. There are bound to be moments of frustration, doubt, and temptation to fall back into old habits. Yet, the call of God will not change to mirror our weaknesses or emotions. We are called to believe in Him, to repent of sin, and to seek Him faithfully through His Word. Unsurprisingly, this includes choosing to take the high road on occasions where we feel a pull back into disobedience or God-dishonoring pursuits. Most people find that vices like pride and selfish ambition remain a thorn in their sides long after they give their hearts to Christ. However, sanctification is a process we need to embrace. It also requires an understanding that there will be hard days and moments where we feel like giving up on the call of God.

Thankfully, the joy of the LORD is our strength at these times of uncertainty. We are free to pursue a personal relationship with Jesus Christ, the very Person who is willing to share that everlasting joy we need so desperately. If the joy fuel tank is low, giving us a sinking feeling as an indicator, we need to return to the source and tap into the Vine's nourishment for our souls. Like eagles, we can soar above pettiness and entanglements as we joy-up in Jesus. Fly free, shine bright, and find rest in the presence of the LORD.

Why does salvation bring more joy to us than we could ever imagine? Because Jesus' gift of life is free, and His victory is secure. Salvation is a shower of blessing that we do not deserve, and the Savior Himself provides all we need to thrive in our designated roles. He has given us life so that we may live free of sin and walk in abundance; in joy, love, peace, kindness, and all that is of eternal value. We must joy-up in Jesus' love and mercy because our blood-bought freedom holds only beauty and wholeness in its future. We do not need to go through life despondent, fearful, or trapped in weakness; we can soar like eagles and rejoice in every good and perfect gift that comes from above[353].

As we allow the Holy Spirit to reveal more of God's character, purpose, and love for us, miracles start to happen in our hearts and minds. A deeper knowledge of God brings increasing joy to the fore, allowing us to press into the Savior's love without hindrance. It is easier to measure our worth when we see our value in heavenly terms: the King of the Universe was willing to die for us. We have no right to insinuate that we are worthless. We have no reason to lie to ourselves that life is meaningless when this undeserved, gut-wrenching sacrifice stands as an eternal testament of just the opposite. God's children are not worthless, and life is not meaningless. The Bride of Christ, His church, was worth every drop of blood and every tear shed by the groom. He kept His eyes on us, on our freedom and joy, while He bled, suffered, and cried out that the work was finished. There is no greater joy than knowing the One who created us for it, and who wants to pour it out on us forever and ever. Rejoice, Christ has overcome!

---

[353] James 1:17 ESV

How to Joy-UP and Ship Out for the Glory of God

As we have unpacked the need to rejoice at all times in our Savior, it seems natural to want to apply joy in real ways as we live out God's calling. It may be injecting joy to daily tasks or community-based interactions like the joy ringers do. Or it may look like intentional focus on gratitude to ensure our smiles are genuine.

- Here are some ideas for how to joy-up when distractions or doubts seem to rise up out of nowhere:
- When darkness looms, gaze at Jesus Christ and rejoice in the privilege of this intimacy. He is the source of joy and the reason we exist. He fills us with joy so that we may share it with others and experience the fullness of doing what we were made to do.
- How can we take joy in the God of our salvation when the chips are down? By reminding ourselves that a joy-filled spirit comes from continuously seeking to know God, love Him, and praise Him. Joy-up and fall on your knees in worship of the One who rejoices in every soul that returns to the fold.
- Has affliction, temptation, or a global pandemic diluted your ability to rejoice lately? Joy-up and shake off the remnants of sin that Jesus has loosed on your behalf. Refuse to be bound and let joy rush in to light up the way forward.
- Like Paul, you may find yourself doing the very thing you do not want to do. All Christians experience this same challenge, but there is hope. Meditate on the Word of God with careful introspection and let the Holy Spirit reveal the deepest, darkest corners of your heart. Trust in God's love for you and watch how the giver of joy makes room for many blessings in your new heart of flesh.

- Conquering the duplicity of the mind takes some effort, and it is always helpful to remember that with God, anything is possible. You can conquer negativity as it spirals up; the Holy Spirit's power is at your disposal. Joy-up and love God with everything you've got, and the Gardener Himself will help you plant joy-producing seeds that bloom and spread salvation's sweet fragrance.

- Focus on giving joy-producing seeds priority in the mind so that they bloom into godly words that speak life to all. Bury the Word in your heart that you might not sin and know when to stay silent for the sake of preserving joy. With our eyes on Jesus, we can joy-up and control our speech--a golden tongue honors God and shows how much we love Him.

- A battle is inevitable because 'in this world' we will have trouble. Yet, the King of glory makes it possible to fight for our joy, and with joy, while we follow Him through the highs and lows. Trials can be 'pure joy' when we let the Holy Spirit change our perspective to that which matters for eternal value. Don't give up; the armor of God comes with full access to His power, love, and a burst of supernatural joy in the face of trouble.

- Life's troubles have a side benefit for the children of God: an opportunity to joy-up and embrace an attitude of resilience that transcends earthly understanding. No matter what happens, walking with God takes us through it intact and ready to serve Him in even greater ways. Be faithful in the little things and watch as He pours out blessing and favor upon your life to increase your joy tenfold.

- Obedience breeds joy, and adversity breeds resilience if we submit to the LORD and trust Him with the details. Stand strong, good triumphs over evil.

- A busy schedule is no excuse; God's call is relevant in every season. If we pay attention to all that He wants to show us, in His Word, and by His Holy Spirit's whispers into our hearts, we will thrive wherever He plants us. Go forth in boldness, as you joy-up for all the exciting developments God will place along your path, one by one. Soften your heart, and He will empower you to spread lasting, God-honoring joy to everyone you meet, like Jesus.

Finally, brothers and sisters, the high road's twists and turns are sure to require much grace to keep us on track. Thankfully, we serve a loving, faithful God who is always at hand. Trust Him, spread your wings, and keep your eyes on the joy set before you: eternity in the presence and favor of the LORD. Joy-up, it is going to be the best ride of your life! In all of this, the key to joy is a direct connection with the source, the Vine, and a desire to deepen that bond daily.

Let the Earth Receive Her King

Remember why you are here.

Before time began, the earth was dark and formless. Nothing moved upon the face of the deep before God's gift of life sparked things into being. Intimacy with the Creator held for a moment before the stubbornness of sin ripped away generations from that crucial connection. The Vine waited, but the branches could not find a grip while the chasm of sin held them in bondage. Yet, on the other side of the great divide, God was moving pieces into place. He poured out hope and favor upon His chosen people, His holy nation. He made promises, sent prophets, and patiently breathed life into the story He had been writing since that first shaft of light. Joy waited in anticipation; it was almost time to open the floodgates of mercy and pour out joy onto the universe that was writhing in pain. God's tears flowed for the suffering that the world had unleashed upon itself through the choice to disobey, an eye for an eye, a tooth for a tooth. Where was the Savior? When would He come?

Pieces fell into place. The veil started to dance in the breeze.

And then, Jesus walked through it "unto us" as He brought the gift of joy to the world. The plan was in motion, the child was born, and all of heaven and earth knew that something had changed in the universe. Nobody was exempt as joy broke through the darkness to bring light to all; not the continents of the earth, the body of Christ, the weak, the strong, the oppressed, the mighty, the brave, the children, nor anyone else. He came for all, focusing on the joy set before Him as He carried out the next chapter in God's story of love. The birth of that unassuming bundle of joy heralded a day where all creation would lift their voices and worship the LORD for His grace and mercy. The universe, the galaxies, the whole earth, the wise men, two young parents, and an entire cast of witnesses were in place for the day that love showed itself. Everything changed for humanity on that blessed and glorious day. The chasm collapsed, and the door to the throne room was opened to those who are called according to the purposes of God.

What joy awaits us as we choose to step into that holy place in repentance and humility. Not by our might, but by the Spirit. Not by our ability, but by the gracious enabling of the Faithful One who loves us so dearly.

It was always about Jesus Christ, from the first rising of the sun to the final return of the King; in Him was life[354]. Those whom He calls have a divine purpose and an intentional God whose steadfast love endures forever. As our Heavenly Father, He takes joy in seeing us happy and blessed. He sent His Son to establish a new throne on every heart because our Creator understood how the creation was made to function. He made us for joy, a holy connection to the source of all life that elevates

---

[354] John 1:4 ESV

our hearts to the highest place of all. Our joy was born as a baby so that we may grasp the fullness of His work in us as His Spirit helps us mature. With each new step, a new level of joy explodes in our hearts, and it does so more fully in those moments we truly comprehend that He resides in us, and we abide in Him.

These 'joy-up moments' are that consciousness of the gift of life we have received and that we can choose whether to accept. If we do, we should prepare Him room and wait with bated breath for what He is about to do. And, oh, the joy that will come through the flow of anointing. What joy will flood our newly awakened souls as we see Christ with new eyes!

Joy-UP with Jesus Christ for the Kingdom is Near

Jesus Christ is the LORD, the Vine on which we abide, and the Living Water that gives us access to wells of joy in the exact moment we need them. A personal relationship with Him is where it all begins for us, but it started long before that for the Son of God. He was there in the beginning, forming us in the image of God and breathing life into our dry bones. He fashioned each hair and wove together each string of our DNA. He breathed life into us to create a unique, beloved child of God whose soul was of eternal value.

Joy lies in the presence of God because it is here that we finally realize the vast beauty, awesome power, and pure love of our Creator. When we see Him, there is nothing else to do but fall to our knees, sing out praises, and rejoice at the privilege of witnessing His perfection firsthand.

Isn't it a captivating picture to read about Jesus' final return at the end of God's Word to us? Imagine the joy that must saturate heaven, which already sees the Almighty One in all His glory. Our current perspective '*through a glass darkly*[355]' is enough to get us through anything that we may have to overcome here on earth. Yet, His fullness will come into stark clarity as He descends on the clouds on that final day. If His joy overflows in our hearts now, there can be no words to describe what we will experience at seeing our bridegroom face to face. *"For from him and through him and to him are all things,*[356]*"* and His love endures forever![357]

Relying on the joy of the LORD is the right way to live; we were made for it because we were made to know Jesus. All this is for Him, the Alpha and the Omega. Every effort we make to honor His call will store up treasure in heaven[358] that moth and rust will never touch. That is how Paul could admonish us to 'rejoice always' despite his endless suffering for the sake of the Gospel. It is why David could accept a full restoration of the joy of his salvation after he made terrible choices and had to live with the consequences for the rest of his days. Joseph held onto his knowledge that God's love for Him was real and that the promises of the LORD are always fulfilled. He rejoiced in each opportunity to honor the LORD, even when it seemed like there was silence from his Savior.

The death and resurrection of Jesus Christ, the Son of God, secured victory over death and sin for all who believe it. We can live forever in the presence of the LORD, where joy resides, if we believe with our hearts and confess with our mouths that He is King. And, He is King, whether we choose to acknowledge it or stubbornly resist. As the blood of Jesus washes over our guilt and cleanses us of all unrighteousness in the eyes of God the Father, joy bubbles up from the depths of our hearts and humble adoration glistens in our eyes. Let the earth receive her King; time is almost up.

If you have not yet chosen to take hope as your anchor, joy as your strength, and love as your portion, you may not yet realize how different

---

[355] 1 Corinthians 13:12 ESV
[356] Romans 11:36 ESV
[357] Psalm 118, 136 ESV
[358] Matthew 6: 19 ESV

life could look. If the Holy Spirit's whisper is rising, consider whether it is time to answer that call and see Him write your name in the Book of Life. There is no other way to know joy than to know Jesus Christ. We do not have to live under guilt or shame any longer; Jesus has taken care of all our transgressions by His blood, and He stands waiting for us to take His gift of salvation with both hands. Our Savior lifts us up when we stumble and rejoices as He presents us blameless before the throne of God.[359] The same Person who has all glory, majesty, dominion, and authority[360], from the beginning of time to the end of it, has extended love toward us and wants to offer us a relationship with Himself!

Don't you want to joy-up and see your life bloom as it was meant to? Reach out to Jesus Christ. Tell Him your desire, your longing to know Him, and acknowledge all that He has done for you. Repent of your sin and declare that Jesus is your King and Savior, because *"if you confess with your mouth that Jesus is Lord and believe in your heart that God raised him from the dead, you will be saved."* **Romans 10:9 ESV**.

The 'Sinner's Prayer' is one we all need to pray, and there is no harm in reminding ourselves of the commitment it represents. Whether we are at the beginning of this journey or well into the battleground, the forgiveness of sins is a daily gift that God is willing to bestow upon His children. When we turn to Jesus for the first time, or after years of getting to know Him, all we need to do is lift our voices and humble our hearts. He accepts us, just as we are. He embraces us as we turn from our sin and agree to follow His lead. Jesus is the Way, the Truth, and the Life[361], and the only one in the universe who can save us. Believe in Him. Ask Him to show you what is truly means to rejoice with joy that is inexpressible and filled with glory[362] as He rescues you from darkness.

---

[359] Jude 24 ESV
[360] Jude 25 ESV
[361] John 14:6 ESV
[362] 1 Peter 1:8-9 ESV

Pray,

"LORD Jesus Christ, I am a sinner living in disobedience to Your Word. I am sorry. Forgive me. I believe that You died for me, that You rose again, and that You are the LORD of all, King of Kings. I believe that Your sacrifice paid the full price for my salvation, and I humble myself before you. Please accept me as your child, pouring grace, mercy, and love over me as I seek to know You. There is nothing I can do to earn your love, and I thank you for offering it to me freely. I accept it by faith, Jesus, Son of God. Here is my heart, please fill it with the joy of MY salvation! Amen"

Now, brothers and sisters in Christ, it is time to celebrate with the angels. There is abundant joy to be found in a relationship with the Savior, more than we could ever ask for or imagine. Outside of Jesus, happiness is as fleeting as the pains and disappointments we face in life. You and I have only one life to steward, and it may be that God has placed us exactly where we are for such a time as this[363]. If we are faithful to follow where He leads, we will know joy all our days.

Will you fight for joy and with joy because our Redeemer lives? Will you embrace the full benefits of salvation in Jesus Christ and open your heart to receive His joy to overflowing? The world needs joy, and we can be the ones to provide it as we keep ourselves firmly rooted in the Vine Himself. We can live as elated believers that shine brightly in a dark, lost world.

Get up, rejoice! Prepare for Christ to fill you with a joy that will last throughout eternity. Our eternal souls learn each day what it means to live in step with their awesome, unfailingly kind and patient Creator. We serve a God who rules the world with truth and grace, and it is time that we lift our voices with the heavenly hosts and live joy to the world!

---

[363] Esther 4:13-14 ESV

Bibliography and References

Reference List by Chapter

Chapter 1

1. ESV Study Bible. English Standard Version, Crossway, 2011.
2. Kelly, Douglas F, Philip B. Rollinson, and Frederick T. Marsh. The Westminster Shorter Catechism in Modern English. Phillipsburg, N.J: Presbyterian and Reformed Pub. Co, 1986. Print.
3. Lewis, C.S. (1963-64) Letters to Malcolm: Chiefly on Prayer. Harcourt, Brace, and World.

Chapter 2

1. Bloom, Jon. (2021) You Can't Fake What You Love - How a Sentence Exposed and Delighted Me. *DesiringGod.org*. Sep 5, 2021. https://www.desiringgod.org/articles/you-cant-fake-what-you-love Accessed Sep 6, 2021
2. Kelly, Douglas F, Philip B. Rollinson, and Frederick T. Marsh. The Westminster Shorter Catechism in Modern English. Phillipsburg, N.J: Presbyterian and Reformed Pub. Co, 1986. Print.
3. Piper, John (2021) "God Is Most Glorified in Us When We Are Most Satisfied in Him." Desiring God, March 31, 2022. https://www.desiringgod.org/messages/god-is-most-glorified-in-us-when-we-are-most-satisfied-in-him.

Chapter 3

1. Deibert, B. What is Yoke in the Bible? Meaning & Importance of Jesus' Teaching. *Chistianity.com*. Feb 12, 2019. https://www.christianity.com/jesus/life-of-jesus/teaching-and-messages/the-yoke-of-jesus-biblical-meaning-and-importance.html Accessed: Aug 23, 2021

2. Coert Rylaarsdam. 2020 J. David king of Israel. *Britannica.* https://www.britannica.com/biography/David Accessed Aug 20, 2021
3. Crossway. Psalms based on Incidents in David's Life. *ESV.org* https://www.esv.org/resources/esv-global-study-bible/chart-19-01/ Accessed Aug 22, 2021
4. Huebert, B. What is Spiritual Bondage? A Biblical Definition. *Bradhuebert.com* 11 Apr 2011. https://bradhuebert.com/what-is-spiritual-bondage/ Accessed Aug 24, 2021
5. Kelly, Douglas F, Philip B. Rollinson, and Frederick T. Marsh. The Westminster Shorter Catechism in Modern English. Phillipsburg, N.J: Presbyterian and Reformed Pub. Co, 1986. Print.
6. Mandela, N, Long Walk to Freedom. New York :Flash Point/Roaring Brook Press, 2009.

Chapter 4

1. Kelly, Douglas F, Philip B. Rollinson, and Frederick T. Marsh. The Westminster Shorter Catechism in Modern English. Phillipsburg, N.J: Presbyterian and Reformed Pub. Co, 1986. Print.
2. Pulpit Commentary. Psalm 51. *Bible Hub* *https://biblehub.com/commentaries/pulpit/psalms/51.htm* Accessed Sep 27, 2021

Chapter 5

1. Calvin, J. 1555 Commentary on a Harmony of the Evangelists, Matthew, Mark, and Luke, Volume 3. *Christian Classics Ethereal Library.* https://www.ccel.org/c/calvin/comment3/comm_vol33/htm/viii.htm Accessed Oct 1, 2021

Chapter 6

1. Britannica. (2021) Agape--Christian feast. Britannica. Oct 3,2021. https://www.britannica.com/topic/agape Accessed: Oct 1, 2021.

2. Dodds, A (2018) On Saying "Everything's Fine," When It's Not: Our Solidarity with the Shunammite Woman. Abigail Dodds. May 5th, 2018. https://hopeandstay.com/2018/05/05/on-saying-everythings-fine-when-its-not-our-solidarity-with-the-shunammite-woman/ Accessed: Oct 4, 2021
3. The Holy Bible, King James Version. Cambridge Edition: 1769; King James Bible Online, 2021. www.kingjamesbibleonline.org. Accessed Oct 9, 2021.

Chapter 7

1. Keeth, J. (2008) 3. Smyrna--The Suffering Church. *Bible.org.* Jan 25,2008. https://bible.org/seriespage/3-smyrna-suffering-church#P4_989 Accessed: Nov 17, 2021
2. Piper, J. (2021) Can Joy Come in Sorrow? Lessons for an Authentic Christian Life. *DesiringGod.org* May 2, 2021 https://www.desiringgod.org/messages/can-joy-come-in-sorrow Accessed Nov 23, 2021

Chapter 8

none

Chapter 9

none

Chapter 10

1. Glenn, J (1994). *Walk Tall, You're a Daughter of God*. Salt Lake City. Deseret Book Co.
2. Lewis, C. S. (2001). *The weight of glory and other addresses*. 1st HarperCollins ed. San Francisco. HarperSanFrancisco.

Chapter 11

none

Reference List Alphabetically

- Bloom, Jon. (2021) You Can't Fake What You Love - How a Sentence Exposed and Delighted Me. *DesiringGod.org.* Sep 5, 2021. https://www.desiringgod.org/articles/you-cant-fake-what-you-love Accessed Sep 6, 2021
- Britannica. (2021) Agape--Christian feast. Britannica. Oct 3, 2021. https://www.britannica.com/topic/agape Accessed: Oct 1, 2021.
- Calvin, J. 1555 Commentary on a Harmony of the Evangelists, Matthew, Mark, and Luke, Volume 3. *Christian Classics Ethereal Library.* https://www.ccel.org/c/calvin/comment3/comm_vol33/htm/viii.htm Accessed Oct 1, 2021
- Coert Rylaarsdam. 2020 J. David king of Israel. Britannica. https://www.britannica.com/biography/David Accessed Aug 20, 2021
- Crossway. Psalms based on Incidents in David's Life. ESV.org https://www.esv.org/resources/esv-global-study-bible/chart-19-01/ Accessed Aug 22, 2021
- Deibert, B. What is Yoke in the Bible? Meaning & Importance of Jesus' Teaching. Chistianity.com. Feb 12, 2019. https://www.christianity.com/jesus/life-of-jesus/teaching-and-messages/the-yoke-of-jesus-biblical-meaning-and-importance.html Accessed: Aug 23, 2021
- Dodds, A (2018) On Saying "Everything's Fine," When It's Not: Our Solidarity with the Shunammite Woman. Abigail Dodds. May 5, 2018. https://hopeandstay.com/2018/05/05/on-saying-everythings-fine-when-its-not-our-solidarity-with-the-shunammite-woman/ Accessed: Oct 4, 2021
- ESV Study Bible. English Standard Version, Crossway, 2011.

- Glenn, J (1994). *Walk Tall, You're a Daughter of God.* Salt Lake City. Deseret Book Co.
- Huebert, B. What is Spiritual Bondage? A Biblical Definition. Bradhuebert.com Apr 11, 2011. https://bradhuebert.com/what-is-spiritual-bondage/ Accessed Aug 24, 2021
- Keeth, J. (2008) 3. Smyrna--The Suffering Church. *Bible.org.* Jan 25, 2008. https://bible.org/seriespage/3-smyrna-suffering-church#P4_989 Accessed: Nov 17, 2021
- Kelly, Douglas F, Philip B. Rollinson, and Frederick T. Marsh. The Westminster Shorter Catechism in Modern English. Phillipsburg, N.J: Presbyterian and Reformed Pub. Co, 1986. Print.
- Lewis, C.S. (1963-64) *Letters to Malcolm: Chiefly on Prayer.* Harcourt, Brace, and World.
- Lewis, C. S. (2001). *The weight of glory and other addresses.* 1st HarperCollins ed. San Francisco. HarperSanFrancisco.
- Mandela, N, Long Walk to Freedom. New York :Flash Point/Roaring Brook Press, 2009.
- Piper, J. (2021) Can Joy Come in Sorrow? Lessons for an Authentic Christian Life. *DesiringGod.org* May 2, 2021 https://www.desiringgod.org/messages/can-joy-come-in-sorrow Accessed Nov 23, 2021
- Pulpit Commentary. Psalm 51. *Bible Hub* https://biblehub.com/commentaries/pulpit/psalms/51.htm Accessed Sep 27, 2021
- The Holy Bible, King James Version. Cambridge Edition: 1769; King James Bible Online, 2021. www.kingjamesbibleonline.org. Accessed Oct 9, 2021.

***Reader, I pray that you enjoyed reading this book. As a new first indie author, it is difficult to acquire visibility. So, with all humility, if you enjoyed this book, please consider writing a review on Amazon, to spread the word and influence the algorithm.

To deepen your joy-up experience, the companion guide is now available for small groups Joy-up with a group of like-minded believers in your church or community and fortify your joy-up experience with others! Together, let's reverberate a resounding joy that reaches the four corners of the earth! The world needs it!

New releases by Dr. Candi Dukes

14 – Lesson Companion Study Guide

Stay Calm & Joy-Up! Pre-teens, Teens, & Young Adults!!! New Releases!!!

Order the Book & Study Guide:

For wholesale prices of bulk orders e-mail: cdukes71@outlook.com

www.ingramcontent.com/pod-product-compliance
Lightning Source LLC
Chambersburg PA
CBHW070838160426
43192CB00012B/2227